US Foreign Policy after the Cold War

The second edition of *US Foreign Policy after the Cold War* provides a comprehensive introduction to the main actors and machinery of American foreign policy. It also offers an assessment of the foreign policy records of the Clinton and the two Bush administrations. It examines how America struggled to find a defining role in the decade after the Cold War and then assesses the revolution in US foreign and security policy brought about as a result of the 9/11 terrorist attacks. It charts the unilateralist trends in the first George W. Bush administration and suggests that there may be some changes in foreign policy during the second four years as a result of the experience of going-it-alone on Iraq.

The book provides an inside account of the major actors in US foreign policy – the White House, the State Department, the Pentagon, intelligence agencies, Congress, media and public opinion. It then considers the priorities of US foreign policy including:

- Terrorism
- Rogue states
- The promotion of democracy
- Trade
- The Middle East
- Europe
- Asia

It also contains an overview of the debate about the direction of US foreign policy within the US and analyses the implications of American power for the rest of the world. This book is essential reading for professionals and academics with interests in the United States, international politics and international relations.

Dr Fraser Cameron is Director of Studies at the European Policy Centre, a leading think tank in Brussels. He is a former academic, British diplomat and adviser in the European Commission. He has published and lectured widely on European and transatlantic political and security issues.

US Foreign Policy after the Cold War

Global hegemon or reluctant sheriff?

Second edition

Fraser Cameron

Routledge
Taylor & Francis Group

LONDON AND NEW YORK

First published 2002
Second edition published 2005
by Routledge
2 Park Square, Milton Park, Abingdon, Oxon OX14 4RN

Simultaneously published in the USA and Canada
by Routledge
270 Madison Ave, New York, NY 10016

Routledge is an imprint of the Taylor & Francis Group

Typeset in Garamond and Helvetica by Taylor & Francis Books
Printed and bound in Great Britain by MPG Books Ltd, Bodmin

British Library Cataloguing in Publication Data
A catalogue record for this book is available from the British Library

Library of Congress Cataloging in Publication Data
Cameron, Fraser, 1947-
    US foreign policy after the Cold War / Fraser Cameron.– 2nd ed.
        p. cm.
    Includes bibliographical references (p.   ) and index.
    ISBN 0-415-35864-7 (hardback) – ISBN 0-415-35865-5 (pbk.) 1. United States–Foreign relations–1989–
I. Title: United States foreign policy after the Cold War. II. Title.
    E840.C345 2005
    327.73'009'049–dc22

                                                    2005004160

ISBN 0-415-35864-7 (hbk)
ISBN 0-415-35865-5 (pbk)

Taylor & Francis Group is the Academic Division of T&F Informa plc.

Contents

Figures

Tables

Preface

At the start of the twenty-first century, the United States (US) is the world's only superpower, or "hyperpower," as former French Foreign Minister, Hubert Vedrine, famously described it. The use of "hyper" aroused considerable controversy in the US but if one takes the analogy of a French *hypermarché* being so much bigger and stocking far more goods than a *supermarché* then the comment is justified and is not pejorative. The US has the largest and most productive economy in the world, a long history of democracy, political stability, a highly educated and inventive population and a military power unequalled and unrivalled in the history of the world. Yet even this hyperpower could not prevent the horrendous terrorist attacks on New York and Washington on 11 September 2001.

Following the change in the White House from Bill Clinton to George W. Bush in January 2001, the new administration seemed to take delight at rejecting many previous policies and mapped out a unilateralist approach in foreign policy. It sent a clear message that it preferred to establish its own policies without reference to its international partners. America would lead while others should follow. In its first nine months in office the Bush administration rejected a host of international treaties, much to the consternation of the rest of the world. The terrorist attacks in September 2001 brought about a major reassessment of US foreign policy as President Bush recognized the importance of building a broad-based international coalition to tackle the terrorist threat. Six months after the attacks, however, there was little evidence that the President's new-found desire for multilateral cooperation to tackle terrorism was being reflected in other policy areas. Indeed other policy areas were largely neglected as US foreign policy was focused completely on the war on terrorism and in particular the "axis of evil."

President Bush made it clear that the US was prepared to act alone if necessary in tackling threats from states, such as Iraq, suspected of having links to Al Qaeda and seeking to acquire weapons of mass destruction (WMD). His doctrine of pre-emptive strikes led him to invade Iraq in March 2003, even though there was no hard evidence of Iraq having WMD. The swiftness of the US military victory contrasted with the lengthy period pacifying and reconstructing Iraq. The US invasion led to a major crisis in transatlantic relations and a dramatic fall in support for the US throughout the world. The Bush foreign policy, style and substance, was a major theme of the 2004 presidential elections which saw the President re-elected by a substantial margin of the popular vote.

While America is divided about its international role, many non-Americans view the US as a hegemonic power, using its military as well as political and economic levers to increase its global influence. The recurring metaphor of recent US foreign policy conjures up a sheriff and a posse. The sheriff rides out of town to round up the bad guys. Willing deputies such as Britain's Tony Blair are welcome to ride along. But the sheriff calls the shots.

The motive for writing this book arose from the fact that US foreign policy after the end of the Cold War has undergone important changes and that given the overwhelming power and influence of the world's only superpower these changes have important implications for the rest of the world. From my vantage point in Washington DC at the start of the new millennium, I was able to observe at first hand the debate among America's foreign policy elite about the direction that the US should move in the new century. Following the 11 September 2001 attacks there was a significant change in the direction of US foreign policy with the emphasis placed firmly on a military response to "the war on terrorism" and the promotion of "God given values of freedom" around the world. These changes, with their implications for the rest of the world, made a second edition highly desirable.

President George Herbert Walker Bush (President from 1989 to 1993 and the father of George Walker Bush who took office in January 2001) coined the phrase "new world order" in the aftermath of the collapse of communism and shortly before the successful Gulf War campaign. President Bill Clinton talked of "expanding democracy and free markets" as the hallmarks of his foreign policy. President George W. Bush pledged in his inauguration speech "to keep America strong and free." But at the start of the twenty-first century there was no real consensus on what role the US should play in the face of a new terrorist threat and in a world shrinking continually as a result of globalization. The domestic political splits revealed during and after the 2000 and 2004 presidential elections (the first which George W. Bush won despite gaining fewer popular votes than Al Gore and the second which saw him defeat Senator John Kerry with more votes than any previous president) were also reflected in divisions on foreign policy. These divisions crossed party lines and touched on issues such as unilateralism versus multilateralism, free trade versus protectionism, how to tackle "rogue states" and terrorists, what importance to attach to human rights and when to intervene for humanitarian reasons (see Glossary for explanation of these terms). Some of these issues surfaced in the 2004 presidential election campaign when for the first time for many years foreign policy was a major theme.

The views expressed here are my own, but in writing this book I was helped by many individuals in the policy and think tank communities in Washington DC and Brussels. It would be invidious to single anyone out and many who spoke with me wish to remain anonymous. I would, however, like to thank Karen Donfried, Jonathan

Greenwald, Charles Kupchan, Kori Schake, Simon Serfaty, James Steinberg and John van Oudenaren for their valuable input. I am also grateful for the stimulation and support of many colleagues in the European Commission, particularly Ambassador Guenter Burghardt. My wife, Margaret, has been a constant support in this enterprise.

Fraser Cameron
January 2005

List of abbreviations

ABM	Anti-Ballistic Missile
ACDA	Arms Control and Disarmament Agency
AIDS	Acquired Immune Deficiency Syndrome
AIPAC	American Israeli Public Affairs Comittee
APEC	Asia-Pacific Economic Cooperation
CBO	Congressional Budget Office
CIA	Central Intelligence Agency
CINC	Commander-in-Chief
CNN	Cable News Network
CTBT	Comprehensive Test Ban Treaty
DEA	Drug Enforcement Agency
ESDI	European Security and Defense Identity
ESDP	European Security and Defense Policy
EU	European Union
FAA	Federal Aviation Authority
FBI	Federal Bureau of Investigation
FDI	Foreign Direct Investment
FTAA	Free Trade Area of the Americas
GATT	General Agreement on Tariffs and Trade
GMO	Genetically Modified Organism
HIRC	House International Relations Committee
IADB	Inter-American Development Bank
ICC	International Criminal Court
IISS	International Institute of Strategic Studies
ILSA	Iran–Libya Sanctions Act
IMF	International Monetary Fund
IRA	Irish Republican Army
MAD	Mutual Assured Destruction
NAFTA	North American Free Trade Agreement

NATO	North Atlantic Treaty Organization
NEC	National Economic Council
NGO	Non-Governmental Organization
NIC	National Intelligence Council
NMD	National Missile Defense
NSA	National Security Agency
NSC	National Security Council
NTA	New Transatlantic Agenda
OAS	Organization of American State
OECD	Organization for Economic Cooperation and Development
OPIC	Overseas Private Investment Corporation
PFIAB	President's Foreign Intelligence Advisory Board
PNTR	Permanent Normal Trading Relations
QDR	Quadrennial Defense Review
SALT	Strategic Arms Limitation Talks
SFRC	Senate Foreign Relations Committee
TPA	Trade Promotion Authority
UN	United Nations
UNSC	United Nations Security Council
USAID	United States Agency for International Development
USIA	United States Information Agency
USTR	United States Trade Representative
WMD	Weapons of Mass Destruction
WTO	World Trade Organization

Introduction

The US occupies a unique position in world affairs. Never in history has a country dominated the international scene to the extent that the US does today. No matter what the indicator – military power, economic strength, political influence, technological prowess, cultural model – the US is in a league of its own. It is the only nation on earth able to project power in every part of the world, and since 1990 it has been involved in resolving conflicts on every continent. As former Secretary of State, Madeleine Albright, stated in 1996, "the US is the indispensable nation whose work never stops." There are, however, very different images of this "indispensable nation" around the world, ranging from admiration to envy and hatred. It was clearly hatred of the US that motivated the terrorist attacks of 11 September 2001 or 9/11 in the American vernacular.

Until 9/11 there was little consensus on what the US should do with its power. There was also remarkably little debate on the priorities of US foreign policy and whether the US was developing the right instruments to further its external interests. The Republican chairman of the House International Relations Committee (HIRC), Henry Hyde, voiced a widespread concern on the occasion of Secretary of State Colin Powell's first testimony before the committee on 7 March 2001.

> The principal problem [for the US] is that we have no long-term strategy, no practical plan for shaping the future. The fall of the Soviet empire has removed the central organizing principle of our foreign policy for the past half-century. For all our undoubted power, we often seem to be at the mercy of the currents, carried downstream toward an uncertain destination instead of moving toward one of our own. We must resist the temptation of believing that we can fix every problem.

Six months after Hyde spoke, the US was faced with a new enemy – Al Qaeda. The devastating attacks in New York and Washington were to lead to a fundamental change in American foreign policy. The post-Cold War era ended on 9/11. The Bush administration henceforth only had one priority – the war on terrorism. Containment was dismissed as a guiding principle. Pre-emptive strikes moved to the top of available policy instruments. The President divided the world into "those who are with us and those who are against us." The US was no longer a reluctant hegemon nor a reluctant sheriff.

The US-led victory over communism had helped to create an impression at home that the stakes involved in foreign and security policy issues were reduced. 9/11 witnessed an upsurge in interest about foreign policy, Islam and the wider Middle East. Globalization also brought changes to the political forces in favor of free trade and tore down barriers between "foreign" and "domestic" policy. Meanwhile the shift in population to the south and southwest of the US as well as the rapidly expanding access to information, from CNN to the internet, led to an increase in the number of players outside the traditional East Coast establishment that had controlled US foreign policy for decades. In the post-Cold War era, one could speak of a "democratization" of the foreign policy process in America.

How does one define foreign policy? Stated simply, foreign policy refers to a consistent course of actions followed by one nation to deal with another nation or region, or international issue. A country's foreign policy is usually based on values (such as democracy, rule of law), interests (such as defense of or expansion of territory) and may reflect broad national objectives or be a very specific response to a particular situation. A country can achieve its foreign policy goals by employing a variety of instruments ranging from political, diplomatic, and military to economic, social, and cultural. Foreign policy is often influenced by many different variables, including a country's historical ties to other nations, its culture, type of government, size, geographic location, economic strength, and military power. A country's foreign policy is usually aimed at preserving or promoting its economic and political interests abroad and its position in the world.

The analysis of foreign policy has traditionally focused on government actions, particularly those related to political and military issues, but in recent decades the focus has changed. Today, many non-governmental organizations (NGOs) play an important role in foreign policy. Furthermore, in recent years, there has been a sharpening interest in many aspects of a country's domestic policy. For example, the energy policies of the US and other countries have become the object of international scrutiny as the world attempts to deal with the problems related to climate change and global warming. The chemicals and genetically modified organisms (GMOs) used in agriculture have become the subject of international controversy, as have the levels of aircraft noise, corporate taxation, and investment regimes, the death penalty and human rights. These developments have made the definition and practice of foreign policy much more difficult than in the past.

Although there is no significant threat to the US (apart from terrorism) it has had to confront a number of difficult issues in the post-Cold War world. How is the US to relate to a world that is no longer bipolar (i.e. dominated by the two superpowers, the US and the Soviet Union) but increasingly complex? How is the US to meet the new security threats, including terrorism? How does it deal with failed states? Under what circumstances should it intervene overseas? When should it act alone, and when with allies? How does it deal with the rapid pace of globalization? Given the importance of America in world affairs it is important to understand how the debate on the global role of the US is evolving, how foreign policy decisions are made, what US priorities are and how the US exercises its power and influence on the world stage.

This textbook seeks to provide the reader with a comprehensive introduction to these issues and debates as well as a guide through the maze of US foreign policy preparation and decision-making. The book focuses largely on contemporary events and draws on the author's experience of operating in the Washington policy milieu. It is a user-friendly textbook with the inclusion in each chapter of key facts. There are a number of case studies, a glossary of terms used in foreign policy, several tables and charts, a chronology and a comprehensive bibliography including numerous websites for further reading and research. It deliberately does not discuss international relations theory but suggestions are given at the end of Chapter 1 for students who wish to explore further this field.

Chapter 1 charts the slow but steady rise of the US to global power. A brief historical review highlights some of the issues that have characterized US foreign policy since the founding of the republic. It then examines the domestic and external pressures that propelled the US to intervene in two world wars and, after 1945, to establish a worldwide network of alliances and military bases to fight the Cold War. Chapter 2 examines the record of the three Presidents in office since 1989 and looks at how they coped in attempting to define a new post-Cold War paradigm for American foreign policy. President George H. W. Bush was the most experienced of the three in terms of foreign policy but this experience did not help him chart a new course for US foreign policy nor help him win re-election in 1992. Both Bill Clinton and George W. Bush were more interested in domestic affairs but each swiftly found out that the President of the United States cannot ignore foreign policy. The events of 9/11 led to a major change in US foreign policy. Chapter 3 looks in some detail at the role of the President and the executive agencies involved in foreign policy. It examines the rise of the National Security Council (NSC), both as an agency and in terms of staffing, and considers how its role has evolved in recent years. The State Department has had mixed fortunes in terms of bureaucratic infighting. It has seen its budget decline during the 1990s and has struggled to assert itself as the natural lead agency to cope with the new issues that have thrust their way onto the global agenda. The Department of Defense (Pentagon) and the intelligence community also faced cuts following the end of the Cold War but there was no fundamental reassessment of their size, structures, or mission until after 9/11 and the painful experience of the war in Iraq. An acrimonious debate took place in 2001 on the reform of the military and on the importance and urgency to attach to national missile defense (NMD). A further such debate took place in 2004 on how the intelligence agencies should be reformed to deal with terrorism. President George W. Bush established a large, new Department of Homeland Security to coordinate domestic policies on terrorism.

Chapter 4 looks at the role of Congress in making foreign policy. It examines the constitutional checks and balances governing the executive and legislative branches of government and suggests that while there are many real benefits to this system, the fatigue, frustration, and mistrust engendered in the process can often have serious consequences for the formulation and execution of US foreign policy. It is argued that the increased partisanship on display in Congress during the 1990s has had a negative impact on US foreign policy. Chapters 5 and 6 consider the changing domestic political environment and examine the increased influence of other actors involved in the foreign policy process including the role of interest groups, the media, and public opinion. Powerful domestic interests that bring money and votes to both political parties often drive US foreign policy. In the 1992, 1996 and 2000 presidential elections, foreign policy played a negligible role, unlike the situation during the Cold War when several elections had foreign policy issues high on the agenda. This changed in 2004 when foreign and security policy issues, notably the wisdom of the Bush administration's policy on Iraq, was a major theme. Chapter 6 examines the role of the media and provides an analysis of the latest polling data on public opinion. The "CNN effect" and rise of Fox News is considered and the changing public interest in foreign affairs analyzed.

Chapter 7 reviews the development of and examines the interests driving US trade policy. It considers the American role in international financial and economic organizations and how the US has been affected by and responded to globalization. Chapter 8 examines the US-led war on Iraq and American response to the terrorist attacks that dominated political life after the tragic events of 11 September 2001. It discusses the issue of "rogue states," three of which (Iraq, Iran and North Korea) were described as forming an "axis of evil" by President George W. Bush in January 2002, and the dilemmas America faces in responding to terrorism. It examines the nature and implications of the US-sponsored international coalition to fight terrorism, the Bush preemptive doctrine and raises the question why so many people hate America. Chapter 9 considers the lack of consensus in setting American foreign policy priorities and assesses how recent administrations have responded to new challenges in Europe, Asia, and elsewhere. It also looks at missile defense, US relations with the UN and expenditure on international affairs. Chapter 10 considers the debate on what role the US should play in the world and examines the question of continuity and change in US foreign policy. What were the defining features of US foreign policy before, during, and after the Cold War? What is the legacy of American internationalism? Is isolationism a real threat? Could the US withdraw in any meaningful way from today's world? What is the balance between the unilateralists and the multilateralists – those who favor going it alone and those who prefer working with others when possible? What is the balance between the idealists and the realists – those who would like to make the world "safe for democracy" and those who take a more cautious approach to tackling the outside world's problems? Is the US more a global hegemon than a reluctant sheriff? Have the neo-conservatives passed the zenith of their influence? Is "new realism" a sufficient doctrine for the challenges ahead? A concluding chapter reviews the making of US foreign policy and looks at the world in which the US will have to operate in during the next two decades. It suggests that America might best face the new challenges and change its image as "the ugly American" by modifying its behavior and spending priorities. It also asks whether 11 September has meant the end of the post-Cold War era? While there is unlikely to be an early resolution to the debates on the future direction of US foreign policy, one thing is clear – the US will remain the most important global actor for the foreseeable future. But what kind of leadership will it offer the world?

1

From colony to superpower

Key facts

- The twentieth century was "the American century." Since 1945, America has enjoyed, and continues to enjoy, a unique role in the world as the pre-eminent political, military, and economic power. The contemporary debates on what global role the US should play are rooted in American history.
- A large majority of the Founding Fathers did not wish the US to become involved in global affairs. Blessed by geographical position and abundant natural resources, the US maintained a low foreign policy profile during its first hundred years. The gradual expansion of territory during the nineteenth century was followed by an imperial scramble at the turn of the century. Presidents Theodore Roosevelt and Woodrow Wilson represented competing visions of realism and idealism.
- The First World War intervention in 1917 was decisive in securing an allied victory but the US rejected the League of Nations and reverted to isolationism and protectionist economic policies in the inter-war years. The Japanese attack on Pearl Harbor in 1941 catapulted the US into the Second World War and again its intervention was decisive in ensuring allied victory.
- After 1945, the US began a massive global engagement and arms build-up to ensure "containment" of communism. There was broad bipartisan support for US foreign policy during the Cold War. Superpower rivalry dominated international politics. The Vietnam War divided America and colored later thinking about military interventions.
- The Cold War era saw massive expansion in national security structures and huge budgets for military and intelligence communities. The end of the Cold War was due to freedom and independence movements in Eastern Europe, the internal collapse of the Soviet Union, and US arms spending during the Reagan presidency.

The American century

No country can escape its geography and history when it comes to establishing its foreign policy principles and priorities. The US is not just a country; it is a continent, protected by two vast oceans, the Atlantic and the Pacific. Of course, even its geographical advantages cannot protect the US from terrorist attacks but the enormous size of the US, plus its population and economic base, give it a unique position in the world. True, there are countries larger in size (Russia, Canada) and population (China, India) but no other country enjoys the panoply of resources that befit the term "superpower" or "hyperpower." As can be seen from Table 1.1, the European Union (EU) is already an economic superpower but it is far from being a political and military superpower like the US.

Like all other countries, the US has always acted in defense of its national interests but a continuous thread of idealism has also found a place in American foreign policy. Throughout its history the US has viewed itself as having a unique mission in the world, to promote its values of "freedom, independence, and democracy" and its market economy or capitalist economic system. Other countries, including all other permanent members of the United Nations Security Council (UNSC), France, the UK,

Table 1.1. Comparison of US, EU, Japan, Russia, and China

	US	EU	Japan	Russia	China
Population (millions)	291.0	451.8	127.2	143.4	1,300
Area (millions sq. km)	9.4	3.2	0.38	17.1	9.6
GDP (trillions of $US)	10.9	10.51	4.3	0.433	1.4
Percent of world trade*	13.2	14.5	5.6	1.4	5.5

* excluding intra-EU trade
Source: World Bank & IMF, data for 2003

Russia and China, share, or shared in the past, their own messianic vision. Few have been in a position to promote their values abroad to the same extent as the US, especially in the latter half of the twentieth century. The 1990s were the climax of "the American century." Not only had the US won the Cold War but its economy raced ahead of other industrial nations and its culture and technology had spread to every corner of the globe. Whether studying in China, Russia, Brazil, India or Germany, students were likely to be using Microsoft, listening to Madonna, watching Tom Cruise, drinking Coke and eating Big Macs.

At the start of a new millennium, with a new administration taking over in Washington, there were many debates on the future direction of American foreign policy. A host of reports poured out of Congress, think tanks, and various national commissions seeking to define American external interests and priorities. A central theme of this debate was whether the US should use its extraordinary power only to protect vital American interests, about which there was no consensus, or whether it should play a wider role in the world. In general, those on the left argued that values (e.g. promotion of democracy, protection of human rights) were vital to American interests while those on the right were more skeptical of a values approach to foreign policy. Strangely, at this unique historical moment, there was very little discussion about the external spending priorities of the US nor about the most appropriate instruments the US should be using and developing to maintain its global position. Neither was there any substantive discussion on the kind of image that the US projected abroad. This changed, however, in the aftermath of the 11 September 2001 terrorist attacks on New York and Washington.

The divisions between and within political parties on foreign policy reflected a lack of consensus on what role the US should seek to play in the post-Cold War world. These differences, however, are not new. To some extent they were masked by the largely bipartisan foreign policy approach during the Cold War but divisions over foreign policy have been the norm throughout American history. A brief survey is revealing of such differences.

The reluctant internationalist

The US was not always keen to play a global role. After gaining its independence from Britain, the US sought to limit its involvement in international affairs and avoid competition with foreign powers. In particular, a clear majority of the Founding

Fathers of the new republic insisted that America should avoid involvement in the political intrigues and power rivalries of Europe. (One can imagine how shocked they would be today to learn of the global involvement of the US from Afghanistan to Argentina, from Kosovo to Korea.) In his farewell address in 1796, President George Washington set out guidelines for American foreign policy that found widespread approval. "The great rule of conduct for us in regard to foreign nations is in extending our commercial relations but to have with them as little political connections as possible. It is our true policy to steer clear of permanent alliances with any portion of the foreign world."

This policy of non-entanglement or isolationism from other countries thus has a long historical tradition. Apart from broad agreement on isolationism, there was no consensus among the Founding Fathers as to what principles should guide US foreign policy. Indeed the differences between the idealists and realists led to rival ideological camps that persist to this day. In the idealist camp were the likes of Thomas Paine and Thomas Jefferson, who believed that the new nation could and should make a sharp break with the past and conduct a foreign policy guided by law and reason, not power politics. Jefferson claimed that power and force had been legitimate principles in the past, but that in the new era of democracy and law, relations between nations should be guided by a code of morality.

Representing the realist camp, Alexander Hamilton and John Jay took a quite different perspective. Hamilton attacked the notion that increased trade would lead to perpetual peace. Jay went further in arguing that nations in general would make war whenever they had a prospect of gaining an advantage. As far as Hamilton and Jay were concerned, America would have to be guided by sober national interest just like any other country. Although the US would be sympathetic to other countries seeking freedom, democracy, and independence, its early leaders agreed that it should not become involved directly in such struggles (Kramnick 1987). In the words of Secretary of State, John Quincy Adams, America does not go abroad "in search of monsters to destroy. She will recommend the general cause (of freedom and independence) by the countenance of her voice, and by the benign sympathy of her example" (LaFeber 1965). Adams's words were interpreted as applying to territory outside North America because, in the first half of the nineteenth century, the US was engaged in a military campaign to conquer the western territories from native Americans and Mexico. In another pronouncement that was a mixture of idealism and realism, the US let it be known that it would not welcome any outside interference in the western hemisphere, a policy statement made by President Monroe in 1823 that later became known as the "Monroe Doctrine."

Developing a foreign policy for the new republic entailed reconciling not just the divide between idealists and realists, but also the competing interests of the country's different regions. Northerners were interested in developing an industrial base and therefore sought tariffs (taxes on imports) to protect their manufactured goods. Southerners depended heavily upon the export of cotton and other crops and thus opposed the protective tariffs sought by the north. In addition to divergent foreign trade policy priorities of the north and south, there were also fundamental social and cultural differences (e.g. over the issue of slavery) that culminated in the Civil War of 1861–5. In the aftermath of the Civil War, in which over half a million Americans lost their lives, the US concentrated on re-building the devastated south, expanding its economy, and healing social divisions. But as the turn of the century approached, the US began to flex its muscles. It started to construct a formidable navy and simultaneously began to push its weight around in the Caribbean and Pacific. In 1898 it provoked a conflict with Spain over Cuba and then in the same year proceeded to establish colonial rule in Puerto Rico, Hawaii, Guam, and the Philippines.

The reasons for this change in policy were complex. For some Americans, it was simply time for their country to enjoy the fruits of being a great power. The US had developed a strong economy; it should therefore have an international voice commensurate with its new status. Others argued that the US was "a nation apart" and had a "manifest destiny," which involved a moral mission to promote liberty and democracy around the world, and to protect Latin America from European imperialism. According to one historian, many influential Americans of the time simply liked

> the smell of empire and felt an urge to range themselves among the colonial powers of the time, to see our flag flying on distant tropical isles, to feel the thrill of foreign adventure and authority, to bask in the sunshine of recognition as one of the great imperial powers of the world.
>
> (Kennan 1984: 17)

The increased power of the federal government after the upheaval of the Civil War also played a role. National leaders were able to allocate more resources to support the military, a necessary buttress to a more assertive foreign policy (Zakaria 1998). Throughout the nineteenth century the US continued to proclaim that its ideas were universal but did little to export them to other countries. This would change in the twentieth century. President Theodore Roosevelt was the first occupant of the White House to acknowledge the importance of the balance of power and a keen proponent of a more robust American approach to world affairs. During his presidency (1905–09), the US intervened in Haiti (as it would do at the end of the twentieth century) and helped Panama secede from Colombia, thus paving the way for the Panama Canal to be completed. In a first effort at global mediation, in 1905, Roosevelt invited representatives from Japan and Russia to sign a peace treaty, the Treaty of Portsmouth, in the US.

The two world wars

If Theodore Roosevelt was a "realist" in foreign policy, President Woodrow Wilson was more of an "idealist." With the outbreak of the First World War, involving initially Britain, France, and Russia on one side and Germany and Austria-Hungary on the other, Wilson's initial response was to remain neutral. Public opinion strongly opposed entry into what many Americans viewed as a European civil war and there was solid support for the President's policy of neutrality. After German submarines began sinking American merchant ships, however, Wilson's strategy proved untenable, not least because the war threatened to do serious harm to the US economy by shutting down transatlantic trade. The President did not, however, seek to win support for the war by appealing to American national interests. Rather he sold the war to the American public in idealist terms, speaking of the US "making the world safe for democracy." America was unlike other powers pursuing narrow national interests. Wilson saw the war as an opportunity "to end the failed balance of power system and replace it with a community of power and an organized peace."

At the President's urging, Congress declared war on Germany in April 1917, and the US was thereafter directly involved in just the type of conflict it had avoided successfully since the founding of the republic. Given American military and economic resources, the US intervention in the war was to prove decisive. Once an allied victory appeared inevitable, Wilson devoted his presidency to negotiating the Versailles peace treaty and designing the League of Nations, the organization that he hoped would ensure America's permanent involvement in safeguarding global stability. The debate on America's participation in the League was revealing of attitudes toward a wider US international engagement.

Wilson made much of America's idealist traditions setting out in 1918 "fourteen points" or principles that should guide US policy. These included a call for open diplomacy, self-determination, general disarmament, and the abandonment of the balance of power principle in favor of a system of collective security. His opponents argued that the US should look after its own interests and not become involved in settling disputes around the world. Despite his huge personal efforts Wilson was unable to convince the Senate, or a majority of Americans, that they should become permanently involved in world affairs through the League of Nations. His unwillingness to compromise on the treaty's provisions, as some senators demanded, was also a serious error. Many senators were opposed to the automatic and binding provisions of the treaty. The Senate's rejection of the treaty in 1919 by fifty-five votes to thirty-five not only dealt a fatal blow to Wilson's hopes but also revealed the country's doubts about becoming a global power (Cooper 2001). Warren Harding, who won the 1920 presidential election, campaigned on an "America First" slogan and rejected Wilson's view that the US should play a prominent internationalist role in foreign and security policy. The interwar years saw the US retreat into an isolationist and protectionist stance. America largely turned its back on the world and raised tariffs to protect its own industries from foreign competition.

Twenty-five years after rejecting the League of Nations, the US Senate ratified almost without objection (89–2 votes) America's entry into another global collective security organization, the United Nations (UN). This striking turnaround in American policy was the product of years of careful planning and shrewd political maneuvering by President Franklin Roosevelt to build domestic support for America's participation in a postwar security system. The US had again remained neutral at the onset of the Second World War but Roosevelt made clear his sympathy for Britain and its allies fighting against Nazi Germany. It was not until the Japanese bombing of Pearl Harbor in December 1941, however, that the US was able to join the hostilities. Surprisingly it was Hitler that declared war on the US and thus made his own defeat inevitable. As in the First World War, American intervention was to prove the decisive factor in securing an allied victory with American forces fighting in Europe, North Africa, and the Far East. In the latter war theater, the US dropped two atomic bombs on the cities of Hiroshima and Nagasaki in 1945, thus ensuring Japan's defeat. For some, the use of nuclear weapons was more designed to demonstrate American power to Joseph Stalin, the Soviet leader, rather than a device to end the war with Japan (Alperovitz 1994).

President Franklin Roosevelt was determined not to make the same mistake as Wilson in 1919. From late 1943 until the end of the war, the administration carefully mapped out detailed plans for the UN, involving a restricted Security Council of the major powers and an American veto, while working to strengthen the bipartisan consensus supporting US participation. The President's clever political and public relations campaign resulted in overwhelming public and congressional support for American participation in the UN. Support for US engagement was helped by the fact that America had become such a dominant political, military, and economic force in the world. By the end of 1945, and largely as a result of the economic stimulus provided by the war, the US was by far the wealthiest nation in the world with more than half the world's productive capacity. In global affairs, most nations now looked to Washington first, with other capitals such as London and Paris a distant second.

The Cold War

After a century and a half, the US had finally committed itself to play a continuing role on the world stage. But now it was faced with the challenge of communist expansion. As the Soviet Red Army moved toward Berlin in the spring of 1945, it liberated Eastern Europe from the Nazis and became the dominant power factor in the region. The Soviet Union had borne the brunt of the fighting and the losses (20 million) during the Second World War. Given the extent of these losses and the fact that Poland was the traditional invasion route to Russia, Stalin had no intention of allowing Western-style democracy to take root in Poland, Czechoslovakia, or anywhere else under his control, lest these countries adopt an anti-Soviet stance. Partly as a result of Winston Churchill's warning in 1946 of an "Iron Curtain" descending in the middle of the European continent, the US became increasingly concerned at the prospect of a communist takeover in Western Europe as well as Eastern Europe. These rival views about the future of Europe led to a confrontation between the US, which was in the midst of a massive demobilization of its armed forces, and the Soviet Union, which had maintained its huge army, and which would also soon possess the atomic bomb. This confrontation, known as the Cold War, led to an unprecedented arms race between the US and the Soviet Union that would lead to a fundamental change in American foreign policy.

In 1947, the *Foreign Affairs* journal published a famous article signed by "X" (a pseudonym for an American diplomat, George Kennan) that put forward the idea that the US should pursue a patient, but firm, long-term policy of containment of Soviet power. The containment strategy was also designed to destroy Soviet communism over time, by isolating it and exposing its economic and social weaknesses.

President Harry Truman, who recognized the need to build on the new consensus that Roosevelt had created in order to secure domestic support to oppose communism, took up the containment idea. In a speech to a joint session of Congress on 12 March 1947, the President laid down the policy that became known as the "Truman Doctrine."

> It must be the policy of the United States to support free peoples who are resisting attempted subjugation by armed minorities or by outside pressures. The free peoples of the world look to us for support in maintaining their freedoms ... if we falter in our leadership, we may endanger the peace of the world – and we shall surely endanger the welfare of our nation.

This was a blanket commitment by the American President that would define US foreign policy for the next forty-five years. For the first time in its history, the US had chosen to intervene in peacetime outside the Americas. In May 1947, Congress approved $400 million in assistance for Greece and Turkey, the two countries perceived as most threatened by communism. The following month, Secretary of State, George Marshall, announced that the US was also ready to supply Western Europe with economic and financial assistance (the Marshall Plan) in order to help economic recovery and thus stave off the communist threat. American aid had also been offered to the Soviet Union and Eastern Europe but Stalin had rejected the offer. The US also moved decisively away from its protectionist trade policies of the inter-war years and helped to establish international organizations aimed at promoting free trade.

In July 1947, Congress passed the National Security Act, which provided for a single Department of Defense to replace the three independent services and established the Joint Chiefs of Staff. The act also created the National Security Council (NSC) to advise the President, and set up the Central Intelligence Agency (CIA) to gather information and to collate and evaluate intelligence activities around the world. Truman further extended US commitments with the creation of the North Atlantic Treaty Organization (NATO) in 1949, and sent troops to fight in the Korean War in 1950. The US was able to gain UNSC approval to repel the communist, North Korean invasion of South Korea as the Soviet Union was then boycotting UN meetings. Truman worked closely with the Republican chair of the Senate Foreign Relations Committee (SFRC), Arthur Vandenberg, to secure bipartisan support for his radical new departure in foreign policy (Acheson 1969). The President's achievements were quite remarkable. When Truman became President in 1945 he led a nation anxious to return to peacetime pursuits and non-involvement in global affairs. When he left office eight years later, his legacy was an American presence on every continent, an unprecedented number of alliance commitments, and an enormously expanded armaments industry. (The basis for the militarization of US external policy can be found in NSC 68, a famous memorandum of April 1950, stressing the importance of a strong global military posture.)

The Cold War dominated American foreign policy for the next four decades. Leaders of both parties supported the containment strategy and a special American leadership role in world affairs. Speaking at his inauguration in January 1961, President John F.

Kennedy stated that the US "would pay any price and bear any burden, meet any hardship, support any friend, oppose any foes" to keep the world free from communism. President Jimmy Carter reiterated Wilsonian idealism in proclaiming that the US "ought to be a beacon for nations who search for peace, freedom, individual liberty and basic human rights." His successor, Ronald Reagan, was equally eloquent, asserting that "the US was by destiny rather than choice the watchman on the walls of world freedom."

After 1947, opposition to communism thus became the guiding principle of American foreign policy and although there were substantial differences over the conduct of the Vietnam War, there was no serious opposition to the containment strategy that the US followed from the late 1940s until the end of the 1980s. During this period, the US developed into a global superpower, unlike any other in history. It established over 200 military bases around the world and committed several hundred thousand troops overseas to defend both Europe and Asia. It also engaged in a public relations and clandestine battle with the Soviet Union for the hearts and minds of the Third World, spending huge sums in the process. The defense and intelligence agencies expanded enormously and became important players in the formulation as well as the execution of US foreign policy (Ambrose and Brinkley 1997; Andrew 1995). They also had a major impact on domestic policy, not least because of the numbers they employed.

Case study: the Vietnam War

The Vietnam War (1964–73) was a traumatic event for the US with a divided nation losing more than 48,000 dead and 300,000 wounded. The US only intervened after the former colonial master in Vietnam, France, pulled out in 1954 after losing the battle of Dien Bien Phu to the northern, communist, national liberation army (NLA). In 1955 it was agreed at an international conference in Geneva to divide Vietnam into a communist-controlled north and a "free" south Vietnam. After a few years of uneasy truce, the communist guerrilla movement in the south (the Vietcong as the Americans called them) became more active, winning support and controlling large swathes of the countryside. Presidents Kennedy and Johnson increased the number of US troops in Vietnam in the hope that, together with the South Vietnamese army, they could defeat the charismatic North Vietnamese leader, Ho Chi Minh, the NLA, and the Vietcong, thus preventing a communist takeover not only of South Vietnam but all of Southeast Asia. American strategists contended that if South Vietnam fell to communism, then other countries would fall like "dominoes."

As American casualties mounted during the late 1960s, without any sign that the US was winning the war, there were massive student protests around the US. The domestic turmoil did not help President Johnson who, after a poor performance in the New Hampshire primary, announced that he would not seek re-election in the 1968 presidential election. Richard Nixon won the election narrowly on a pledge to end the war (Nixon 1981). He sent his national security adviser, Henry Kissinger, to negotiate a peace agreement with North Vietnam, while simultaneously and secretly widening the war to neighboring Cambodia. As the peace negotiations dragged on for several years, the bitter fighting continued with consequent widespread domestic opposition to the war in the US. Eventually a ceasefire agreement was signed that permitted all American forces to leave Vietnam in January 1973. Two years later, with President Nixon having in the meantime resigned in disgrace over a domestic political scandal (the Watergate affair that involved concealing a break-in at Democratic party offices), the war finally ended with the fall of Saigon resulting in victory for the North.

The fall of Saigon signified an ignominious American defeat that left scars for more than a generation. It showed that massive protests could bring about a change of policy although some argue that the protests actually lengthened the war as they inhibited American leaders from using all means (nuclear weapons, invading North Vietnam) that might have won the war (Garfinkle 1995). It also showed the influence of the media as Vietnam was the first television war. Democrats and Republicans alike bore responsibility for the failure to understand that the National Liberation Front had wide appeal in the south and that military force alone could neither subdue nor win the minds and hearts of the population. The US bombing of Vietnam and associated atrocities brought widespread condemnation around the world and caused considerable, lasting harm to America's image abroad. At home, the term "Vietnam syndrome" entered the vocabulary, meaning that the US should never again engage in military conflict far from home without clear, viable, political objectives, public support and an exit strategy for the military.

There were various stages of the Cold War that resulted in periods of high tension and periods of détente between the US and the Soviet Union. One of the most dangerous periods was the "thirteen days" of the Cuban missile crisis in 1962 when President Kennedy faced down the Soviet leader, Nikita Khrushchev, over the issue of Soviet missiles being installed in communist Cuba (R. Kennedy 1966; Allison and Zelikow 1999). One of the most significant periods of détente was during Richard Nixon's presidency when the US engaged in several rounds of arms control negotiations with the Soviet Union (Kissinger 1979). The Soviet invasion of Afghanistan in 1979 gave rise to a further period of confrontation with the US supporting groups in Afghanistan fighting to restore the country's independence. (This policy would later come back to haunt the US as it armed the Mujaheddin resistance whose numbers included Osama bin Laden. When the Soviet Union pulled out in 1989, the US did not provide any significant economic assistance to Afghanistan and it dissolved into semi-anarchy allowing the Taliban to take control.) There was also renewed tension in Europe leading to the installation of short- and intermediate-range nuclear weapons on both sides of the Iron Curtain and the US and the Soviet Union boycotting the respective Olympic Games in Moscow in 1980 and Los Angeles in 1984.

In 1985, however, the accession to power in Moscow of Mikhail Gorbachev opened the prospect for an end to the Cold War. He withdrew Soviet forces from Afghanistan; stated that Moscow would not use the Red Army to support communist governments in Eastern Europe; and his policies of *glasnost* (openness) and *perestroika* (economic reform) led to fundamental changes in the Soviet Union. President Reagan, who branded the Soviet Union "the evil empire," also contributed to the collapse of the Soviet system by being ready to launch a new space arms race (star wars), something he knew that the bankrupt Soviet economy could not afford (LaFeber 2002). Strangely, the US was not directly involved in any of the seminal events that led to the end of the Cold War, the fall of the Berlin Wall in November 1989, the "velvet revolutions" in Eastern Europe, and the collapse of the Soviet system in 1990–1. The end of the Cold War was a demonstration of the new-found importance of "people power." Indeed the US, and its huge, expensive intelligence agencies, had failed to predict the sudden collapse of communism. It was rather a stunned Washington that surveyed the new post-Cold War world, free from the Soviet threat (Beschloss and Talbott 1993).

Many wondered how the US would react after it was suddenly deprived of the enemy that had dominated US foreign policy thinking and structures for over forty years. Perhaps because the collapse of communism came so quickly, and perhaps because President George H. W. Bush was such an establishment figure, there was no questioning of the continuing rationale for the Cold War national security structures that had been established back in 1947. There were no substantial changes either to the military or to the intelligence services. There was no re-organization of the NSC, the State Department, and other executive branch agencies. Nor was there any real pressure from Congress or the public to do so. According to one member of the Bush administration, "there were too many vested interests in maintaining the status quo." Even the think tanks found it difficult to adjust to the new world that was no longer black and white but different shades of gray. The US had established a small army of Cold War specialists, Russian linguists, Red Army analysts, nuclear deterrence theorists, professors of communism, agents and double-agents. They had devoted their life to the Cold War. What would they do now?

Conclusion

The US moved from being a British colony to being a major international actor in less than a century. After a further fifty years in which the US played a decisive role in securing allied victories in two world wars, the new republic was the number one power in the world. Unlike post-1918, when it turned its back on the world, the US became actively engaged in world politics after 1945. It became the principal opponent of communism, engaged in a continuing ideological battle with the Soviet Union (and communist China), and built up a massive national security apparatus to deal with the threat. With the collapse of the Soviet Union in 1991, the US had clearly won the Cold War. But could it change the mindset developed during these four decades? What kind of world would await the sole remaining superpower? Would the end of the Soviet threat usher in a "new world order" or would the end of bipolarity lead to more conflict in the world? Throughout its history, the US had veered between isolationism and inter-nationalism, between idealism and realism, between protectionism and free trade. How would it respond to the challenges of the post-Cold War world, especially terrorism?

Selected further reading

Kramnick (1987) *The Federalist Papers* provides a good overview of the debates between the Founding Fathers of the republic. Cooper (2001) *Breaking the Heart of the World* examines Woodrow Wilson's fight for the League of Nations treaty. LaFeber (2002) *America, Russia and the Cold War* offers a detailed account of superpower rivalry. Halberstam (1983) *The Best and the Brightest* provides an excellent analysis of the motives behind US involvement in Vietnam. The inside story of the end of the Cold War is recounted in Beschloss and Talbott (1993) *At the Highest Level* and Bush and Scowcroft (1998) *A World Transformed*. Ambrose and Brinkley (1997) sketch out America's growing power in *Rise to Globalism* as does Brown (1994) in *The Faces of Power*. The uncertainties surrounding US foreign policy at the end of the Cold War are considered in Scott (1998) *After the End* and in Oye, Lieber, and Rothchild (1992) *Eagle in a New World*. The various works of Henry Kissinger offer a detailed, if partial, view of US foreign policy in the 1970s and 1980s.

For an introduction to the basic concepts of international relations theory see the texts by Art, Booth, Doyle, Nye, Viotti and Kauppi, Weber, and Waltz, listed in the bibliography.

2

The post-Cold War years

Key facts

- The end of the Cold War led to renewed questioning of the US global role and in particular its involvement in peacekeeping and humanitarian interventions (Somalia, Rwanda, Kosovo) and in nation building. However, there was little real national debate on foreign policy interests and priorities.
- The US responded to the Iraqi invasion of Kuwait by massing a huge military force for "Operation Desert Storm." In the wake of a rapid Gulf War victory, President Bush's optimism about a "new world order" was short-lived as the US struggled to deal with conflicts in the Balkans and elsewhere.
- President Clinton's priorities were expanding democracy, free markets, and preparing the US for the challenges of globalization. His emphasis on multilateral institutions should not hide the fact that his administration was also prepared to go it alone on many issues. Republican control of Congress from 1995 onwards made life difficult for Clinton.
- George W. Bush appointed an experienced team to run foreign policy. He began by rejecting many of Clinton's policies and adopted mainly a unilateralist approach during his first term in office. Several international treaties were rejected and "new realism" was proclaimed as the guiding principle.
- The September 2001 terrorist attacks led to a major change in US foreign policy. The overwhelming priority was now "the war on terrorism" and other issues were downgraded. The invasion of Iraq, supposed to herald a new era of democracy in the wider Middle East, was hugely controversial. Bush's foreign and security policy was a central issue of the 2004 presidential election.

President George H. W. Bush

The end of the Cold War did not lead to any rejoicing in Washington. There were no victory speeches, celebrations, or medals. A certain justified, quiet satisfaction was apparent, but President George H. W. Bush rightly held that there was no need to rub Soviet faces in the mud, particularly as there were many daunting problems to overcome, including the reunification of Germany and the Iraqi invasion of Kuwait. George H. W. Bush was the last US President to have direct experience of the Second World War. He also came to office with an excellent pedigree in foreign affairs, having been a former envoy to China and the UN as well as director of the CIA (Bush 1999). Despite his considerable experience, Bush did not find it easy to articulate what the US role should be in the post-Cold War world. One of those who did try and set down some guidelines was Francis Fukuyama. In a widely read and highly influential article (later a book), *The End of History*, Fukuyama postulated that the collapse of communism meant that liberal democracy had triumphed. Not all states were democratic or had market economies but that was their common goal. This meant the end of history in the sense of searching for the best system and the end of major wars. The Fukuyama thesis was challenged by many, including Samuel Huntington, who predicted that the new fault lines in the world would be cultural and religious leading to a "clash of civilizations" (Huntington 1996).

Even if there were to be no more major wars, there were numerous smaller wars that posed difficult choices for the US. One of the problems Bush faced was a reduced budget to buttress his foreign policy efforts. Largely as a result of the massive arms expenditure during the Reagan years (1981–9), the US had moved from being a creditor nation to being the largest debtor nation in the world. As the treasury coffers were empty, albeit not for the Pentagon, Bush could not offer the new emerging democracies in Eastern Europe anything like the Marshall Plan that had benefited Western Europe after 1945. Nearly all US assistance in the early 1990s was directed to Israel and Egypt plus the small countries of Central America.

Case study: the Gulf War

The lack of finance was also an important factor in the US response to the Iraqi invasion of Kuwait in the summer of 1990. The invasion took the US and the rest of the world by surprise. The Iraqi leader, Saddam Hussein, had made threatening noises before toward his oil-rich neighbor but nothing had happened. Iraq had also benefited from US weaponry during the 1980s and Saddam Hussein did not believe that the US would go beyond imposing sanctions on his country. President Bush, however, was not prepared to allow such naked aggression to go unpunished, especially as it would irreparably damage any prospect of a "new world order" being established. The President also argued that it was essential to protect America's vital oil interests in the region. If the Iraqi invasion of Kuwait was ignored, then neighboring Saudi Arabia, with a sixth of proven world oil reserves and a main supplier to the US, might be next in line.

Despite these arguments, there were considerable doubts in Congress as to whether the US should respond militarily as Bush wished. Many argued that the imposition of sanctions would be a sufficient response. The decisive vote in the Senate was only 52–47 in favor of using force at that time. Meanwhile, Bush had succeeded not only in securing UN approval for a military response, but also stitched together a coalition that financed the war (especially the large contributions from Japan, Germany, and Saudi Arabia). Former Secretary of State, James Baker, has described how Bush was keen to ensure that American action had the widest international support in order to disprove the impression that American foreign policy followed "a cowboy mentality" (Baker 1995). With a broad international coalition, including the Soviet Union, supporting the US, the American military, under the leadership of General Norman Schwarzkopf in the field and Colin Powell as chairman of the Joint Chiefs of Staff, was free to launch a massive attack on the Iraqi forces in February 1991. Within a matter of days, the US military, complete with the latest weaponry and aided by contingents from Britain and France, won an overwhelming victory in "Operation Desert Storm." Courtesy of CNN and the BBC, millions of television viewers around the world were able to see American cruise missiles strike targets in Baghdad and elsewhere with amazing precision.

President Bush decided to end the war when Iraqi forces retreated from Kuwait. This decision was then, and later, widely criticized as it left Saddam Hussein in power and free to persecute the minority Kurds and Shiite groups in Iraq. As a consequence of his defeat, Saddam Hussein had to accept the presence in Iraq of UN inspectors who had a mandate to search for weapons of mass destruction (WMD). The inspectors faced innumerable problems in carrying out their activities and eventually Saddam Hussein ordered them out of Iraq under the pretence that they were spying. The UN had also imposed a strict sanctions regime on Iraq and a "no-fly zone" covering the north and south of Iraq. The sanctions regime did not lead to any weakening of Saddam Hussein's grip on power but it was blamed for the deaths of many children through malnutrition and lack of medicines. The Iraqi leader used this suffering to considerable propaganda effect against the US. The no-fly zone was monitored by the US and British air forces that regularly bombed Iraqi military installations if there was a violation of the zone. This game of "cat and mouse" continued throughout the 1990s.

When George W. Bush took office there was a hardening of the US stance toward Iraq with a number of senior officials, led by Deputy Defense Secretary, Paul Wolfowitz, arguing that this Bush administration should finish what the previous Bush administration had failed to do – topple Saddam Hussein. These arguments increased in the wake of the terrorist attacks of September 2001. The opponents of this policy, led by Secretary of State Colin Powell, argued that overthrowing Saddam Hussein would be a highly risky operation involving massive American forces operating alone as the international coalition to counter terrorism (with the exception of Britain) had made clear its opposition to any invasion of Iraq. Furthermore, there was no certainty that removing Saddam Hussein would lead to a more stable or democratic Iraq (see chapter 8).

President Bush, with approval ratings topping 90 percent, was delighted at the military success in the Gulf, believed that the Vietnam syndrome had been buried in the desert sands, and considered that the world was on the verge of a new era. In his State of the Union address in January 1991, the President proclaimed

> that there was the very real prospect of a new world order in which the principles of justice and fair play protect the weak against the strong . . . a world in which freedom and respect for human rights find a home among all nations . . . a world in which the United Nations – freed from Cold War stalemate – is poised to fulfill the historic vision of its founders.

Bush rejected the idea that the US should become the world's policeman but in the wake of the Cold War, "as the only remaining superpower, it is our responsibility – it is our opportunity – to lead."

This vision of a "new world order" had echoes of Wilsonian idealism but Bush did not maintain his grandiose rhetoric for long. His administration was faced with numerous pressing problems, including the break-up of the Soviet Union, the unification of Germany (a task it managed with considerable skill), a humanitarian catastrophe in Somalia, and the tragedy of Yugoslavia. The break-up of the Soviet Union was a major headache for the US as there were around 30,000 nuclear weapons spread around the constituent republics of the former communist superpower. It became a top priority to ensure that these weapons remained under safe control. Washington helped Moscow financially to secure the return of these weapons to Russian territory and their eventual destruction.

Despite having won a spectacular victory in the Gulf War that demonstrated US military dominance, Bush was reluctant to become involved in the Balkans. 1992 was an election year and Bush, already under attack by his Democratic rival, Bill Clinton, for spending too much time on foreign policy, was not willing to commit American troops in a precarious situation. In a reference to the Yugoslav conflict, James Baker, his Secretary of State, said that the US "did not have a dog in that fight" and despite protests from some members of the administration, Washington refused to get involved in the early years of the conflict (Zimmerman 1996). Apart from the lack of an agreed policy on the Balkans, the US was also afraid of taking any action that might have a negative impact on Mikhail Gorbachev's chances of survival. Although Bush was slow in coming to trust Gorbachev, his later support for the Soviet leader dwarfed all other foreign policy considerations, including support for Ukrainian independence and readiness to intervene in Yugoslavia (Halberstam 2001). The refusal to become involved in the Balkans led some observers to suggest that the US was guilty of double standards. It was ready to act quickly and decisively when its oil interests were threatened, but not otherwise. Others criticized the new US formula for warfare that required massive firepower, followed by a speedy withdrawal from the scene of destruction, regardless of the havoc and anarchy that followed (Ambrose and Brinkley 1997: 377–8).

In dealing with the reunification of Germany, Bush displayed a sure touch. He quickly recognized the geopolitical importance of securing a united, democratic Germany in the center of Europe, and ensured that the US was in the driving seat of the four-power (US, Soviet Union, Britain and France) negotiations that dealt with German reunification. He dealt firmly with Soviet attempts to weaken the new German state, rejecting the idea that it should be neutral and not fully in NATO. He also dealt firmly with a highly skeptical British Prime Minister, Margaret Thatcher, and a reluctant French President, François Mitterrand, both of whom would have preferred to slow down and even postpone German reunification (Rice and Zelikow 1997).

The sudden collapse of communism and the swift success of "Operation Desert Storm" raised a number of questions about America's post-Cold War role. Would the US be willing to continue playing the role of world cop or sheriff? If so, would it continue to adopt a selective approach? What should be the criteria for intervention? Who would foot the bill? Surprisingly, there was little real debate among the foreign and security policy elite as to what role the US should play and whether the massive resources devoted to external affairs should be reduced. In 1991–2, Bush, supported by a powerful coalition of entrenched bureaucratic interests, arms producers and a Congress reluctant to accept military base closures, rejected calls for a substantial cut in the defense budget. Indeed the Pentagon, in a famous leaked report of 1992 entitled *Defense Policy Guidelines* and drafted by Paul Wolfowitz, argued that the US should do everything possible to maintain its sole superpower status and prevent the emergence of a rival regional or global power.

During his four years in office, President Bush managed a huge and complex agenda of difficult foreign policy issues with a sure touch. He found it difficult, however, to explain the changed international environment to the American public and did little to transform the US military and intelligence communities to deal with the changed world. Although his preoccupation with foreign policy may have cost him re-election, his defeat in 1992 ultimately led to his son occupying the White House eight years later. In the intervening years the White House was in Democratic hands under the leadership of William Jefferson Clinton, largely a novice in foreign policy, and the first truly post-Cold War President. Meanwhile Bush had presented a poisoned chalice to the new President. Africa had hardly figured during the Bush presidency but at the very end of his administration, the President agreed to send a small military force to war-torn Somalia, to support UN humanitarian assistance programs. Somalia was to become a major factor in the development of post-Cold War US foreign policy.

President Bill Clinton

Foreign policy played little or no role in the 1992 election apart from Bill Clinton's criticism of President Bush for paying too much attention to foreign as opposed to domestic policy. Clinton's informal campaign slogan was "It's the Economy – Stupid." Clinton had also sniped at the Republicans for failing to do more on the human rights front in China and in the Balkans but in reality there were no major foreign policy differences between Clinton and Bush. Perhaps as a sign of the public's lack of interest in foreign affairs, neither candidate was prepared to launch a national debate on what role the US should play in the post-Cold War world. Clinton's victory occurred when there was much speculation about America's decline. A headline in *Time* magazine on 15 October 1992 asked "is the US in an irreversible decline as the world's premier power?" In the same month the French newspaper *Le Monde* published a twelve-part series on America in eclipse. A distinguished historian wrote a best seller depicting the likely decline of US power (Kennedy 1993). Americans were worried about the economic challenge from Japan. The glory of the Gulf War had faded fast and brought no lasting political benefits to George H. W. Bush.

As a former governor (like Carter, Reagan and George W. Bush), Clinton had no foreign policy experience when he took office in January 1993. He made clear that domestic issues would have priority and appointed a foreign policy team (Anthony Lake as his national security adviser, Warren Christopher as Secretary of State) with clear instructions to keep foreign policy problems away from his desk. One public relations adviser, who served both Republican and Democrat Presidents, estimated that Clinton spent less than 25 percent of his time on foreign affairs, unlike Bush who had spent 75 percent of his time on foreign policy (Gergen 2002). When Clinton assumed office, however, the US faced no serious threats and there was no domestic pressure on the new President to take a more active role in foreign policy. There were, however, numerous foreign policy challenges awaiting Clinton, including the spreading conflict in the Balkans, the economic collapse in Russia, the breakdown of law and order in Haiti, several "rogue states" attempting to develop weapons of mass destruction and rising tension in the Middle East.

Clinton seemed to recognize that he was heading into uncharted waters. In his inaugural address in January 1993 he stated that "not since the late 1940s has our nation faced the challenge of shaping an entirely new foreign policy for a world that has fundamentally changed." The President promised "bold new thinking" and a bipartisan approach in foreign policy. A few weeks later, speaking at the American University on 26 February, Clinton elaborated on these challenges and introduced globalization and cyberspace as two central features of his foreign policy. The President said that his priorities would be:

- to restore the American economy to good health, "an essential prerequisite for foreign policy";
- to increase the importance attached to trade and open markets for American business;
- to demonstrate US leadership in the global economy;
- to help the developing countries grow faster;
- to promote democracy in Russia and elsewhere.

The President acknowledged that there were other challenges.

> The dangers we face are less stark and more diffuse than those of the Cold War, but they are still formidable – the ethnic conflicts that drive millions from their homes; the despots ready to repress their own people or conquer their neighbors; the proliferation of weapons of mass destruction.

Clinton added drugs, crime, AIDS and the environment for good measure.

Clinton's principal advisers reiterated these priorities in all their speeches. The administration's three primary policy objectives were promoting democracy, promoting prosperity, and enhancing security. Enlargement of the world's "free communities of market democracies" was the stated rationale for the Clinton administration's global posture. Given the fragility of emerging markets and democracies in Russia, Asia, and Latin America, especially during the late 1990s, the theme lost some of its appeal, only to make a strong comeback toward the end of the Clinton presidency. In two speeches, at Nebraska on 8 December 2000 and Warwick, in England, on 14 December 2000, Clinton sought to claim a mantle of "progressive internationalist pragmatist" for his foreign policy legacy.

The President's apparent lack of interest in foreign affairs caused some apprehension with America's allies in Europe and Asia. To Asians, Clinton seemed preoccupied with NATO and Russia. To Europeans, however, Clinton seemed obsessed with correcting trade imbalances and opening markets in Asia. Despite his emphasis on domestic policy, Clinton soon found that there was no escape from the world outside. The new President could hardly have been confronted with three more difficult issues during his first months in office than Haiti, Somalia, and the Balkans, problems that he inherited from Bush. The basic dilemma Clinton faced in all three cases was whether or not the US should intervene militarily to redress worsening humanitarian situations.

With Haiti, Clinton faced a breakdown in law and order, after the ousting from power of the democratically elected President Aristide by General Raoul Cedras. Apart from some interest by the Black Caucus (black members of Congress), there was no significant American domestic constituency interested in Haiti. What prompted Clinton to intervene was the prospect of thousands of refugees seeking shelter and a permanent home in the US as a result of the violence on the island. The first attempt at landing a small military force in October 1993 was foiled by an unruly mob which led one historian to comment that "rarely had the US looked so impotent, its mighty military driven away from a banana republic by a pip-squeak dictator and a hired mob" (Halberstam 2001: 271). A year later, Clinton ordered a larger invasion force to Haiti but just before the deadline for their landing, former President Jimmy Carter brokered a deal with General Cedras that allowed him to leave the island. This enabled American troops to land unopposed in order to restore order and to carry out peacekeeping duties, pending the return of Aristide. Clinton was able to proclaim a foreign policy "success" but Haiti would remain a problem country for the remainder of the decade and beyond.

Case study: the US and Somalia

The US intervention in Somalia, 1993–4, launched by one President and completed by another, had profound consequences for American foreign policy. For most of the Cold War, Somalia had sided with the Soviet Union and had been largely ignored by the US. But after the Soviet Union sided with Ethiopia against Somalia in the Ogaden War, a US–Somali rapprochement began in 1977 and culminated in a military access agreement in 1980 that permitted the US to use naval ports and airfields in exchange for military and economic aid. During the 1980s, the US viewed Somalia as a defense partner and many Somali officers were trained in America. Toward the end of the 1980s, however, Somalia disintegrated into civil war. The economy was in shambles, and hundreds of thousands of Somalis fled their homes.

During 1992 the fighting worsened and the images of homeless, starving women and children began to fill television screens, thus increasing pressure on President Bush to send American troops to Somalia. This would later be cited as a good example of "the CNN effect." A month after losing the 1992 presidential election to Clinton, Bush made a televised address to the nation officially announcing US participation in "Operation Restore Hope." The former President stated that

> our mission has a limited objective – to open the supply routes, to get the food moving, and to prepare the way for a UN peacekeeping force to keep it moving. This operation is not open-ended. We will not stay longer than is absolutely necessary.

He stated further that the US had no plans to dictate political outcomes in the war-torn East African nation.

Just days before President Bush's announcement, Smith Hempstone, the US ambassador to Kenya, cautioned in a confidential cable to his State Department superiors that the US should think "once, twice, and three times" before getting involved in Somalia. He warned that Somalis are "natural-born guerrillas who would engage in ambushes and hit-and-run attacks. They will not be able to stop the convoys from getting through. But they will inflict – and take – casualties." Referring to the ill-fated US intervention in Lebanon in 1982–3 that ultimately cost the lives of more than 260 marines, Hempstone concluded, "if you liked Beirut, you'll love Mogadishu." There was also considerable opposition within Congress to the administration's decision to send American troops into a civil war situation. The Pentagon offered assurances, however, that American forces would not get bogged down in a Somalian quagmire. Colin Powell, chairman of the Joint Chiefs of Staff, compared the US mission to having the cavalry ride to the rescue and then transferring responsibility to the "marshals" (i.e. UN peacekeepers) once the situation stabilized. The Pentagon also hoped that intervening in Somalia would ease the pressure to intervene in the much more difficult Balkans arena. In responding to the public's demand "to do something," the administration made sure that the initial military units that landed in Somalia in January 1993 were greeted by a blaze of television cameras.

There were indeed ominous similarities between the situation in Lebanon during the early 1980s and the environment in Somalia: for example, politically fractured societies with an assortment of heavily armed militias backing various factions. As in the Lebanon, the US gradually became involved in the internal politics of Somalia – with equally fatal consequences. Although the US was in Somalia under UN auspices, its forces were never under UN command. Washington was also unwilling to coordinate its political and military objectives with UN headquarters. President Clinton, however, was persuaded to move from a policy objective of supporting humanitarian assistance to one of "nation building," i.e. promoting democracy and political stability. As a result, Clinton agreed to a more robust military posture, at first with a view to disarming some of the local militias, and then capturing one noted warlord, Mohamed Farah Aideed. After a number of attacks on US forces in August 1993, Clinton ordered the elite Delta Rangers to capture Aideed. The attempt to do so, on 3 October, went horribly wrong with hundreds of Somalian casualties killed and wounded in a fierce gun battle in downtown Mogadishu. Eighteen American soldiers died, and seventy-seven were wounded. In the confusion Aideed escaped.

The urban battle and loss of American lives resulted in sharp criticism of the President and his national security team. Public attitudes also changed overnight as the naked body of a US Ranger was shown on television being dragged through the streets of Mogadishu. The President was in a difficult position. He warned "that if US troops were to leave now, we would send a message to terrorists and other potential adversaries around the world that they can change our policies by killing our people. It would be open season on Americans." At the same time he set a deadline of 31 March 1994 for a political settlement in order that US troops could be withdrawn. In hoisting a diplomatic white flag, the President sought to place the blame on the United Nations. "We cannot let a charge we got under a UN resolution to do some police work – which is essentially what it is, to arrest suspects – turn into a military mission." Republicans were highly critical of Clinton's policy. Senator Nancy Kassebaum said, "I can think of no further compounding of the tragedy that has occurred there for our forces than to have them withdraw and see what started out to be a very successful, noble mission end in chaos." Congressman Dellums stated that "a terrible mistake was made. Rather than maintaining a neutral peacekeeping role for a famine-relief effort implemented by Bush, Clinton became enmeshed in urban combat. Cardinal rules were violated. We chose sides, and we decided who the enemies were."

The American involvement in Somalia (later turned into a film, *Black Hawk Down*) had a major impact on US foreign policy, particularly on relations with the UN and on whether or not to intervene abroad for humanitarian purposes. The Clinton administration's initial reluctance to become involved in the Balkans and its refusal to respond to the genocide in Rwanda that began in April 1994 was due in large part to its humiliating experience in Somalia. President Clinton issued a policy directive shortly after US forces left Somalia that implied a sharp curtailment of American involvement in future armed humanitarian interventions and that marked a retreat from his administration's earlier rhetoric of assertive multilateralism. The efforts by Congress to cut or restrict US contributions to UN peacekeeping were also a direct response to the perceived failures in Somalia.

Meanwhile Clinton was actively pursuing an expansive foreign policy agenda on the trade front. The President sought to increase the economic dimension of America's foreign policy and gave top priority to the negotiation of new trade deals, opening new markets for American business and encouraging Americans to take advantage of globalization. In Clinton's view, the US was like a large corporation competing in the global market place. As a sign of the increased attention the President gave to trade and economic affairs, Mickey Kantor, the US trade representative (USTR), enjoyed much better access to the President than Warren Christopher, the Secretary of State. One of the President's major successes was securing passage through Congress of the North American Free Trade Agreement (NAFTA) between the US, Canada, and Mexico that served, *inter alia*, to reduce tariffs and promote investment in and between the three countries. The NAFTA was strongly opposed by Ross Perot, the maverick businessman and presidential candidate, some right-wing Republicans, the labor unions and many of their supporters in Congress. As a result of the wide opposition within his own party, Clinton was forced to rely on Republican votes to secure passage of the agreement through Congress. The final vote in Congress on 17 November 1993 was 234–200 in favor of NAFTA.

Clinton could claim a number of other successes on the international economic front. Despite widespread unease in Congress and even within his administration, Clinton swiftly recognized the importance of helping Mexico when America's neighbor faced a major financial crisis in 1994. As one writer put it, "Mexico was the test for what became the signature change in American foreign policy" (David Sanger, *Washington Post*, 28 December 2000). Apart from leading the rescue of Mexico after its financial crisis and securing passage of NAFTA through Congress, Clinton oversaw the completion of the Uruguay Round of trade negotiations, moved China closer toward membership of the World Trade Organization (WTO), negotiated new trade deals for African and Caribbean States, and supported debt relief for poor countries.

Clinton's supporters would also claim many other achievements for his presidency. On the European front, the President had upgraded relations with the EU, re-vitalized, adapted and expanded NATO, and led the alliance in military operations to end the killing in Bosnia and Kosovo. In Asia, the President had reduced the North Korean threat through a mixture of deterrence and diplomacy and helped bring China into the global mainstream. As regards Russia, Clinton had supported its transition to a market economy and its membership of the G8 and the Asia-Pacific Economic Cooperation forum (APEC), and helped it establish a new relationship with NATO. Clinton also helped secure the removal of nuclear weapons from Ukraine, Belarus, and Kazakhstan.

Clinton also made major efforts to promote peace in the Middle East, the Balkans, Northern Ireland, the Andes (border dispute between Peru and Ecuador), East Africa as well as tackling a host of new international issues (see A *National Strategy for a Global Age*, published by the White House in December 2000). Sandy Berger provided a robust defense of the Clinton record just before the 2000 presidential election. The President's national security adviser contrasted the concerns about America's place in the world in 1992 with the situation in 2000 when the US

> was not only the unrivalled military and economic power in the world, but was also a catalyst of coalitions, a broker of peace and a guarantor of financial stability. Furthermore, the US was widely seen as the country best placed to benefit from globalization.
> (Berger, *Foreign Affairs*, November/December 2000)

Many critics, however, saw Clinton's foreign policy as lacking in strategic focus and essentially reactive. Former Secretary of State, Henry Kissinger, charged the President with intermittent attention to foreign affairs and pursuing "band aid diplomacy." Republican Senator John McCain complained that Clinton had no conceptual vision for US foreign policy (but failed to produce one himself). Clinton was also criticized for having "lost" Russia, for policy inconsistencies toward China and excessive demonization of foreign leaders such as Iraq's Saddam Hussein and Yugoslavia's Slobodan Milosevic. One critic alleged that Clinton "stumbled from crisis to crisis, trying to figure out what was popular, what would be effective, and what choices would pose the lowest risk to his presidency, and, especially, to his reputation." The same critic alleged that Clinton delegated too much to his subordinates who hijacked his foreign policy in the name of "neo-Wilsonian internationalism" that led to a series of failures and disasters. Clinton had missed a "magnificent historical opportunity to mold a new international order" (Hyland 1999: 203–4).

At a Brookings Institute seminar in December 2001 to review the Clinton presidency, Jonathan Clarke of the Cato Institute gave Clinton "a less than stellar grade," arguing that at the end of the Cold War there was an enormous opportunity to build a new relationship with Russia, restructure US security policy with Europe and East Asia to reduce America's burdens and exposure and revisit the troubled relationships with Cuba, Vietnam, and North Korea. Instead of seizing the opportunity "we were given an alternating diet of overheated rhetoric, inattention, and, if the going got tough, bombs. Against this background, the record is acutely disappointing" (Clarke 2000). Yet another critic alleged that although the Clinton team succeeded in blending realism and idealism in practice, it never articulated a set of guiding principles that could serve as the conceptual foundation for their actions. Without such conceptual coherence, "the whole of Clinton's foreign policy ended up being much less than the sum of the parts." Furthermore, precisely because Clinton failed to arm himself with a clear set of guiding strategic principles that he could impart to the electorate, "he was not able even to begin the task of laying the foundation for a new American internationalism" (Kupchan 2002).

In an interview with the author, James Steinberg, deputy national security adviser during Clinton's second term, rejected these charges, claiming that the administration worked hard to develop a new foreign policy concept based on a judicious mixture of defending American interests and support for humanitarian interventions. Clinton was in favor of working through multilateral institutions to achieve greater results. His problem was that for most of his administration he had to deal with a Congress vehemently opposed to his occupation of the White House. There were certainly a large number of Republicans in Congress who let their hatred for Clinton color their attitudes on foreign policy. This was clear from the vote to reject the Comprehensive Test Ban Treaty (CTBT), to withhold American UN dues and to micro-manage Balkan policy.

Case study: the US and the Balkans

The US was never a willing participant in the entire Balkan imbroglio of the 1990s. During the latter part of the George H. W. Bush administration, there was a marked reluctance to become involved as Yugoslavia disintegrated into civil war. Despite clear evidence that several constituent republics (Slovenia, Croatia, Bosnia-Herzegovina) wanted independence from Belgrade, the Yugoslav President, Slobodan Milosevic, was determined to maintain control of the federation by force. The Pentagon argued that vast numbers of troops would be required to engage in meaningful peace enforcement duties. It would be too much even for NATO to handle. This did not stop some, however, arguing that the EU should take care of the Balkans as it was their back yard. During the election campaign, Clinton had criticized Bush for failing to protect human rights in the Balkans, but on taking office he did not choose to pursue a more robust policy, even as the killings increased and the world watched in horror at the ethnic cleansing that was being blatantly perpetrated. In the eyes of many Europeans, the US sought to maintain the moral high ground while refusing to participate in the UN forces overseeing humanitarian aid distribution in Bosnia. In 1993, Washington effectively vetoed the EU-supported Vance–Owen peace plan (drawn up by former US Secretary of State, Cyrus Vance, and former British Foreign Secretary, David Owen) that would have ended the fighting. The US vetoed the plan because it would have meant accepting a re-drawing of state boundaries as a result of force. Both these actions angered their European partners and transatlantic relations were severely strained during 1993–5.

Eventually Slobodan Milosevic overreached himself in February 1994 when the Yugoslav army killed nearly seventy Bosnian civilians in the marketplace in Sarajevo. This prompted a diplomatic mission by Richard Holbrooke, a senior US ambassador and renowned troubleshooter, to try and dissuade Milosevic from further aggression. When this failed, Clinton authorized US air strikes on Yugoslav targets (opposed by many congressmen as overstepping presidential authority) that eventually led Milosevic to agree to peace talks with the other parties (Croats and Bosnians) at the Dayton air force base in Ohio. The negotiations were an opportunity for Holbrooke to show his diplomatic skills and press the warring parties to sign the Dayton agreement. To most observers, the Dayton agreement was very much along the same lines as the Vance–Owen plan of 1993 but meanwhile two years had been lost and thousands more had died (Owen 1995; Holbrooke 1998).

Although the Dayton accords brought peace to the central Balkans, there was one noticeable piece of unfinished business – Kosovo, a province of Yugoslavia that had enjoyed considerable autonomy before Milosevic came to power. Its population was very largely Albanian and desired independence from the rest of Yugoslavia. Milosevic rescinded Kosovo's autonomy and attempted to quell rising civil disobedience with force. This led to an escalation of violence which the international community, including the US, could not ignore. Once more, Holbrooke was sent to persuade Milosevic to agree on a political settlement for Kosovo. When Milosevic refused to comply with the political agreement that had been worked out by the local parties under strong international pressure, the US again launched air strikes on Yugoslav targets. It was several weeks before Milosevic capitulated with much of Yugoslavia's infrastructure in ruins. The Kosovo campaign was nominally under NATO control but the US military commander chafed at the interference of political leaders and NATO lawyers (Clark 2001). This negative experience would later influence US attitudes during the Afghan War when NATO political support was welcomed but the alliance was not asked to participate in any military operations.

Following Yugoslavia's capitulation, the Clinton administration argued that the US had achieved all its overriding objectives in Kosovo. It had forced Milosevic to accept NATO's terms including the return of the Kosovo-Albanian refugees while preserving alliance solidarity, avoided an irreparable break in relations with Moscow, and contained the fall-out in Beijing from the accidental bombing of the Chinese embassy in Belgrade. Other critics were less sanguine about the outcome, despite the ostensible success of the American bombing campaign (Mandelbaum 1999). In a speech at the Woodrow Wilson Center on 30 September 1999, Lee Hamilton, former chair of the HIRC, pointed to the troubling implications of exclusive reliance on an air campaign with zero tolerance of allied casualties. He said that it had been an error to forego the use of ground forces and to signal this in advance to the enemy. There had been insufficient efforts to secure the support of Moscow and Beijing. Furthermore, the NATO mandate was no substitute for an UNSC resolution authorizing intervention.

In the months following the conclusion of the Kosovo campaign, there was an unseemly row between the US and EU over peacekeeping troop levels and who should pay for the reconstruction of the province. The fact that the EU contributed over 70 percent of the troops and 80 percent of the budget for reconstruction was usually forgotten or ignored by most congressmen. Clinton had never been able to secure broad public or congressional support for American peace enforcement and peacekeeping duties in the Balkans. When George W. Bush took office, there were fears that the US would pull out completely from the Balkans but Colin Powell won the battle in Washington to ensure that American troops would stay as long as required. But as the US reacted to the terrorist attacks in September 2001 it became clear that Washington expected the EU to continue to take the lead and shoulder even more of the burden in dealing with the problems in Bosnia and the southern Balkans (Kosovo, Macedonia, and Montenegro). In December 2004 the EU took over command of the stabilization (SFOR) peacekeeping mission in Bosnia from NATO.

Clinton did not help his case, however, by becoming involved sexually with Monica Lewinsky, a White House intern. To most Americans, including the media, Kosovo was a sideshow compared to the developing sex scandal that engulfed Washington in 1998–9. As the Kosovo crisis was developing, Clinton was embroiled in an effort to save his presidency following his admittance of an affair with Monica Lewinsky. Even before the Kosovo conflict, there had been considerable apprehension in foreign capitals that the sex scandal would impair the President's ability to provide international leadership. The headline in the *Economist* of 19 September 1998, referring to Clinton, was "Just Go." Although as a result of the impeachment proceedings the President had little time to devote to foreign policy, he seemed to appreciate the opportunity of a foreign policy crisis to divert attention from the scandal. This in turn led to "wag the dog" accusations, some critics suggesting that Clinton was prepared to order military action in order to divert attention from his domestic political problems.

Notwithstanding domestic criticism for his handling of Kosovo and other foreign crises, Clinton craved a legacy as a peacemaking President. He invested a large personal stake in the Northern Ireland peace process and made Balkan stability a personal priority. His main efforts were toward the Middle East, hoping that a comprehensive settlement could be agreed during his term. In his final months, weeks, and hours in office he immersed himself in the intricacies of the Middle East peace negotiations, inviting PLO chairman Yasser Arafat and Israeli Prime Minister, Ehud Barak, to Camp David, the presidential weekend home outside Washington DC in rural Maryland. But despite the marathon sessions and the undoubted progress toward a deal it was not to be. To most Americans, Arafat was to blame for the failure to reach an agreement. The President found it hard to hide his disappointment.

Clinton thus deserves mixed marks for his conduct of US foreign policy. After a rocky start, when his focus was almost exclusively on domestic policy, he recognized that he could not simply ignore problems and hope that they would disappear. Like his predecessor, he hesitated to use military force, most notably in the early years of the Yugoslav conflict, and when he authorized such usage the top priority was to avoid American casualties. The main items on his foreign policy agenda were partly forced by events (Bosnia/Kosovo) and partly by domestic lobbies (Middle East/Ireland). Clinton upgraded the importance of trade and economics in foreign policy and arguably succeeded in his aim of promoting market democracies around the world. He was always mindful of domestic opinion and would often consult focus groups before taking decisions.

Clinton might also take some credit for keeping the US engaged globally while the public and Congress were largely uninterested in foreign affairs. In the absence of a coherent "new world order" following the dissolution of the old bipolar world, Clinton struck a reasonable balance between committing US forces and resources where vital interests were at stake, and staving off pressures to become the world's policeman. In light of his successor's policies, it should be noted that while Clinton was instinctively in favor of multilateralism, he did not shrink from unilateral action. His administration was divided on the Kyoto Protocol on greenhouse gas emissions with the result that it never reached the Senate for approval, and it was reluctant to sign up to the International Criminal Court (ICC) and the land-mines convention. Clinton only signed the ICC treaty on his last day in office. He also decided unilaterally to launch cruise missiles at Afghanistan and Sudan following the bombings of the American embassies in East Africa. His Republican critics, however, were later to accuse him of "taking his eye off the ball" when it came to the threat from Al Qaeda.

Party differences

Although foreign policy played only a small role in the 2000 presidential election campaign (unlike 2004), there was an open and often acrimonious debate in the US before and after the election as to how the world's only remaining superpower should conduct its external relations in the twenty-first century. The Senate's rejection of the CTBT in 1999, the arguments surrounding the proposed national missile defense (NMD), the ICC, and the Kyoto Protocol were testimony to American internal divisions as well as revealing of the significant differences between the US and most of its allies. According to the *Financial Times*, 15 October 1999, the rejection of the CTBT was "the clearest indication yet of the radical change in US politics and the country's view of its role in the world. Thumbing its nose at the rest of the world was not an option open to the US during its struggle with communism."

In election year 2000, two articles by Condoleezza Rice and Bob Zoellick, both of whom would figure in key posts in the George W. Bush administration, provided an opportunity for a detailed Republican critique of Clinton's foreign policy. Rice attacked Clinton's "Wilsonian multilateralism and fondness for symbolic international agreements and attachment to the illusory norms of international behavior." A Republican administration would most certainly be internationalist, but it would proceed from the firm ground of American national interest. It would embrace power without arrogance, and pursue American interests without hectoring or bluster. Rice also criticized Clinton's lack of a guiding vision, absence of any strategy, and the "devastating military cuts, the damage of which was compounded by a furious pace of overseas deployments, on average one every nine weeks." The next President would have to build a force structure for the twenty-first century – lighter, more lethal, more mobile and agile, capable of firing accurately from long distances. Military force was intended to be lethal. It was not meant to be a civilian police force, nor a political referee, and most certainly not intended to build civil society.

A Republican administration would devote more attention to its traditional allies. For Rice, the main issues in Europe were NATO enlargement and redefining NATO's structure and mission. The US welcomed a greater EU military capability as long as it strengthened NATO. Trade liberalization with China was necessary, but China was a "strategic competitor," not a partner, whose regional ambitions must be contained. US defense relations with Japan and South Korea should therefore be strengthened. The "one China" policy was wise, but Taiwan required more assurance. As regards Russia, Clinton had a blind spot about Yeltsin and corruption. The US must be resolute and decisive in dealing with rogue regimes. Deterrence required a credible threat of national obliteration in the event anyone used weapons of mass destruction (Rice, *Foreign Affairs*, January/February 2000).

Zoellick's article (in the same edition of *Foreign Affairs*) was along similar lines but emphasized more the economic dimension. He identified five key Clinton flaws – drift on trade, erosion of credibility, inability to frame strategies, uncertainty as to when and how to use power, and driven too much by polls and political calculations. The Republicans would respect power, acknowledge the importance of allies, judge international agreements as means to achieve ends, embrace globalization and recognize that there was still evil in the world.

Both these articles as well as the one major campaign speech on foreign policy made by George W. Bush, which focused heavily on the need for missile defense, signaled a more muscular, at times more truculent, tone. But stripping the rhetoric aside, the Rice and Zoellick articles were not arguing for a fundamental change in foreign policy. Their views were mainstream internationalist and anti-protectionist, far from the semi-isolationist and nationalistic views of Republican Senator Jesse Helms and other right-wing Republicans. Although the Republicans called for the overarching vision that they complained was so lacking in Clinton's administration, they were unable to articulate a vision or a concept any more compelling than the Clinton administration's efforts to cope with an untidy post-Cold War world in which the US sought to strike a balance between its global responsibilities and the risk of over-extending its reach.

Many observers, therefore, thought that Clinton's national security adviser was per-haps on target when he argued that there was generally a bipartisan consensus on American leadership.

> That doesn't mean that the consensus isn't threatened, or that there aren't com-peting visions of our role ... the duty of internationalists in both parties is not to agree on every matter of policy, but to come together around the basic principle that Americans benefit when nations coalesce to deter aggression, to resolve con-flicts, to open markets, to raise living standards, to prevent the spread of dangerous weapons, and to meet other dangers that no nation can meet alone.
>
> (Berger 2001)

A year later, however, it seemed that Berger's hopes for a bipartisan consensus on for-eign policy were in danger of being dashed. Moises Naim, editor of *Foreign Policy* magazine, echoed widespread opinion when he suggested that under George W. Bush, "no country was doing more to undermine the multilateral approach to issues of global concern" (*Washington Post*, 23 July 2001).

President George W. Bush

Like Clinton, George W. Bush had little foreign policy experience when he moved into the White House. His world views were simple and reflected the fact that he is a born-again Christian. On taking office on 20 January 2001, George W. Bush named two Afro-Americans to the most senior foreign policy positions in his administration. He appointed Condoleezza Rice as his national security adviser. She had been a staffer in the NSC during the first Bush administration and later became provost of Stanford University. She had also become a personal friend of the Bush family, spending con-siderable time at their Texas ranch tutoring George W. Bush in foreign policy. The President was widely praised for naming former general Colin Powell as Secretary of State. Powell had had an illustrious military career, serving as national security adviser under President Reagan, and ending up as chairman of the Joint Chiefs of Staff. He had also been a board member of America On Line (AOL) which gave him valuable business experience. Given his immense popularity in the country, Powell had been courted by both political parties as a potential presidential candidate. More surprisingly, Bush chose Donald Rumsfeld to be Secretary of Defense, a post he had held more than twenty years previously. Another former Secretary of Defense, Dick Cheney, became his Vice President, with an enhanced role in foreign and security policy. In the second-tier appointments there were also many experienced hands such as Richard Armitage at State, Paul Wolfowitz at Defense, Stephen Hadley at the NSC. The Republicans made much of these experienced hands dealing with foreign and security policy. Bush, a self-acknowledged amateur in foreign policy, made clear that he would normally defer to these seasoned hands but that the final decisions would be his and his alone.

To many observers it seemed as if the new administration was determined to set its foreign policy in opposition to the course charted by the Clinton administration. There was little evidence of support for multilateral institutions or global engagement. In the early months of his administration, Bush announced that there would be no continuing US engagement in the Middle East peace process (or Northern Ireland); that there would be a suspension of the talks with North Korea; that there would be no new troops sent to the Balkans (and Rumsfeld suggested that those there should leave); that the US would press ahead with national missile defense regardless of the views of others; and that the Kyoto treaty on climate change was "dead on arrival."

The *Washington Post* summed up the thrust of these unilateralist moves in its headline on 17 March 2001, "Bush Retreats from US Role as Peace Broker." Another critic suggested that in his first hundred days Bush had succeeded in antagonizing old friends and pushing potential partners into adversaries (Walter J. Clemens Jr, *Washington Post*, 20 May 2001). Morton Abramowitz, senior fellow at the Century Foundation, criticized the lack of clarity in the Bush foreign policy team which he attributed to divisions within the ranks, uncertainty about the basic orientation and skepticism about whether action and rhetoric coincide.

> It is hard to think of another administration that has done so little to explain what it wants to do in foreign policy. One day China was a "strategic competitor" and a threat to all of Asia; the next, the US had "to engage" with China and deepen its involvement in the world. Even more confusion existed toward North Korea – initially an unfit negotiating partner, and then moving to a posture of talking without preconditions. Did the administration want to remove Saddam Hussein? If so, how? Or did it want to tinker with "smart sanctions"? Did the administration want to extricate itself from all peacekeeping missions, or just some? It started off abhorring all IMF bailouts but ended up supporting them.
>
> (*Washington Post*, 11 September 2001)

Several leading figures in the Clinton administration were critical of what they considered the hasty ditching of their policies. Madeleine Albright, interviewed for an article in the *Financial Times* on 30 June 2001, said that she did not expect the new President's determination "to obliterate all that happened during Clinton's two terms."

Sandy Berger, in the same article, also criticized the excessive reliance on military power at the expense of global issues as "fundamentally misconceived."

In an interview before becoming President in January 2001, George W. Bush seemed acutely aware of the need for a country as powerful as the US to show restraint. "If we are an arrogant nation, they will resent us. If we are a humble nation, but strong, they will welcome us." Yet on the eve of his first visit to Europe in June 2001, the headlines could hardly have been worse. The European press castigated Bush for his alleged arrogant behavior and readiness to defy international opinion whether on arms control, climate change, or the death penalty. Typical headlines referred to "The Texas Executioner," "Bomber Bush," "Bush Rejects Kyoto," "US Says No to World Court" (Roger Cohen, *The New York Times*, 7 May 2001). The world had become accustomed to US participation in and general support for multilateral institutions during the Bush senior and Clinton administrations. Many world leaders, therefore, found it difficult to accept the new Republican view that international organizations often reflect "a consensus that opposes American interests or does not reflect American principles and ideas" (Senator Trent Lott, CNN, 20 June 2001).

In his initial meetings with European leaders, Bush made a favorable impression by stating that he wished to hear their views on a number of controversial issues. But as one commentator noted, "although the President says 'no' with a smile and offers consultations on nearly every issue, the conversations are aimed at conversion, not compromise" (Theo Sommer, *Die Zeit*, 20 July 2001). European critics were soon followed by further criticism from across the Atlantic. The respected veteran columnist of the *Washington Post*, Jim Hoagland, wrote on 29 July 2001 of the danger of Bush's unilateralism. "In six months the US has rejected, in aggressively stated fashion, a half-dozen important global treaties and negotiations strongly favored by the rest of the world. Bush leaves a first impression that while his government is not deliberately isolationist, it is comfortable with being isolated." Hoagland went on to criticize Bush's foreign policy as beholden to domestic interests and electoral needs. "It is hard to recall an American President who has been this open and unapologetic about mixing domestic political needs with foreign policy initiatives." This was clearly a reference to the powerful energy lobby influencing the Bush administration's response to the Kyoto Protocol on greenhouse gas emissions. In another editorial on 6 September 2001, Hoagland wrote:

> there must be a better way to win friends and influence nations than walking out of conferences, denouncing treaties or sitting on your hands while the Middle East burns. Whether by design or by failing to anticipate the cumulative impact of their actions, Bush and his foreign policy aides have created the theme of America the Absent in world affairs.

Another critic, Thomas Friedman of *The New York Times*, wrote on 8 June 2001, "there is nothing wrong with coming in and saying we're going to be tougher than the previous lot. But there is a fine line between a tougher effective foreign policy and a tougher ineffective foreign policy with no allies." In another article on 30 July 2001, the same author regretted that the US was now perceived as "a rogue state."

Many people around the world look to America as the ultimate upholder of rules and norms. But the message that we have been sending to the world lately is that we do not believe in rules, we believe in power – and we've got it and you don't.

The Bush administration's preference for unilateralism was also criticized by Democrat Tom Dashle, the Senate majority leader. "We are isolating ourselves and in so doing we are minimizing ourselves."

President Bush was stung by this sustained criticism and responded that he was "plenty capable" of conducting US foreign policy (*Washington Post*, 20 July 2001). A more detailed defense of the administration came from national security adviser, Condoleezza Rice, who countered that the Bush administration "was one hundred percent internationalist" and criticized policies under which "internationalism somehow becomes defined as signing on to bad treaties just to say that you have signed a treaty." While accepting that the rejection of the Kyoto Protocol "could have been handled better," she described the administration's policy as the "new realism" (CBS *Face the Nation*, 29 July 2001). Richard Haass, the State Department's policy planning director, also defended the administration's approach, arguing that the new policy was "*à la carte* multilateralism." The US would assess each treaty or agreement on an individual basis and decide on participation purely on national interest (speech at Nixon Center, 26 July 2001).

It was clear that Secretary of State Colin Powell was not happy with some of these initial policy stances and there was much media speculation about rifts between the State Department and the Pentagon (*Time*, 9 September 2001). But gradually the administration reversed or modified their initial policy pronouncements. This was done partly due to pressure from allies, partly due to widespread critical media coverage in the US and abroad, and partly due to recognition that there were not so many alternatives to the policies of the previous administration. For example, the new Treasury Secretary, Paul O'Neill, let it be known that he was opposed to bailouts for countries in financial distress. Yet the US participated in the IMF rescue package for Argentina in 2001. The talks with North Korea were re-started and there was a round of consultations with allies on missile defense.

The debate and criticisms of American foreign policy ceased, at least temporarily, on 11 September 2001, the day of the tragic terrorist attacks on New York and Washington. As Bush and Powell prepared to assemble an international coalition to fight terrorism, the President's father, George H. W. Bush, called for an end to unilateralism. In a speech at Boston on 14 September 2001, Bush senior said:

Just as Pearl Harbor awakened this country from the notion that we could somehow avoid the call to duty and defend freedom in Europe and Asia in World War II, so, too, should this most recent surprise attack erase the concept in some quarters that America can somehow go it alone in the fight against terrorism or in anything else for that matter.

There was little sign, however, that Bush senior's remarks were taken to heart by his son or his son's foreign policy advisers. There was no change in US views on the Kyoto

Protocol, the ICC, CTBT or other arms control treaties (see International Agreements rejected by US on p. 184). A fortnight after the attacks, Colin Powell said that the US would not let terrorism hijack American foreign policy. The US would continue to pursue a full international agenda. But it was clear that foreign policy henceforth would be conducted through a new prism. According to the President, the US would assess each country on the basis of whether it was with the US or against it in fighting international terrorism. This would lead the US into some strange alliances.

Initially there was broad international support for the President's measured response in attacking and defeating the Taliban regime in Afghanistan even though many NATO members were upset that the US declined the offer of alliance assistance. Countries such as Uzbekistan that had recently been criticized for their poor record on human rights overnight became partners in the war on terrorism. Pakistan, a country that had been condemned for joining the nuclear club, was suddenly a key ally in the search for Osama bin Laden, the leader of Al Qaeda.

During 2002 the neo-conservatives (neocons) in the Bush administration tried to establish a link between Saddam Hussein and Al Qaeda and alleged that Iraq possessed WMD that might be used by terrorists to attack the US. As the momentum for war against Iraq built up in the US there was mounting international concern. Tony Blair, a staunch Bush supporter, helped persuade the President to go to the United Nations and seek the authorization of the Security Council for any invasion of Iraq. But opposition in the UNSC, led by France, Russia and China, led to an impasse and in March 2003 President Bush decided to wait no longer and ordered the attack on Baghdad, a decision that led to a serious rift in transatlantic relations. The official war did not last long, a few weeks, but the aftermath proved vastly more complicated and difficult than the President had forecast (see chapter 8). As the problems mounted there was a steady fall in American support for the war, giving Presidential candidate, Senator John Kerry, who had supported the decision to invade Iraq, an opportunity to attack President Bush during the election campaign. Former President Clinton also attacked Bush for alienating so many friends and allies. "Our paradigm now seems to be: something terrible happened to us on 9/11, and that gives us the right to interpret all future events in a way that everyone in the world must agree with us – and if they don't they can go to hell. We cannot kill, jail or occupy all of our adversaries."

The 2004 Presidential election featured Iraq and the war on terrorism high on the agenda. Bush sought to portray himself as a wartime commander-in-chief best suited to defend America from terrorist threats and to stay the course in Iraq. Kerry made some telling criticism of the President's deception about why the US invaded Iraq and for his failure to plan for the peace. His views were supported by most foreign policy analysts but in the end Kerry lost to Bush. The world then wondered whether the second Bush administration would pursue the same foreign and security policy as before or whether it would modify its course, and if so, in what direction. Given the domestic support for Bush and in light of his personal convictions, it was doubtful that there would be any radical shift in policy. The resignation of Colin Powell and the appointment of Condoleezza Rice as Secretary of State was widely seen as confirmation of this view.

Conclusion

If one looks back at American history, it is not surprising that the US struggled to find a set of guiding principles for its foreign policy after the end of the Cold War. The differences and debates that may be observed throughout the nineteenth and twentieth centuries as regards idealism v. realism, unilateralism v. multilateralism, are still on display today and it is unlikely that they will be resolved quickly even in the aftermath of the September 2001 terrorist attacks. All three post-Cold War presidents found it difficult to articulate a new strategy for the US. All were ready to intervene overseas to protect American interests. George H. W. Bush ensured public support for the Gulf War by linking it to American oil interests. Clinton was also ready to use military force, albeit reluctantly, for a mixture of motives, including humanitarian purposes. Clinton and George W. Bush differed in their approach toward multilateral institutions but the differences narrowed somewhat in the wake of the terrorist attacks and the need to secure international support to combat the terrorist threat. George W. Bush, however, accepted the neocon thesis that American military power could resolve most foreign policy problems. The Iraq war was to demonstrate both the potency and the impotency of US military power.

Selected further reading

Zimmerman (1996) *Origins of a Catastrophe* discusses the dilemmas facing the Bush and Clinton administrations over the Balkans. For a European perspective see Bildt (1998) *Peace Journey* and Owen (1995) *Balkan Odyssey*. The political issues are covered in Daalder (1999) *Getting to Dayton* and the military issues are covered in Clark (2001) *Waging Modern War*. Clinton's presidency is assessed in Woodward (1994) *The Agenda*, Walker (1996) *The President We Deserve*, Hyland (1999) *Clinton's World: Remaking American Foreign Policy* and in articles by Berger, Chege, Clarke, Haass, Rice, Walt, and Zoellick (see bibliography). For the George W. Bush presidency there have been several critical volumes published including Brzezinski *The Choice: Global Domination or Global Leadership* (2004), Prestowitz *Rogue Nation* (2004), Halper and Clarke *America Alone: The Neo-Conservatives and the Global Order* (2004).

3

The executive branch

Key facts

- Post-Cold War, US foreign policy has become more complex involving many more domestic agencies that are often engaged in "turf wars" for influence. In the wake of the 11 September 2001 attacks a new department of Homeland Security was established.
- The President is the most important actor with the ability to set the agenda. But his influence depends as much on his political standing with Congress and the public as on the constitution. The role of the Vice President varies with each occupant and wishes of the President.
- The President relies on the NSC staff for advice and briefing. The national security adviser is one of the key figures in the US foreign policy machine and the NSC plays a vital role in coordinating bureaucratic inputs into US foreign policy.
- The State Department is constitutionally the lead agency for US foreign policy but its influence varies from issue to issue and according to the standing of the Secretary of State with the President. Its funding was sharply reduced during the 1990s.
- The Pentagon, with its enormous resources, and the various intelligence agencies, are also important actors in national security and foreign policy issues. The Pentagon assumed responsibility not only for the war on Iraq but also for the post-war reconstruction efforts.

Increasing number of actors

The US system of government is characterized by a strongly functioning separation of powers. The constitution states that power is shared between the presidency and a bicameral Congress plus a Supreme Court. In practice, power depends very much on the strengths and weaknesses of the President as well as the political and ideological balances in Congress. Before examining the powers of Congress, it is important to understand the role of the various actors within the executive branch. The complexity of US foreign policy was well illustrated at a State Department briefing on "Plan Colombia" in March 2001. Plan Colombia is the name given to the policy of the Colombian government, supported militarily and economically by the US, to tackle the problem of illegal drug production in that country. Most drugs are produced in areas of the country controlled by anti-government guerrillas. The US has a vital interest in the success of "Plan Colombia" as 80 percent of the cocaine on American streets comes from this Andean country. Although the briefing was given by officials from the State Department, the Justice Department, and USAID, officials from several other agencies, including the Federal Bureau of Investigation (FBI), the Drug Enforcement Agency (DEA), the Inland Revenue Service (IRS), the US Treasury, the US Marshal's office, the US Customs Service, the Secret Service and the US Attorneys' office, were also on hand to answer specific questions.

As American foreign policy has grown increasingly complex and distinctions between foreign and domestic policy have lessened, foreign relations are no longer solely, or even principally, the domain of the State Department. In some of the larger US embassies there may be representatives from upwards of twenty different agencies present and an increasing number of executive branch departments and agencies have international responsibilities and overseas programs. The Treasury, with its lead responsibilities toward the International Monetary Fund (IMF), was the dominant player throughout the Russian, Mexican, and Asian financial crises. The Department of Commerce promotes American exports while the Department of Agriculture looks after the particular external interests of American farmers. The USTR plays the lead role in international trade negotiations such as the Uruguay and Doha Rounds. The Environmental Agency is involved in international environmental negotiations such as the Kyoto Protocol. Since the end of the Cold War these economic branches of the government have increased their role and influence in US foreign policy.

Along with the new Department of Homeland Security, the Department of Justice and the FBI lead terrorism investigations, such as the investigation of the 11 September 2001 attacks and the Khobar Towers bombing in Saudi Arabia. The FBI also has a growing number of overseas programs and training activities, particularly in Eastern Europe and the former Soviet Union. The Defense Department often supports humanitarian assistance operations, disaster relief, and has numerous cooperation and training programs with foreign militaries. The intelligence agencies also liaise with their counterparts around the world and have a significant input into the foreign policy process. The liaison efforts increased significantly as a result of the September 2001 terrorist attacks.

There are thus many, often competing, executive branch actors engaged in the formulation of US foreign policy. Within the administration, the President, operating mainly through the NSC, the State Department, the Department of Defense and the intelligence agencies, are traditionally among the most important actors. It is useful, therefore, to look at these structures in more detail.

The President

The President is the most important actor in the foreign policy decision-making process. The famous inscription on President Truman's desk "The Buck Stops Here"

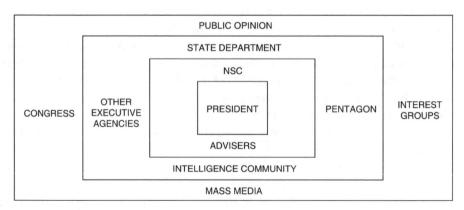

Figure 3.1. US foreign policymaking

remains true today. Foreign governments, lobbyists, ethnic groups and the media have the White House as their principal target in trying to influence American foreign policy. The President has to weigh all the political ramifications of any decision they make. For example, in the spring of 2001, the White House, under strong pressure from the energy lobby, decided not to make any effort to reach a compromise on the Kyoto Protocol on global warming. A year later the President decided to impose tariffs on imported steel to protect American steel producers. The White House knew that these decisions would cause widespread dismay abroad but it considered domestic interests should take priority.

Although Presidents rely mainly on the NSC for briefings and advice, they also listen and often take into account the views of family and close advisers. President Reagan admitted that his wife's reading of the stars influenced him. President Kennedy relied heavily on his brother, Robert, who was Attorney General, during the Cuban missile crisis. President Clinton discussed domestic and foreign policy issues with his close friend, Vernon Jordan. President George W. Bush received advice on foreign policy from his father as well as Karen Hughes and Karl Rove, his media and political advisers. All Presidents have friends in the business, labor, religious or ethnic communities that are not reticent about offering advice, particularly when their interests might be affected.

Everyone wants to meet the President, and if possible have a photograph taken with the occupant of the White House. Following each presidential election, there is a mighty scramble among foreign leaders to meet the new President and his top advisers. Similarly after the terrorist attacks of September 2001, there was a procession of world leaders to Washington to offer sympathy and support to the US. To symbolize the strong Anglo-American ties and instant British support for US military action, President Bush invited Prime Minister Tony Blair to attend his speech to the joint session of Congress on 20 September 2001. Tony Blair was also the first foreign leader to meet with President Bush after his re-election in November 2004.

The constitution makes the President commander-in-chief of the armed forces but does not allow him to declare war on his own authority, send envoys overseas without Senate approval, or raise money for foreign operations without congressional agreement. Traditionally, Americans have granted considerable latitude to their Presidents in foreign policy, compared to domestic policy. But since the Vietnam War, Congress and the public have pressed for tighter controls on the occupant of the White House. One leading authority on the presidency has even argued that unless the President exercises his informal powers of persuasion, then he may often be in a weak position to secure his goals (Neustadt 1990). As in other domains much depends on the political landscape in which the President operates as well as the personality and political skills of the President. A popular President enjoying a high reputation with a compliant Congress can achieve much more than a damaged President with a hostile Congress. An important aspect of the President's powers is his ability to set the agenda and to use the prestige of the office as a "bully pulpit" to explain and seek public support for his policies. It has been shown how President Wilson failed to persuade Congress of the merits of the League of Nations while President Roosevelt was able to win a huge majority to support US membership of the United Nations. President Clinton's problems started in 1994 when for the first time in almost fifty years the Republicans won control of both the House and the Senate, while a Democrat occupied the White House. For most of the 1998–2000 Congress, that voted to impeach the President in 1999, Clinton was the lamest of lame ducks, and the Republicans saw no reason to cooperate with him, either on foreign or domestic policy. This desire to punish the President was one important reason for the Senate's rejection of the CTBT and its unhelpful attitude on other issues such as payment of dues to the United Nations.

The qualities needed to ensure an effective presidency include the ability to communicate, persuade, and rally public support. Presidents Reagan and Clinton were clearly much better communicators than President Carter or either of the two Bush Presidents. Carter and Clinton were "hands-on" Presidents, interested in every detail of policy. Reagan and George W. Bush preferred a more laid-back approach. The Clinton White House was characterized by a certain amount of chaos both as regards meetings and timetables. The author recalls one meeting on Yugoslavia that lasted over five hours. The George W. Bush White House was a much tighter, business-like, operation, perhaps befitting the first MBA to occupy the Oval Office. A President is also more effective if he understands how to operate the system, sets clear priorities, and has a team of strong, prudent advisers. Presidents also set the tone for the administration. Jimmy Carter felt very strongly about human rights and thus pushed the issue to the top of the foreign policy agenda. Ronald Reagan felt equally strongly about the evils of communism and made its defeat his top priority. Not even the strongest President, however, has complete control over the foreign policy agenda. Presidents are constantly buffeted by unforeseen events and have to react in an increasingly reduced timeframe.

A four-year presidential term also imposes its limitations. It can take almost a year before the President's full foreign policy team is in place. Senate confirmation hearings may take months to confirm a nominee, whether as an ambassador or senior State Department official. By the summer of 2001, six months after the new Republican administration took office, the State Department had only managed to secure the confirmation of 50 percent of its senior nominees. Usually a President has more opportunity to push his agenda in the early period of his administration, although he may require some time to work himself in and to disengage from unworkable campaign promises. During the 1992 campaign, Clinton criticized Bush for "coddling dictators" in China and inaction in the Balkans. In office, Clinton pursued policies little different to Bush. In the first nine months of his administration, George W. Bush pursued quite different policies to those of his predecessor but then he too was forced to retreat. Rarely has a President been able to chalk up any foreign policy successes in his final year. If running for re-election, foreign leaders will wait until they see who wins. If leaving office, foreign leaders will want to deal with his successor. Clinton made a determined effort in the last months of his presidency to secure a Middle East peace deal but it was probably illusory to set such a tight timetable, particularly at the end of a presidency. Another observer of the presidency has stated that:

> The price we pay [for the four-year electoral cycle] is a foreign policy excessively geared to short-term calculations, in which narrow domestic political considerations often

outweigh sound strategic thinking, and where turnover in high positions is so frequent that consistency and coherence are lost.

(Wittkopf and McCormick 1999: 108)

An American President is not free to formulate and implement foreign policy to the same extent as European leaders. This is not due to Cabinet interference – indeed the Cabinet rarely meets under the American system – but rather because of a constant battle with Congress, with much depending on the political balance between Congress and the White House. Although foreign policy experience was often regarded as an important requirement for a presidential candidate during the Cold War, it became less so after 1990. President George H. W. Bush was an acknowledged foreign policy expert, but his very expertise and interest in foreign policy worked against him in the race for re-election. Al Gore had a far greater grasp of foreign policy than George W. Bush but his experience in this field made little difference to the outcome of the 2000 presidential election.

Clinton began his presidency by focusing almost exclusively on domestic issues. No President, however, can completely ignore foreign policy and Clinton, as a confirmed policy wonk, was soon able to master the intricacies of Northern Ireland, Bosnia, and the Middle East. George W. Bush was also an acknowledged amateur in foreign affairs when he took office in January 2001 but he assembled a strong team of advisers and gradually began to play a more assertive role. His preference was for a one-page memo outlining the major points rather than a detailed policy brief. One staffer told the author in spring 2001 that the President had requested a new policy toward Russia that should be on one page, contain no more than four points, and be comprehensible to a farmer from Texas.

History demonstrates that one should not rush too early into assessments on how Presidents handle foreign policy. Many Presidents in recent times have had little or no foreign policy background, particularly those with gubernatorial backgrounds, such as Reagan, Carter, and Clinton. European voices were heard complaining about Carter's plans for the neutron bomb, at Reagan's description of the Soviet Union as "the evil empire," and at Clinton's lack of decisiveness on Bosnia. By contrast, the President with the most foreign policy experience, George H. W. Bush, was unable to win re-election for a second term, despite having "won" the Cold War and the Gulf War. His son, George W. Bush, with an acknowledged lack of interest in foreign policy, nevertheless had foreign policy thrust upon him as a result of the September 2001 terrorist attacks. His response to the terrorist threat was an important element if not the defining feature of his presidency. In the 2004 election, he sought to portray himself as the military commander-in-chief most able to defend Americans from the terrorist threat. John Kerry, the Democratic challenger, and a Vietnam war hero, also attempted to sell himself to the American electorate as a military leader.

The Vice President

Traditionally Vice Presidents have played a supporting role in foreign policy with their overseas travel limited to attending the funerals of foreign leaders. Those with a strong background and interest in foreign affairs, such as George H. W. Bush under Reagan, were able to carve out a niche for themselves. In contrast, Dan Quayle, the Vice President under George H. W. Bush, was almost invisible on the foreign policy front. Clinton's Vice President, Al Gore, played a prominent role in relations with Russia through the Gore–Chernomyrdin Commission, and he was also influential in international environmental issues, an area of high personal interest.

Dick Cheney, a former Defense Secretary, enjoyed a sweeping role as Vice President under George W. Bush, involving himself in all major foreign policy decisions and building an unprecedentedly strong team of advisers. With concerns about his health he did not undertake any substantial foreign travel as his predecessors had done. But he was a prominent supporter of the neocons' views on foreign policy and very influential in encouraging the President to invade Iraq (Woodward 2004:175). Paul O'Neill, who was secretary to the Treasury and resigned from the Bush administration, alleged in his memoirs that "the real power behind the throne was Dick Cheney." Although George W. Bush encouraged this more prominent role for Cheney, no President wishes to be overshadowed by his deputy and gradually the President began to play a more prominent public role himself in foreign policy. This became unavoidable after the 11 September terrorist attacks and the importance of selling the Iraq War to the American people.

The National Security Council

The formal National Security Council comprises the President's main external relations advisers including the Vice President, the Secretaries of State and Defense, the chairman of the Joint Chiefs of Staff, the director of the CIA, and the national security adviser. It is the NSC staff, however, that provide the steady stream of briefing papers for the President. The national security adviser is the hinge between the formal NSC and the working machine. Over the past few decades, the national security adviser has often emerged as the most important foreign policy aide to the President. This role has sometimes been exercised largely outside of public view, as was the case with Brent Scowcroft, who served under Presidents Ford and George H. W. Bush, or in a more high-profile manner, as was true for Henry Kissinger, Zbigniew Brzezinski, Sandy Berger and Condoleezza (Condi) Rice.

A piano-playing child prodigy, Rice had a role in the first George W. Bush administration going beyond foreign policy. She served on strategy groups dealing with race, education, and the environment. One White House staffer told the author in 2001, "when Bush speaks on foreign policy he reiterates what Condi prepares for him." She herself described the job as "working the seams and stitching the connections together tightly." There were however criticisms of her performance in failing to bang heads together in the run up to the Iraq War. The same staffer said that "she did not know how to fight the 'big beasts' in the jungle," a reference to Powell, Cheney and Rumsfeld. Nevertheless she was rewarded for her loyalty to the President by being appointed the first black, female Secretary of State in the second George W. Bush administration.

Unlike their Cabinet counterparts, the position of national security adviser is neither rooted in law nor accountable to Congress. As with members of the Cabinet, the national security adviser serves at the pleasure of the President. While the adviser heads a small staff, his/her managerial duties are quite limited compared to the huge departmental responsibilities of the Secretaries of State, Defense, Treasury, and others with a role to play in the formulation and implementation of foreign policy. There is little doubt, however, that the national security adviser and the NSC staff have become steadily more influential in the Washington power game. The long queue of foreign ministers, ambassadors, and diplomatic advisers seeking appointments with the national security adviser (and his/her deputy) is testimony to this increased influence. One staffer told the author that Condoleezza Rice only accepted about one in forty requests for an audience and her deputy only accepted about one in twenty. The competition for the President's attention between the NSC and State Department has been likened to a duel between the "courtiers" and the "barons" (Destler *et al.* 1984). The White House "courtiers" nearly always win the battles not only because of their proximity to the President, and can thus respond quickly to his needs, but also because Presidents increasingly use foreign policy for political purposes.

Over the years the NSC has expanded its staff from one of less than fifteen policy people in the early 1960s to what is today an organization of some 200 people, including about 70 to 100 substantive professionals. Inevitably the NSC has its own

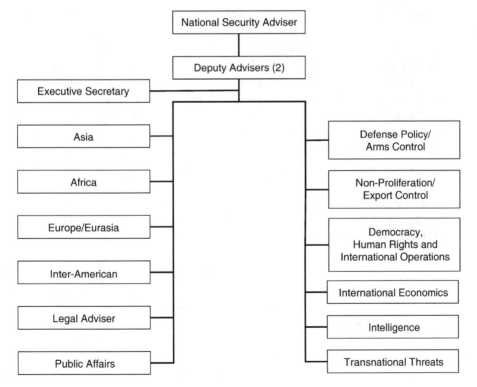

Figure 3.2. Organization of the National Security Council

views on the myriad of national security issues confronting the administration. There are various reasons for the growing importance of the NSC. First, as can be expected of any organization that has operated for many decades, the NSC has become institutionalized and even bureaucratized. The White House situation room, established under Kennedy, has become the focal point for crisis management. The NSC communications system, also inaugurated under Kennedy but progressively more technically sophisticated, allows staff to monitor the overseas messages sent to and from the State Department, to have access to major intelligence material, and to communicate directly and secretly to foreign governments. Over time, these capacities, together with continuing presidential need, have built the NSC into a powerful agency.

Second, the kinds of foreign policy issues that need to be addressed have both expanded in number and become more complex in nature. As a result, the number and type of players concerned with each issue has grown – placing a premium on effective organization and integration of different interests. Of all the players in the executive branch, it is usually only the White House that has the trust and confidence of the agencies necessary to manage these disparate interests effectively; and within the White House only the NSC has the capacity to coordinate them as was demonstrated during the US response to the September 2001 terrorist attacks. In the weeks following the attacks, the NSC met three times a week, with the President usually attending, listening to positions, and taking decisions on the war against terrorism (*The New York Times*, 23 December 2001).

The structure and functioning of the NSC depends in no small degree upon the interpersonal chemistry between the President and his national security adviser. Under President Nixon, Henry Kissinger drew on an expanded NSC staff that rivaled the State Department in policymaking and implementation. As Nixon recalled in his memoirs: "From the outset of my administration, I planned to direct foreign policy from the White House. Therefore I regarded my choice of a national security adviser as crucial" (Nixon 1981). The NSC under Kissinger coincided with an extremely active period of American foreign policy and contributed to Kissinger's growing power. Kissinger wrote later that "in the final analysis the influence of a Presidential assistant derives almost exclusively from the confidence of the President, not from administrative arrangements" (Kissinger 1979). He might have added that the location of the national security adviser's office, just a few paces from the President's study, is also an important factor. Although the office is small, barely seating six people, the location is perfect. He or she oversees all papers going to the President and is always present when the President meets or telephones with foreign leaders.

The NSC continued to play a major role under Jimmy Carter's presidency with Brzezinski adopting a high-profile role like Kissinger. Policy differences between Brzezinski and President Carter's Secretary of State, Cyrus Vance, eventually led to the latter's resignation. During the Reagan administration, the NSC was heavily criticized over its role in the "Iran-Contra affair." This was a clandestine effort, carried out without knowledge of the State Department, to provide Iran with arms in return for Teheran's help to secure the release of American hostages in the Middle East. The profits from these arms sales were then used to fund the right-wing "Contras" who were fighting the left-wing government in Nicaragua. The Iran-Contra affair severely damaged the reputation of the NSC and led to a thorough reform including a reduction of staff and the appointment of a legal counsel. President George H. W. Bush further reformed the NSC by establishing a principals' committee, a deputies' committee, and eight policy coordinating committees with the aim of ensuring a unified front by all parts of the administration in national security affairs.

President Clinton expanded the NSC to include the Secretary of the Treasury, the US representative to the UN, the assistant to the President for economic policy (who was also head of a newly-created national economic council (NEC) parallel to the NSC) and the President's chief of staff. The NEC was to deal with foreign and domestic economic issues in much the same way as the NSC coordinated diplomatic and security issues, and the assistant to the President for economic policy was to be included in meetings discussing international economic issues. One senior official in the Clinton administration appealed for an integrated international staff as one could no longer pigeonhole complex policy problems.

> Today, the "international" element of US policy is organized around four separate structures: traditional national security (centered on the NSC); international trade and finance (centered on the NEC); law enforcement and counter terrorism (largely centered on Justice, the FBI and CIA); and science (the office of science and technology policy and the council on environmental quality).
>
> (James Steinberg, *Washington Post*, 2 January 2001)

According to Steinberg, the bureaucratic divisions led to a lack of coherence and weakened US foreign policy. There was further pressure for a more integrated structure following the terrorist attacks in September 2001. On taking office, George W. Bush had simplified the NSC structure. The economic side was downgraded; three formerly separate regional offices were combined in a European and Eurasian affairs directorate. Offices dealing with health, the environment, refugees, and other humanitarian issues were consolidated in a single directorate for democracy, human rights, and international operations. Support offices were sharply reduced and some activities (legislative affairs and communications) were given back to the main White House machine. Bush also agreed to establish a second NSC deputy post, responsible for international economic issues, and who reports both to the national security adviser and the national economic adviser. The officials working in the NSC are a mix of political appointments and officials on secondment from other agencies.

The national security adviser has a number of tasks including advising and briefing the President, managing the decision-making process, and explaining and defending the policies of the administration in public. Each morning the adviser is present when the CIA director or his representative provides the President with the "daily brief," a short, global intelligence assessment. The adviser may see the President several other times during the day but he or she must try and minimize imposition on the President's time. This requires careful judgment on what issues should be brought to the President's attention and what can be resolved at a lower level.

Before any recommendation is sent to the President, the adviser must ensure that all executive branch agencies with strong stakes in the issue are included in the policy process; and that all realistic options have been considered and fully analyzed – including options not favored by any agency – before they reach the President. The adviser also has to mediate between departments should they come to the table pushing contradictory positions. The adviser must try and reach a compromise that reflects the political wishes of the President rather than the NSC or any department. It is not always an easy task to decide when to become involved in such mediating sessions. There is a danger that the NSC becomes bogged down in details rather than concentrate on the big picture. Moreover there will often be a temptation to seize control of an issue, even to the point of becoming responsible for policy implementation. As the Iran-Contra affair revealed, this can be a dangerous road to travel.

The adviser also must ensure that decisions are made in a timely manner and that they are implemented. In short, the national security adviser must balance the role of adviser and honest broker by both earning the trust of his or her colleagues in presenting their views fully, fairly, and faithfully to the President and giving the President his or her best advice on every issue. Certainly Rice made a major effort to ensure that there were as few disputes as possible reaching the President's desk. She made a point of meeting with Powell and Rumsfeld every week to try and iron out differences of opinion.

Another important task is briefing the President and assisting him when he is meeting foreign leaders. Meetings may be formal state visits, or working visits, or informal meetings in the margins of summits. But whatever type of meeting is scheduled, the bureaucracy requires a briefing book and the NSC will usually chair an interagency meeting before the President meets with the foreign leader to iron out any differences in approach and to agree the main messages to deliver. The competition for foreign visits to Washington is intense but usually varies little from President to President. The top candidates are close allies such as Britain, France, Germany, Italy, Japan, Israel, Egypt, Canada and Mexico. They are then followed by Russia, China, and South Korea and since the end of the Cold War by the East Europeans. The schedule for presidential visits abroad is partly determined by fixed summits such as the G8, EU, APEC, FTAA, NATO, and partly by the importance of business to transact. George W. Bush was less keen on state visits and dinners than Clinton. He did not schedule his first, with Vicente Fox of Mexico, until nine months into his administration.

Visits to the White House usually follow a set pattern. The visitors arrive at least ten minutes in advance of the scheduled meeting to pass through security and line up outside the Oval Office. When the line is ready, the door is opened and the visitors file in to meet the President. If there are too many in the overseas party, some may be asked to wait in Blair House, the government guesthouse situated across the road from the White House. A normal meeting would be 30–45 minutes but sometimes a foreign guest might only have 15–20 minutes with the President. In most cases there is a "photo opportunity" after the meeting followed by a press conference, or, more likely, press availability. This means that the President will take a few questions, usually on domestic rather than foreign affairs, while saying goodbye to his guest. For special guests the President may use his weekend retreat at Camp David or his own home. In

November 2001, President Bush invited Russian President Putin to his ranch in Crawford, Texas. In April 2002, British Prime Minister Tony Blair and Crown Prince Abdullah of Saudi Arabia received similar invitations. Other guests at the ranch have included the former Spanish (Aznar) and Italian (Berlusconi) prime ministers, both supporters of Bush's invasion of Iraq.

Although, since the Iran-Contra affair, the NSC has largely performed a coordinating and oversight function, Presidents have sometimes called on their national security adviser to undertake special missions. Both Berger and Rice had separate tracks with their Russian counterparts. And during Clinton's term the adviser also had direct links with the British and Irish governments to deal with Northern Ireland. It is understandable that Presidents will always want to make some operational use of their adviser, as this is normally someone they know and trust. The same is not always true for the Secretary of State and certainly not for the State Department, which is largely staffed by career officials.

As the national security adviser is not subject to congressional confirmation, he or she has no obligation to appear before Congress. But public speeches and media appearances have become more and more important. This reflects a change from earlier times when Brent Scowcroft counseled that the national security adviser "should be seen occasionally and heard even less." In recent years, the increasing politicization of foreign policy has made defense of the President's policies by his principal adviser more important. The second reason for the greater public exposure of the national security adviser in recent years is the rapidly expanding media landscape and continuous pace of the news cycle. There are more and more demands for the national security adviser to be seen and heard, in addition to the Secretary of State.

Rice herself played a more visible and operational role than some of her predecessors, meeting many foreign visitors and appearing on the major television talkshows. This reflects both a desire to sell the administration's policies and an acceptance that most foreign visitors view the White House as the real locus of power when it comes to foreign policy. Following the departure of Rice to the State Department, the President appointed her deputy, Stephen Hadley, as national security adviser. He had a much lower profile than Rice, reflecting his background as a bureaucrat and lawyer. Although much depends on the personality holding the title "national security adviser," it can be seen that he or she has played an increasingly important role in the making of US foreign policy over recent decades. This is unlikely to change in future as the political focus, at home and abroad, is likely to remain firmly fixed on the White House. The NSC is thus a highly developed and efficient system to coordinate and manage US national security policy. Its relations with other agencies vary according to the issues and the personalities involved. In day-to-day business it deals principally with the State Department and the Department of Defense.

The State Department

Constitutionally, the State Department is the lead executive agency for the conduct of US diplomacy, a mission based on the role of the Secretary of State as the President's principal foreign policy adviser. The State Department has the primary role in:

- leading and coordinating US representation abroad;
- conducting negotiations and concluding agreements and treaties;
- managing the international affairs budget;
- coordinating and supporting international activities of other US agencies.

It would also like to see itself as the lead department in interagency coordination in developing and implementing foreign policy but it has a strong rival in the NSC for this task. The State Department was the first executive agency established under the constitution in 1789 and the Secretary of State as the first cabinet officer in line to succeed to the Presidency. (The succession starts with the Vice President, the Speaker of the House, the president of the Senate, and then the Secretary of State.)

Prior to the arrival of Colin Powell in January 2001 the State Department had few friends in Congress and had suffered large budgetary and staff cuts in recent years leading to problems of morale amongst serving Foreign Service officers (these problems are aired regularly in the *Foreign Service Journal*). One American diplomat told the author that "very often Secretaries of State have been interested only in the major political problems facing them and not in the machinery or functioning of the department." The State Department employs some 9000 diplomatic staff and maintains 260 overseas missions in 180 countries. The 2005 budget was $8.1 billion, an increase of 20 percent over 2001, largely to reflect assistance to countries in the war on terrorism and measures to protect US embassies. This figure is tiny compared to most other government departments. For example, the Pentagon had a budget of over $450 billion in 2004. This has led some to describe the State Department as "a bureaucratic pygmy among giants" (Kegley and Wittkopf 1996: 383). Certainly the building in which the State Department is housed has nothing of the style of the White House nor the grandeur of the Pentagon. It could easily be mistaken for an insurance office. Many officials work in cramped offices with poor facilities. When Colin Powell first visited the State Department library in January 2001 he was staggered to find that there were hardly any computers. The State Department also suffers in that it has no domestic constituency to serve. According to some serving diplomats, many Americans are unaware of the State Department's existence or unable to explain what it does. The department has also struggled to escape its image of a snobbish, East Coast, Ivy League, predominantly white, male establishment. Its long-suffering career officers are often described, unfairly in the author's opinion, as "effete, snobbish, striped pants, cookie pushers" (Rubin 1985). According to a number of reports, State also suffers from excessive bureaucracy that leads many of the brightest officers to leave (see the 2000 report of the Advisory Council on US Public Diplomacy. *The New York Times* also highlighted this problem in an article "As Diplomacy Loses Luster, Young Stars Flee the State Department" on 5 September 2000). In addition, the working conditions for foreign service officers overseas has become much more difficult since 9/11. Most US embassies have become fortresses and interaction with the local population more difficult. The US plans to build one of its largest embassies in Baghdad but if its diplomats cannot operate in the country safely one wonders what they can achieve holed up inside a concrete block.

Successful Secretaries of State have usually been those with close access to and the trust of the President. James Baker enjoyed the complete confidence of President George H. W. Bush and was an effective operator around the world. Warren Christopher, Clinton's first Secretary of State and a Californian lawyer, adopted a more managerial style and was under instructions to keep problems away from the President whom he rarely saw. His successor, Madeleine Albright, the daughter of immigrants from Czechoslovakia, was the first female occupant of the office and adopted a higher profile. Prior to her appointment, she had been the US permanent representative to the UN and before that she had been a professor and member of the NSC staff under Brzezinski. Albright won the race to succeed Warren Christopher partly because Clinton considered there would be political gains in appointing the first female Secretary of State and partly because it was felt that Richard Holbrooke, her main rival, might be too flamboyant and difficult to control (Halberstam 2001). She also enjoyed a good working relationship with Senator Jesse Helms, the then chairman of the SFRC, and nemesis of the State Department. Another part of her appeal to Clinton was her knack of explaining foreign policy to the general public in plain language. She too, however, struggled for access to the President.

President George W. Bush chose Colin Powell to be his Secretary of State. Powell was the son of immigrants from Jamaica and had a glittering military career before being nominated for State. With his star charisma, inspiring personal history, and reputation for leadership and integrity, Powell's appointment brought an instant increase in morale at State. One American diplomat told the author that "the moment he set foot in the State Department he was met with rapturous applause." In his first couple of weeks in office Powell invited the President to visit the department and ensured that desk officers carried out the President's briefing for his forthcoming Mexico visit. Many diplomats saw his reliance on the Foreign Service as a rejuvenating tonic to an institution that had felt marginalized. Despite his Washington-insider background, Powell still found it difficult to adjust to the environment at State. In an interview six months into the job, he admitted that he faced "a steep learning curve" (*USA Today*, 19 July 2001). In the fall of 2001 there were still critics. For example, the *Time* magazine cover of 10 September 2001 was "Where Have You Gone Colin Powell?" This would change, however, with the war on terrorism. Powell's experience of the military and diplomatic worlds, as well as the Washington bureaucracy, made him an increasingly powerful figure in the Bush administration but he had to fight a constant battle with Donald Rumsfeld, Secretary for Defense, and other neo-conservative members of the administration. Powell never had the full backing of the President and it was not surprising that he resigned at the end of the first George W. Bush administration. He had few concrete achievements to his name and his tenure included one major embarrassing incident, when, with faulty intelligence information, he tried and failed to convince the UN Security Council in February 2003 that Saddam Hussein possessed WMD.

In appointing Condoleezza Rice as Powell's successor, President Bush placed his closest foreign policy adviser in charge of the US diplomatic machine. With Rice, a close family friend of the President running Foggy Bottom (the slang term for the State

Department as it is located in this district of Washington DC), there would be no splits between State and the White House. Rice is a confirmed workaholic. Unmarried and with no real hobbies she used to spend more than 12 hours each day at the White House. She was the President's mentor on foreign policy for many years and a frequent visitor to his ranch in Texas. A confirmed conservative, the terrorist attacks on 9/11 convinced Rice (as well as the President) that she was helping to preside over nothing less than a titanic struggle between modernity and fundamentalism, good and evil. Few professional diplomats share this black and white view of the world and there was much speculation in early 2005 as to whether she would have more influence on the State Department or whether it would help change her thinking.

The State Department is organized in a pyramid fashion. In addition to the Secretary of State, there is a Deputy Secretary (under Clinton it was Strobe Talbott, a former journalist and university friend of the President; under George W. Bush it was Richard Armitage, a former political appointee at the Pentagon) and five under-secretaries. There are also more than twenty assistant secretaries who are a mix of political appointees and career officials, all of whom require Senate approval, as do all nominations for ambassadorial posts. There is a tendency in the State Department to view the six regional bureaus – African, European and Eurasian, Near Eastern, Western Hemisphere, East Asian and Pacific, and South Asian Affairs – plus International Organizations, as the cream of the crop. They handle the day-to-day emergencies that occur around the world and generally maintain the highest profile. The functional bureaus, by comparison, play a less glamorous role. The State Department has few friends in Congress where many consider that State pays too much attention to the wishes of foreign governments and too little to domestic interests. In an attempt to impose some rationalization in external affairs, Congress insisted that two formerly independent agencies – the US Information Agency (USIA), and the Arms Control and Disarmament Agency (ACDA) – were folded into the State Department in 1999.

The Secretary of State usually has daily meetings with senior staff when decisions are taken on the Secretary's schedule of visits and visitors as well as discussion of priority issues. State has also had to try and meet the challenges posed by new global issues such as climate change, infectious diseases, international crime, drugs and terrorism. Other issues such as patterns of energy consumption, food labeling, corporate taxation, once thought to be exclusively domestic issues, have now become topics of international concern and targets of concerted action. It has not been easy for the State Department or the Secretary to dominate this agenda, or indeed the general foreign policy agenda of the administration. One critic commented that Madeleine Albright had ceded large swathes of the world to the Treasury. The State Department was simply not equipped to handle the new challenges. "Nothing in the foreign policy manual tells you how to deal with financial crises" (Michael Mandelbaum, quoted in *The New York Times*, 28 December 2000). Even with Powell at the helm, one analyst commented that "audiences at home and abroad have been regularly forced to ask what did Cheney say, what did Rumsfeld think, where did Rice stand" (*Time*, 10 September 2001).

Unlike European diplomatic services, the US has a very high percentage of political, ambassadorial appointees which means that there are inevitably fewer top positions for

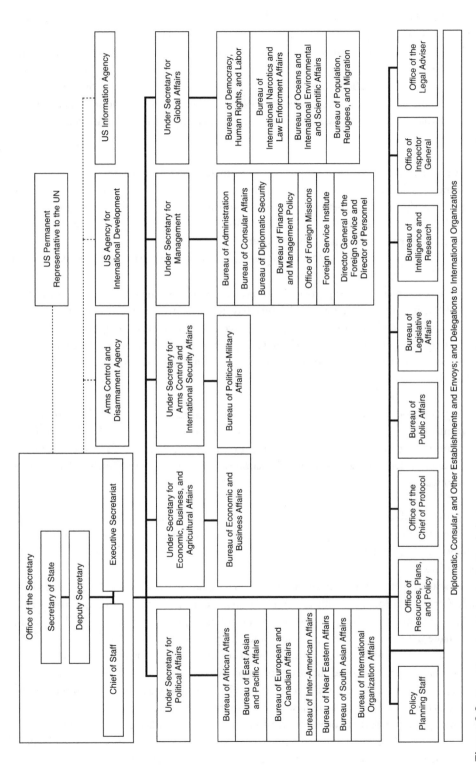

Figure 3.3. State Department – organizational chart

career officials. The number of political ambassadors has steadily increased in recent years, to around 30 percent, perhaps reflecting White House distrust of the career officials from State who may not be such loyal supporters of the President. According to one report in the *National Journal* on 15 June 2001, the minimum qualifications for an ambassadorship in 2001 were campaign contributions of at least $250,000, friendship with and complete loyalty to the President. One former ambassador, Richard Burt, observed that "the system was downright embarrassing." Richard Holbrooke took a similar view.

> We've had some political appointees who made great ambassadors, and we've had some real duds. It's a mixed bag. In the end, however, I don't think we should be particularly proud of this tradition of rewarding campaign contributors, fundraisers and political supporters with ambassadorships. It's clearly one of the last, pure vestiges of the 19th century spoils system.
>
> (*National Journal*, 1 September 2001 [Holbrooke 1998])

In recent years, the State Department, unlike the Pentagon, has been starved of funds. Since 1985, its international affairs budget has declined by almost 50 percent. In 1985 foreign affairs spending amounted to $2^1/_2$ percent of the federal budget – in 2000 it was less than 1 percent. In a speech at Georgetown University on 19 October 2000, Sandy Berger criticized Congress's reluctance to fund American foreign policy. He argued that

> America could not be a first-rate power on a third-class budget. We are at the zenith of our influence, yet our entire international budget for everything – from diminishing the nuclear threat, to preventing conflict, to fighting AIDS, to advancing democracy – is about the same as constructing eight miles of interstate highway.

According to Richard Holbrooke, "if I had to sum up my greatest concern about American foreign policy today, it's the gap between our rhetoric and our resources. We keep proclaiming lofty goals, and then not putting up enough resources to achieve them" (*Financial Times*, 6–7 January 2001).

In a scathing report issued in January 2001, a non-partisan task force chaired by Frank Carlucci, a former Defense Secretary and ambassador to Portugal, warned that the State Department "was in a serious state of disrepair and plagued by long-term mismanagement, antiquated equipment and dilapidated and insecure facilities." If the "downward spiral" was not reversed, the prospect of relying on military force to protect US national interests would increase because Washington would be less capable of avoiding, managing, or resolving crises through the use of statecraft. The report pointed out that the State Department was inadequate in mission, organization, and skills. Personnel policies had left some 700 diplomatic positions unfilled – a staffing shortfall of 15 percent. More than 90 percent of overseas posts were equipped with obsolete equipment to handle classified communications, and 88 percent of all embassies did not meet basic security standards. More than a quarter of all diplomatic posts were seriously overcrowded. These problems rendered US foreign policy increasingly ill-equipped to shape and respond to the realities and challenges of the twenty-first century. Failure to address these shortcomings "would prompt significant negative consequences that will undercut national security."

Madeleine Albright fought strongly but not very successfully for an increased budget. In a speech on 20 November 2000 she argued that the percentage of the federal budget allocated for foreign affairs

> may well determine 50 percent of the history that is written about this era. Every year [the State Department] struggles with Congress for each nickel and dime and this forces us repeatedly to make no-win tradeoffs between such priorities as peace in Kosovo and curbing conflict in the Congo, improving security at our missions and enhancing the skills of our people.

In testimony to the HIRC on 7 March 2001, Albright's successor, Colin Powell, made a strong pitch for increased funds, asking for and securing a 13.8 percent increase from $6.6 billion in 2001 to $7.8 billion in 2002. There were further small rises up until 2005. Powell said that his priorities were hiring new staff (360 extra in 2002), updating

Table 3.1. International affairs expenditure

Fiscal year	Function 150 Constant FY2001 $s	Function 150 Current $s
1981	12.194	22.445
1982	14.222	24.592
1983	16.017	26.443
1984	17.396	27.592
1985	24.057	36.977
1986	20.279	30.326
1987	18.800	27.229
1988	18.079	25.252
1989	18.537	24.873
1990	20.027	25.923
1991	21.321	26.511
1992	20.927	25.258
1993	21.194	24.851
1994	20.854	23.924
1995	20.166	22.599
1996	18.237	20.037
1997	18.333	19.786
1998	18.289	20.583
1999	23.824	24.981
2000	23.776	24.336
2001	23.119	23.119
2002	25.784	26.534
2003	26.975	27.893
2004	27.268	28.962

Source: Office of Management and Budget and CRS calculations

information technology, and improving embassy security and infrastructure. As regards the discretionary budget for international affairs, the figure rose from $23.9 billion for 2002 to $31.5 billion in 2005. This included increased funds for enhanced security measures and a large contribution to the Global Fund to combat HIV/AIDS and to support debt relief for poor countries.

If one examines US discretionary external expenditure during the 1990s one can observe that there has been a steady reduction in funding. The expenditures of the early 1990s were reflective of new aid programs in Nicaragua and Panama in response to the political changes in those countries and the need to provide foreign assistance to the drought- and famine-stricken countries of Africa and to former communist countries in Eastern Europe. During the mid-1990s, Congress worked to balance the federal budget and government expenditures on foreign aid fluctuated from 1993 to 1995 before being drastically cut in 1996. Since 1999, funding increases have resulted from increased humanitarian relief and peacemaking efforts. Support for Israel and Egypt consumes over 80 percent of all security assistance and almost 25 percent of all international affairs spending. Israel, with a per capita GDP of over $12,000, receives over $3 billion in bilateral assistance each year, while the whole of sub-Saharan Africa, with a per capita GDP of under $500, receives a total of about $165 million. This huge support for Israel and Egypt can be traced back to the power of the American-Jewish lobby and the desire of the US to be seen to support the Middle East peace process. The huge imbalance between military and non-military expenditure has been strongly criticized. According to former ambassador Richard Gardner, the resources devoted to preparing for war compared to those for conflict prevention are in a ratio of sixteen to one. In his view, "a realistic assessment of the long-term, trans-border threats to the security and welfare of the American people would argue for a re-balancing of US budget priorities" (*Financial Times*, 6 June 2001). Among the areas that had been cut in the 1990s were funding for public diplomacy and student exchanges. Some observers maintained that these cuts had contributed to the lack of objective knowledge about the US in the Arab world (Stephen Kinzer, *The New York Times*, 11 November 2001).

The decline in the budget for the State Department has been mirrored in other non-military external expenditure. Since the end of the Cold War, US foreign assistance has lost its core political constituency and much of its support, which has led to the steady decline in aid to developing countries. US aid appropriations in 2004 equaled only 0.11 percent of the gross domestic product (GDP), a figure that stands at roughly half of the foreign assistance spending averaged in the 1980s, which amounted to 0.2 percent of GDP. These figures fall well short of the United Nations' recommended 0.7 percent GDP target. As a percentage of the economy, official spending on economic aid is now more than three times greater in the typical OECD country than in the US.

In the aftermath of the September 2001 attacks, there was a significant shift in spending with the focus being on efforts to win the war on terrorism. Increased resources for strategic, development, and humanitarian purposes were approved in record time. The main beneficiary was Pakistan, followed by the countries of central Asia. There was also an increase in funding for the Millennium Goals aimed at tackling poverty. If the anti-terrorism and other foreign aid programs are shown to serve US

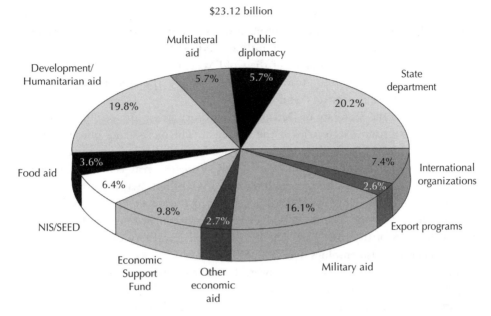

Figure 3.4. Division of international affairs budget

interests, help erode poverty, promote democracy, and stabilize the political situation of coalition partners, public opinion may in future support more robust programs. However, if a large portion of foreign assistance is mismanaged or abused, and/or accountability and impact are marginal, enthusiasm for foreign aid is likely to be undermined further. There is an on-going debate between conservatives who doubt the value of foreign aid programs, believing that free markets and the private sector are the keys to economic growth, and liberals who argue that the US has a moral responsibility to help reduce global poverty.

The Department of Defense (Pentagon)

In constitutional terms, the Department of Defense (DoD) – often referred to as the "Pentagon" because of the huge five-sided building in which it is housed – is responsible for the formulation of general defense policy, in particular the military strategy and the definition of the "mission statement" of the armed forces. In terms of defining an overall approach and policy regarding national security issues, however, the DoD is but one actor and the NSC has increasingly taken the lead in defining the overall national security strategy. Because of its size and enormous resources, the Pentagon plays an increasingly important role in the formulation of US foreign policy. Donald Rumsfeld was never shy about intervening in foreign affairs, famously describing Europe as divided into "old Europe" and "new Europe." Despite some criticism over his handling of the war in Iraq, President Bush reappointed him in December 2004.

The role of the Pentagon has been subject to heated debate at times with concern expressed about the continuing close ties between the military and industry as well as the political implications of bases and contracts in congressional members' districts or states. As far back as 1961, in his farewell address, President Eisenhower warned of the dangers of excessive influence by "the military industrial complex." In the succeeding forty years, fueled by the demands of the Cold War, the influence of the Pentagon in national security policy rose steadily, underpinned by the iron triangle of defense bureaucrats, defense contractors, and Congress.

In addition to the Secretary of Defense and a deputy, there are four under-secretaries and numerous assistant secretaries at the Pentagon. The most senior officer is the chair of the Joint Chiefs of Staff, although he does not formally hold any command position. The four regional commanders-in-chief (CINCs) are the real centers of operational control. The department's budget in 2002 was $340 billion, with a further increase of $48 billion in 2003. This marked a 20 percent increase over 2000, the final year of Clinton's term in office. The 2004 budget saw a further increase to nearly $450 billion due to the costs of the Iraq War. The forces on active military duty total 1,370,000, but the Pentagon also employs over 700,000 civilians.

The American military is more powerful than any armed force in history. In air power the US possesses more jet bombers, more advanced fighter planes and tactical aircraft than all other nations combined. On the seas the US navy boasts twice as many combat ships as Russia and China combined and a dozen super-carrier battle groups while the rest of the world has none. Included in the super-carrier contingent are eight large and sophisticated Nimitz-class floating cities, served by nearly 6000 people and capable of launching more aircraft per minute than London's Heathrow airport. On the ground, the US not only possesses nearly 8000, highly effective, Abrams tanks (more than the combined numbers of modern tanks possessed by Russia and China) but, as both Gulf wars showed, it has the world's best trained troops. In amphibious forces, other nations have service branches called "marines" but none possess anything like the US marines – whole divisions backed by helicopter carriers, floating armor, and jump jets, capable of going ashore anywhere in the world. The US is the only nation that even maintains a standing heavy, amphibious force. In nuclear arms, there is a rough parity between the US and Russia but there are serious doubts about the state of the Russian nuclear forces. Moscow's strategic submarine fleet is in such poor repair that it rarely ventures far from port (and when it does it seems prone to accidents as witness the sinking of the *Kursk*). By contrast, several of America's Ohio-class strategic submarines are at sea at any given moment, and each carries sufficient weaponry to incinerate every major target in Russia and China. Overall, America's strategic deterrent is today stronger in relation to the rest of the world than it has been at any time since the brief American atomic monopoly in the late 1940s.

In technology, as was seen in Afghanistan and Iraq, US "smart" weapons increasingly hit their targets exactly (an improvement on the embarrassing incident of bombing the Chinese embassy in Belgrade during the Kosovo air campaign). Individual American soldiers can receive space-relayed battlefield updates, while US electronic jamming devices have grown so sophisticated that they cause false aircraft to appear on enemy screens while keeping the real ones undetected. The US has three classes of stealth aircraft already in operation, with three more close to production. No other nation even

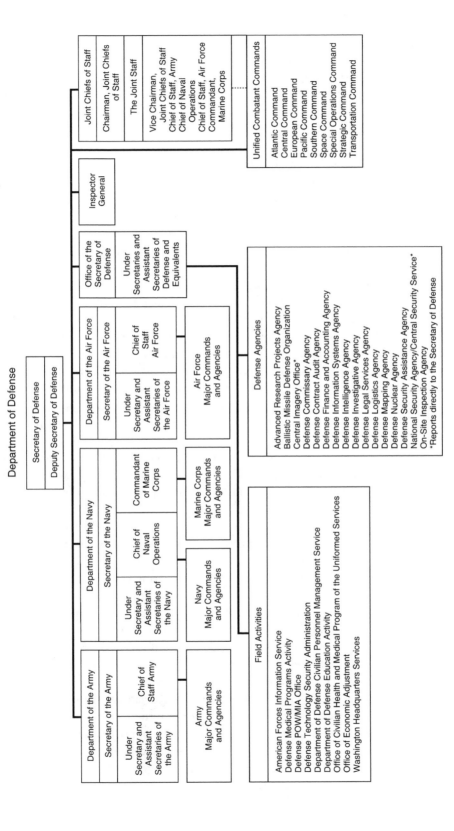

Figure 3.5. Department of Defense – organizational chart
Source: The United States Government Manual

has one on the drawing board. Under development are lasers for shooting down tactical missiles, pilotless fighters, and electro-magnetic rays to destroy enemy electronics.

The US possesses a vast qualitative military advantage over any other nation or group of nations in the world. While such superiority does not come cheap, the amount the US spends on its military is breathtaking. In money, American military spending is three times Russia and China's combined. Or to put it another way, the US spends twenty-three times more on defense than the combined spending of the seven countries or "rogue states" traditionally identified by the Pentagon as its most likely adversaries. In concept, the US is the world's sole military power whose primary mission is not defense. Practically the entire US military is an expeditionary force, designed not to guard American borders, but to project power elsewhere in the world. In day-to-day operations the military spans the world and the scope of its activity is staggering. The US maintains 100,000 troops in Europe, another 100,000 in East Asia and the Pacific, 25,000 in the Persian Gulf, 50,000 on rotation in Latin America and bases and fuel depots across the globe. As one defense staffer told the author, "the US is engaged across the world every day in areas most Americans cannot find on the map." Since 1945, the US has fought, and usually prevailed, in a dozen places thousands of miles from home. Even before the Soviet Union collapsed, America's military power was far ahead of the rest of the world. This relative strength has not declined in the past decade; it has steadily risen. And yet, during the 2000 presidential campaign, the Republicans painted the armed forces in a "serious state of decline" (George W. Bush speech to Veterans of Foreign Wars, 2 August 2000). Even John Kerry criticized the low levels of the armed forces in the 2004 campaign and promised a 40,000 increase in numbers.

Many criticize the armed forces for refusing to modernize. The navy insists on maintaining carrier battle groups to patrol the oceans at a time when no navy on earth is remotely capable of challenging it. The air force has been demanding the very latest in new technology to control and dominate space. The army resists low-intensity operations, such as policing in Bosnia and Kosovo, that happen to be the most frequent tasks of the post-Cold War world. As retired Admiral William Owens put it, "the most difficult obstacle to transition is the culture in which we have been raised and the bureaucracy that we have participated in building." His army colleague General William Nash agreed, arguing that "a fundamental error, both past and continuing, is that we in the US have been slow to redefine the nature of national security in the twenty-first century. The new security threats are more non-military than ever before" (*Foreign Policy*, November/ December 2001). Another critic, Fareed Zakaria, writing in *Newsweek* on 15 October 2001, was even more blunt. "For ten years now, our defense forces have been aligned for everything but the real danger we face."

As a result of the massive arms build up during the Reagan years, there was little need for much new equipment for the armed forces during the 1990s. The total size of the armed forces also declined from 2.1 million in 1989 to 1.4 million in 2001. In terms of strategic rationale, it remained US policy to be able to fight major wars in two regions simultaneously as well as maintaining a US-based force for rapid contingencies. Most scenarios were for wars in the Persian Gulf and the Korean peninsula. There are many critics of the two-war strategy who argue that not only is it highly unlikely that the US would be engaged in two such distant theaters simultaneously but that its likely enemies possess far less and greatly inferior military equipment to that of the US. According to one staffer, this was "an inconceivable response to an implausible threat and no more than a marketing strategy for a high Pentagon budget." Nuclear deterrence continued to be an essential part of US defense posture with both the US and Russia maintaining huge arsenals. In 2004, the US had some 7200 strategic nuclear warheads and Russia about 5800. The 1993 START II agreement calls for cuts to 3000–3500. In a statement following his talks with Russian President Putin in November 2001, President Bush said that he would like to reduce these levels further, assuming the US also proceeds with missile defense.

In a speech at Annapolis on 25 May 2001, President Bush stated that the armed forces of the future "would be defined less by size and more by mobility and swiftness." They would rely "more heavily on stealth, precision weaponry and information technologies." Advances in defense technology must be used "to keep the peace by redefining war on our terms." The President tasked Defense Secretary, Donald Rumsfeld, to undertake a major policy review with the aim of modernizing the armed forces and preparing them for the tasks of the twenty-first century. Rumsfeld set up over twenty panels to provide input into the defense review. He deliberately excluded the interest groups that usually make defense policy – congressional committees, service chiefs, and contractors – from his deliberations. This helped to shield him from those defending the status quo but also left him few friends to support proposals for radical change. As one staffer commented to the author, "Rumsfeld cannot alter the fact that in arms procurement, the Pentagon proposes and the Congress disposes." The initial drafts of his review met significant opposition from military leaders and their allies in Congress who were concerned at the implications of radical changes. It was widely reported that Rumsfeld intended to abandon the two-major-theater-war scenario as the basis for force planning, shift forces from Europe to Asia, reduce forward deployed forces, and reduce overall force levels, in particular, the army.

The Rumsfeld defense review was put on hold in the wake of the September 2001 terrorist attacks. Congress was not in the mood for changes but seemed determined to throw more money at the Pentagon in the expectation that military might alone be

Table 3.2. Comparison of defense spending

Country	Defense spending	Percent of global total	Percent of GDP (billions of dollars)
US	452	3.9	35
Russia	58	5.1	6.9
Japan	42	0.9	5.1
China	41	5.4	4.9
France	38	2.7	4.6
UK	37	2.6	4.5
Germany	32	1.6	3.8

Source: IISS Military Balance, 2004

able to somehow defeat the terrorist threat. There was no discussion of the wider aspects of security policy, including what would be the best approaches, besides the military, to tackle these threats. The Quadrennial Defense Review (QDR), released on 30 September 2001, made only minor changes to existing strategy. The size of the armed forces would remain constant but portions would be reconfigured to combat asymmetrical threats. It recast the two-major-war scenarios into a new concept which envisages having sufficient force capabilities to defend the US, and, second, the ability to fight two contingencies at the same time. Force planning should also be based on current peacekeeping commitments and other global requirements that in practice have proved as demanding as a major theater war. The QDR emphasized the need for the US military to transform itself in order to concentrate on "protecting the US base of operations on tactical, operational and strategic levels; information operations; power projection capabilities; space operations; and levering information technology." The commitment to cooperate with allies in improving regional defense was emphasized although the review did not question the Pentagon's own regional command structure. In light of the war against Afghanistan, and global terrorism, Rumsfeld was keen to promote unified joint regional commands with rapid reaction forces being a top priority. (The QDR is available at www.defenselink.mil/pubs/qdr2001.pdf)

The war against terrorism and in particular the Iraq War may also signal the end of the "Powell Doctrine" – the idea that forces should only be committed where they can be used decisively and with overwhelming superiority to accomplish clearly defined goals. The administration's mission to defeat global terrorism has never been defined precisely. Indeed the commitment to an ongoing, perhaps unending, campaign implies a willingness to engage in a long series of difficult engagements with no guarantee of success, a view of the role of military forces that is quite alien to US military leaders. In the summer of 2004 the President announced that the US would bring home some 70,000 troops stationed in Germany, South Korea and Japan. This was partly a recognition that these countries no longer faced conventional threats and partly to ensure that the US had sufficient troops for a lengthy engagement in Iraq.

While the US military was highly capable of combat operations in Afghanistan and Iraq, post-combat operations in both countries have exposed the reality that US forces are less well trained and prepared for long-term occupation, security and post-war reconstruction tasks, especially in a hostile setting. The defects exposed in Iraq and Afghanistan have raised serious questions about the government's civil–military planning capabilities. Post-war reconstruction in Iraq has also called into question the Pentagon's privatization agenda. A broad range of services, from security to catering to reconstruction projects, have been contracted out, leading to a blurring of the line between core and non-core military functions.

Apart from its seat on the NSC, the Pentagon also plays an important role in US external relations through its foreign bases, its training and assistance programs, and its regional military commanders, or CINCs. The CINCs are a quartet of high-ranking military leaders responsible for managing US military operations in distinct regions of the world: Central, European, Southern, and Pacific. The war against the Taliban regime in Afghanistan was masterminded from Central Command headquarters in

Tampa, Florida. Since their inception in 1986, these command posts have continually gained power and influence within the US foreign policy decision-making process. For example, after the Pakistani army's coup in 2000, the new Pakistani President, General Musharraf, decided to respond to the US criticism by calling General Anthony C. Zinni (the then Central Commander – and later Middle East envoy under Powell) instead of any other administration official. This highlights the active US foreign policy role that these semi-autonomous military commanders play in their respective regions of the world. As one observer notes, "with little oversight, the CINCs have evolved into the modern-day equivalent of the Roman Empire's pro-consuls – well-funded, semi-autonomous, unconventional actors of foreign policy" (*Washington Post*, 28 September 2000).

The massive budgets administered by the CINCs increase their impact on US foreign policy. These budgets have expanded throughout the past decade without congressional scrutiny, while the budget of the State Department has been significantly reduced. The four CINCs combined sustain a budget of $380 million a year, double their budget appropriations at the end of the Cold War, allowing them to host international conferences, maintain large staffs, travel extensively and maintain round-the-clock intelligence centers. Three CINCs have staffs as large as the executive office of the President. More people, about 1100, work at the smallest CINC headquarters, the US Southern Command, than the total assigned to the Americas at the NSC, State, Commerce, Treasury and Agriculture departments.

The CINCs command considerable respect in their regions and have an important input into US foreign policy. But their philosophies on building alliances abroad, developed over long military careers, sometimes clash with civilian views. The most pronounced differences involve how to treat foreign militaries that commit human rights abuses. The administration and Congress routinely press for stopping arms sales and military assistance to countries that violate human rights, e.g. Guatemala, Colombia, Pakistan, Nigeria, and Indonesia. But the CINCs and the Pentagon nearly always advocate using continued engagement to induce change. In Bosnia and Kosovo, General Wesley Clark used the autonomy and resources that have devolved to the CINCs to push NATO troops toward an anti-corruption and a nation-building role often opposed by the Pentagon (Clark 2001; Halberstam 2001). Clark was not rewarded for his efforts, being forced into early retirement shortly after the conclusion of the Kosovo campaign. In the wake of the Afghanistan conflict and the worldwide war on terrorism there was renewed discussion as to whether the autonomous CINCs' command structure was best suited to a global campaign.

The increased role of the CINCs has also been criticized within the military. According to General Nash, "the evolution of the CINCs to pro-consuls is a dangerous trend, both in terms of the image of our democracy, and our larger national security." His naval colleague, Admiral Owens, agreed.

> If you are in China and you ask who is the most important American in the Pacific, the answer is certainly CINC-PAC. As Americans we have to ask whether we want to be represented to our friends and adversaries by a senior four-star officer.
>
> (*Foreign Policy*, November/December 2001)

From this brief review, it can be seen that the US possesses a huge, well-trained, well-supplied, well-supported fighting machine capable of meeting almost any military task it is required to perform. Until Iraq, American leaders have been careful, however, to avoid sending troops into a situation that could lead to a repetition of the Vietnam War scenario. In the post-Cold War world, American forces have been used regularly but for limited purposes. They have either dropped bombs on the enemy from a great height or, with the exception of the Gulf War, confronted small groups of militia on the ground. The Iraqi army scarcely put up any resistance to the US invasion in March 2003. Total American casualties in Iraq up to the end of 2004 were just over one thousand, a politically acceptable number. There were some, particularly in the Islamic world, who argued that the US was a paper tiger as it was so reluctant to take casualties. This argument lost much of its resonance after the American response to the 11 September terrorist attacks. There are also some who argue that America suffers from imperial over-stretch, rather like Britain in the inter-war years. There are too few troops to do the jobs demanded of them. There was certainly much criticism of Donald Rumsfeld for failing to foresee that the US would need a much bigger force to keep the peace in Iraq after the fall of Baghdad. But in the absence of the two-theater war becoming a reality, this assertion is impossible to prove or disprove. One can conclude with some certainty that there are few powers if any likely to be ready, willing, and able to confront the US militarily over the next two decades.

The intelligence community

The US has the largest intelligence apparatus in the world with the 15 different agencies making round-the-clock input into the formulation of US foreign policy. The Director of the CIA is simultaneously director of the intelligence community, of which the CIA is but one component. In 2003–4 the intelligence community was widely criticized for its failure to provide accurate intelligence on whether or not Saddam Hussein had weapons of mass destruction. As a result, the CIA director, George Tenet, resigned in the summer of 2004, to be replaced by Porter J. Goss, a former CIA official and member of the house of representatives.

The intelligence community really began to grow in the early years of the Cold War when the all-consuming effort to defeat communism led to huge resources being devoted to intelligence efforts. It is inevitably difficult to provide an assessment of the effectiveness of these efforts. Scandals often appear in the media but the successes usually go unsung. Some of the more publicized scandals involved the CIA's role in the abortive 1961 Bay of Pigs operation in Cuba, the ousting of socialist President Allende in Chile in 1973, and the violation of US laws in supporting illegally the Contras in Nicaragua (see the 1976 report on the CIA by Senator Frank Church). According to Robert Gates, a former CIA director, the intelligence community did enjoy considerable success during the Cold War although there were also serious lapses of judgment, including the overstatement of Soviet military and economic strength (Andrew 1995).

Oversight of the intelligence community is exercised by the NSC and the President's foreign intelligence advisory board (PFIAB). There are also two congressional oversight committees that have a remit to review operations and the Senate must approve the director of intelligence. The vast budget of the intelligence community (generally estimated at $32 billion in 2004) is largely hidden in the budget of the Pentagon. Most of the budget is spent by the national reconnaissance office on spy satellites that provide photographic imagery and by the national security agency which is responsible for electronic surveillance of all communications. There have been charges in the European Parliament (Echelon report of September 2001) that the NSA also spies on allies and that electronic spying alone cannot supply the US with the intelligence it needs to combat terrorism (Bamford 2001).

The CIA is certainly the most famous or infamous part of the intelligence community, mainly because of its association with "dirty tricks," including numerous plots to assassinate the Cuban leader, Fidel Castro. Covert operations, however, are only a small part of the CIA's remit. By far the largest task is the collation and analysis of intelligence from all sources. The ties between the CIA and the White House vary from administration to administration and generally reflect the importance that each President places on the agency's reports. There was considerable anxiety at the CIA when stories circulated early in the Clinton administration that the new President had little interest in intelligence, though that did not turn out to be true. Under George W. Bush, the agency's access to the White House increased markedly. (CIA headquarters was renamed the George H. W. Bush Center for Intelligence in 1998 in honor of the former President, who was an ex-director of the agency.)

In a television debate in September 2000, two former CIA directors reflected on the relations between the CIA and the White House. According to Gates, "the relationship between the President and the CIA director, if close, can assist enormously in the creation of foreign policy." Gates said he met with the President once or twice a week "if there was something I ought to talk to him about." The best part about meeting face-to-face with the President was to get instantaneous feedback on what his agenda was. "He asked questions and we would get answers to him, and thus had a direct dialogue with the President that is most often missing in the normal daily mix of things." Under Clinton intelligence briefings became more haphazard. Making things worse was the President's poor relationship with James Woolsey, a Washington lawyer whom Clinton had never met before he named him agency director. Woolsey admitted that he saw the President very rarely, except at NSC meetings, and only had two semi-private meetings in two years.

According to one American diplomat, Presidents often attach too much importance to intelligence reports simply because of the way the material is presented. Documents stamped "top secret" and full of code words can give a false sense of importance to the material. Intelligence can thus play a greater role in the President's mind than normal diplomatic reporting. Gates also considers that most Presidents have exaggerated expectations of intelligence.

> Presidents expect that, for what they spend on intelligence, the product should be able to predict coups, upheavals, riots, intentions, military moves and the like with accuracy. Presidents and their national security teams usually are ill-informed

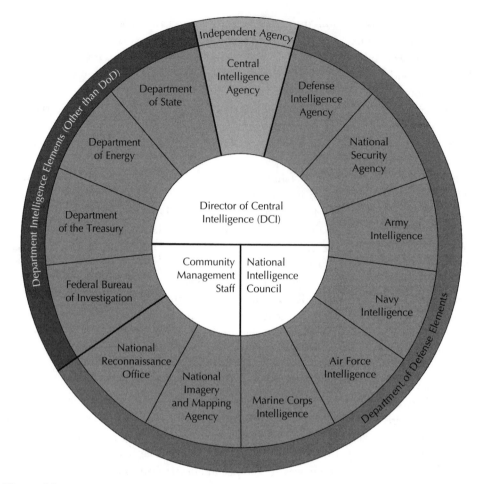

Figure 3.6. Members of the intelligence community

about intelligence capabilities; therefore they often have unrealistic expectations of what intelligence can do for them, especially when they hear about the genuinely extraordinary capabilities of US intelligence for collecting and processing information.

(Andrew 1995: 2)

Gates also alleged that "most Presidents often attach as much – if not more – credibility to the views of family, friends, and private contacts as they do to executive agencies, including the intelligence community" (Andrew 1995: 5). There was considerable criticism of the intelligence community following the terrorist attacks on New York and Washington. But the defenders of the intelligence community responded that the CIA had become a very defensive bureaucracy in light of its experience of the White House failing to support it if things went wrong. Furthermore, Congress had passed legislation in the 1980s that forbade the CIA to recruit unsavory characters who had criminal records. In the aftermath of the terrorist attacks there was a relaxation on many restrictions placed on the CIA and an increased budget for the intelligence community.

Perhaps the biggest intelligence failure in modern times was over Iraq. The CIA was heavily criticized for its wrong assessment that Iraq possessed WMD, a central argument in the US case for the invasion of that country. The CIA also admitted that it did not have a single agent in Iraq. The CIA chief, George Tenet, resigned just before publication of the report by the Commission investigating 9/11. The report said that 9/11 was a shock but should not have been a surprise. There was considerable evidence that Al Qaeda had been planning such an attack for several years. Across the government, however, "there were failures of imagination, policy, capabilities and management." Terrorism had not been the overriding national security concern of the Clinton or pre-9/11 Bush administrations. The US had not updated its capabilities to tackle threats from Al Qaeda and was poor at pooling intelligence. The report pointed to too many priorities, outmoded structures and bureaucratic rivalries. It condemned the fact that there was no national intelligence estimate on terrorism between 1995 and 9/11. The report then stated that US policy should have two ends: dismantling the Al Qaeda network and, in the longer term, prevailing over the ideology that contributes to Islamic terrorism. The Commission concluded by calling for a thorough overhaul of the intelligence agencies, more resources, the establishment of a national counter-terrorism center and the creation of a new post of National Intelligence Director as a sub-cabinet post separate from CIA. It emphasized the need for information sharing rather than "the right to know" and the importance of congressional oversight. (http://www.9–11commission.gov/). In April 2005 Bush appointed John Negroponte as the first Director of National Intelligence

A further Senate committee report criticized the CIA and the other intelligence agencies for "group think." They all assumed that Saddam Hussein had a WMD program and never stopped to consider alternative scenarios. To do so would have been considered heresy which is why Hans Blix, the chief UN weapons inspector, accused America of posting "faith-based intelligence." Although both reports were well received, many CIA staff were angered that the White House later attempted to misuse the intelligence provided on Iraq and blamed the CIA for the intelligence failure. One anonymous officer wrote a devastating critique, *Imperial Hubris*, that claimed the war on Iraq was a major digression from the war on terrorism.

The 9/11 Commission's recommendations were largely accepted by the Congress but in late 2004 both the Senate and the House put forward rival bills that proved difficult to reconcile. Donald Rumsfeld was accused of lobbying to block the proposal to create an intelligence supremo that would direct Pentagon resources. It seemed the wrangle over intelligence structures and budgets would continue into 2005. The focus on terrorism also made the administration aware of the importance of the CIA and FBI's collaboration with foreign intelligence and security organizations. Despite its intelligence superpower status, the US was painfully aware that it was dependent on other countries for assistance.

Department of Homeland Security

In June 2002, President Bush established a new cabinet-level Department of Homeland Security, headed by his old friend, Pennsylvania Governor Tom Ridge. The new department meant a radical shake-up of the Washington bureaucracy as it took over 22 agencies that had previously been located in other federal departments. It also took over some 170,000 staff and had a budget of nearly $40 billion. Its main tasks were border and transportation security, emergency preparedness, chemical, biological, radiological and nuclear countermeasures, and information analysis and infrastructure protection. The new department was also given responsibility for the immigration and naturalization service, the customs service and the coastguard. As it expanded it also took over shared responsibility for cooperation with US allies in protection against terrorism. But inevitably this led it into turf battles with the FBI and CIA. In February 2005 Bush appointed Michael Chertoff as successor to Ridge.

Conclusion

In the post-Cold War world, there are an increasing number of foreign policy actors involved in the executive branch. As foreign policy has become more of a political football, the President has come to depend more and more on his closest advisers in the White House and NSC. The NSC, operating under the direct authority of the President, has steadily increased its authority in recent years and the national security adviser has become the key figure in the US foreign policy machine. Other executive branch actors, including the State Department, have seen their influence decline, although much depends on the personalities holding these positions and their relationship to the President. There are inevitably ongoing rivalries between the national security adviser and the Secretary of State, between the Secretary of State and the Secretary of Defense. It takes a skillful President to ensure that these powerful figures work together as a team rather than pull in opposite directions. The defense and intelligence agencies received more money from Congress following the terrorist attacks of 11 September 2001 and some organizational changes were made. It is likely that their influence will increase as the US continues the war on terrorism. The Pentagon for example assumed responsibility for the reconstruction of Iraq. Despite their central failure on WMD in Iraq, the intelligence agencies were also given substantially more resources. Since the end of the Cold War, Congress has increasingly challenged the White House in foreign policy especially when the incumbent is from a different political party. It is important to examine what powers Congress has in foreign policy and how it uses them.

Selected further reading

Presidential authority is discussed in Neustadt (1990) *Presidential Power and the Modern Presidents*. Shoemaker (1992) examines the role of the NSC in *The NSC Staff*. Kegley and Wittkopf (1996) *American Foreign Policy* provides a comprehensive overview of the making of US foreign policy. Rubin (1985) examines the struggle the State Department has to exert itself as a major player in *Secrets of State*. Proposals to reform the State Department are covered in *The Foreign Service in 2001* (Institute for the Study of Diplomacy, Georgetown University, 1992); Eagleburger and Barry, "Dollars and sense diplomacy: a better foreign policy for less money," *Foreign Affairs*, July/August 1996. The *Foreign Service Journal*, for State Department officials, provides a forum for debating changes in the department (*www.afsa.org*). Destler, Gelb, and Lake (1984) *Our Own Worst Enemy* examines the infighting between State and the NSC. There are also interesting details about the State Department in the memoirs of Baker (1995), Christopher (1998), Albright (2003) and Dobbs's (1999) biography of Madeleine Albright. The role of technology and its impact on the armed forces is discussed in Michael O'Hanlon's (2000) *Technological Change and the Future of Warfare*. The intelligence agencies are well covered in Kessler (1992) *Inside the CIA*, Andrew (1995) *For the President's Eyes Only* and Bamford (2001) *Body of Secrets*. The 9/11 Commission report also provides a vast amount of detail on the intelligence agencies.

All US government agencies have their own websites. The White House and NSC can be accessed at *www.whitehouse.gov*; the State Department at *www.state.gov*; the Pentagon at *www.defenselink.mil*; the CIA at *www.cia.org*; the FBI at *www.fbi.gov* and the Department of Homeland Security at *www.dhs.gov/dhspublic/theme_home1.jsp*.

4

The role of Congress

Key facts

- Congress has significant powers with regard to US foreign policy, including regulating trade, declaring war, approving presidential nominations and ratifying treaties. In addition, Congress must approve all funding for the government's activities.
- Congressional committees are powerful bodies that provide oversight of the executive branch and hold hearings where government officials and experts testify about all aspects of US foreign policy. Staffers play a vital role in preparing briefing papers and speeches for congressmen.
- Throughout American history there has often been friction between the President and Congress. This tension is usually higher when the President's party does not control Congress. At times of national crises there is usually a rallying round the President.
- Since 1992, the overall interest of Congress in foreign policy has declined. Few members travel overseas. There is little interest in serving on the main committees dealing with foreign policy.
- Under pressure from various lobbies, the Congress often resorts to sanctions as a foreign policy tool. Individual congressmen often hold the executive branch to ransom over single issues.

Overview

When Congress is in session Capitol Hill is like a huge bazaar or fairground. The corridors of the Senate and House buildings are thronged with staffers, constituents, lobbyists and assorted visitors all wanting some precious time with an elected representative. As in most legislatures, the main action occurs in the relative tranquility of committee rooms rather than the floor of the Senate or House. Committee chairs invite members of the administration and other experts to testify at hearings on subjects within their area of competence. Usually these meetings are open to the public and can provide useful information about congressional concerns and the response of the administration. The questions and responses of the members are usually prepared by staffers, many with considerable expertise in foreign affairs as a result of previous jobs in the administration, in a think tank, or law firm. A member of Congress may have from ten to twenty staffers working for him or her plus a substantial number of usually unpaid research assistants or interns. Senator Hillary Clinton was alleged to have as many as forty interns working for her. The growth in the number of staffers as well as the excellent reports produced by the congressional research service (CRS) has given Congress a substantial research and analytical capability to draw upon when questioning the administration.

Foreign policy has provoked periodic trials of strength between the President and Congress throughout American history. But traditionally, foreign policy has been less susceptible to high levels of institutional and party competition, with the belief that partisanship ends "at the water's edge" in pursuit of the national interest. In recent years, however, there has been a sharp reduction in bipartisanship, most markedly during the second Clinton administration as the Republican-controlled Congress impeached the President. Anthony Lake, Clinton's first national security adviser, expressed his fear "that US foreign policy strength has been eroded by the poisonous political environment in Washington." In an April 2000 interview with *The Diplomat*, a Washington-based newspaper, he cited the 1999 Senate rejection of the CTBT "as an example of a political culture that has become nasty and dysfunctional." His successor, Sandy Berger, in a speech to the Council on Foreign Relations on 20 October 1999, also complained that

> the internationalist consensus that has prevailed for more than fifty years, increasingly is being challenged by a new isolationism, heard and felt particularly in Congress. The great irony is that we owe our reputation for trying to dominate the world in no small measure to a group of people who are intent on disregarding the world.

Despite these comments from Clinton's two national security advisers, it is worth noting that Clinton failed to secure his party's full backing for "fast track" trade negotiation authority and that there were no major differences between Democrats and Republicans during the Kosovo campaign.

Despite the increasing partisanship in the post-Cold War era, few foreign policy issues divide neatly along party lines. Both the Republicans and the Democrats have faced internal divisions over foreign policy fundamentals such as free trade, foreign aid, alliance expansion and America's role in the world, which limits their ability to impose any kind of party control. Ideology continues to play a greater role in Congress than with most other foreign policy actors. The far right and far left have often joined forces to support more isolationist or protectionist policies, including more allied burden-sharing and reduced foreign aid. The right-wing, North Carolina Senator, Jesse Helms, held up a trade bill offering some concessions to Caribbean countries until he secured greater protection for North Carolina textiles. In trade and international finance, foreign policy priorities such as funding for the International Monetary Fund (IMF) and fast-track trade negotiating authority have been stymied by similarly diverse coalitions. This dynamic also plays an important role in congressional hostility toward China. Liberal human rights activists have joined with religious conservatives concerned about the Chinese persecution of Christian minorities and national security hawks concerned about Chinese military activities. Pro-trade, business interests find themselves squeezed from both directions. The 1998 debate over NATO expansion demonstrated this "strange bedfellow" phenomenon. The nineteen senators who voted against expanding the NATO alliance to include Poland, Hungary, and the Czech Republic included ten Democrats and nine Republicans representing a wide spectrum of political views. There has thus been an increasing fragmentation of foreign policy in Congress with changing coalitions often able to block administration policies or even the majority position in Congress.

Case study: organization of Congress

The House of Representatives has 435 members, with a simple majority of 218 needed to pass most legislation, and a two-thirds majority needed to override a presidential veto. The Senate has 100 members, with a simple majority needed for passage of most bills and 67 needed for a "super majority" to override a presidential veto. Three-fifths or 60 are needed to shut off a "filibuster" (unlimited debate by one senator or a small band of like-minded senators to delay legislative action). In 2004–6 the House was composed of 231 Republicans, 200 Democrats and four independents. The average age of members of the House is fifty-three, with women constituting 14 percent of the members. For the Senate, the average age is fifty-nine, with women accounting for 13 percent of senators. Every two years the members of the House must run for re-election. This means that they are constantly searching for campaign funds as the cost of elections has risen steeply in the past decade. The members represent districts based on the population of their states, with each district composed of roughly 600,000 people. Very few seats are really contested. The vast majority, 80–90 percent, are either firmly Democrat or Republican. This tends to make congressmen's politics more extreme. In 2000–2 there were 50 senators from each party (every state has only two senators). Each senator serves a term of six years, and approximately one third of the Senate is up for re-election during each congressional election (every two years). Senate seats are unaffected by population changes. In May 2001, Republican Senator Jim Jeffords left his party and sat as an independent member, thus allowing control of the Senate to pass to the Democrats. In November 2002, partly due to the then popularity of President Bush, the Republicans won back control of the Senate and the House. For the first time for many years one party had control of the White House and both Houses of Congress. In November 2002 the balance in the Senate was 51 to 48 in favor of the Republicans. This increased to a 55/44 split in 2004. The Republicans also increased their majority in the House.

The end of the Cold War has also helped to create an impression in Congress that the stakes involved in foreign policy have declined. Senator Pat Roberts, speaking in Texas on 10 April 1998, lambasted Congress for its lack of interest in foreign affairs, stating that "not since the 1930s, when Congress passed the neutrality acts just as the world was going up in flames, not since the Smoot–Hawley tariff helped create the Great Depression, has Congress been so insular and isolationist in its view of the world." The senator added that "the internationalist wing of the Republican party, once the bulwark of US engagement abroad, is now barely represented on Capitol Hill. Meanwhile, Democrat members of Congress are becoming more and more protectionist over the excuse of losing jobs." The impact of individual legislators on foreign policy has also increased. Although never particularly strong, the decline in party discipline and the congressional committee system has created the opportunity for individual members of Congress to push their own agendas. This is in marked contrast to the parliamentary systems of most European countries.

The main foreign policy committees

The main committees dealing with foreign affairs are the Senate Foreign Relations Committee (SFRC) and the House International Relations Committee (HIRC). For many years the SFRC chair was Republican Senator Jesse Helms, a thorn in the flesh to the Clinton administration. With the change in control of the Senate in 2001, Democrat Joe Biden became chair of the SFRC. After the 2002 elections Republican Richard Luger became the chair. The SFRC has seven subcommittees:

- African Affairs;
- East Asia and Pacific Affairs;
- International Economic Policy, Export and Trade Promotion;
- International Operations and Terrorism;
- Near Eastern and South Asian Affairs;
- Western Hemisphere, Peace Corps, and Narcotics Affairs.

The HIRC, chaired by Republican member Henry Hyde in the 109th Congress, 2004–6, has six subcommittees, with slightly differing responsibilities to those of the SFRC:

- Middle East and South Asia;
- East Asia and the Pacific;
- Europe;
- International Operations and Human Rights;
- Africa;
- Western Hemisphere.

The Senate Armed Services Committee also plays an important role in national security policy and, more importantly, has spending clout. During the 1990s, in addition to the general decline in party discipline, seniority played a lesser role in determining committee assignments. Both the SFRC and the HIRC have found it difficult to recruit members. According to Senator Chuck Hagel, speaking on 14 March 2001, "foreign relations has been a kind of wasteland. It is not a particularly strong committee to fundraise from." Though Senator Jesse Helms and Congressman Henry Hyde in 2001 became chairs of the SFRC and HIRC, respectively, based upon their seniority, many other senior members passed up the opportunity to chair subcommittees. This is particularly true in the SFRC, where in 1999 all seven subcommittees were chaired by first-term senators.

The declining prestige of the foreign policy committees has been accompanied by the growing perception that most foreign policy issues do not interest the voters, thus giving most members of Congress little incentive to take an active role in this area. Exceptions are most likely to exist where members have a large constituent ethnic group with a keen interest in policy toward their country of origin. Moreover, as responsibilities for foreign affairs proliferate throughout the executive branch, each government agency brings its oversight committee further into the fray. As a result, the Commerce, Finance, Judiciary, Banking and Ways and Means committees, that authorize expenditure, are playing a greater role in international affairs than ever before. Members can thus work on foreign policy issues from almost any committee.

Congressional powers

The framers of the constitution and the debates surrounding the constitutional convention reveal that the Founding Fathers intended to divide power relating to foreign policy between the executive and legislative branches. In terms of the constitution, it produced "an invitation to struggle for the privilege of directing American foreign policy." Four specific powers related to foreign relations are given to Congress in the American constitution:

- Congress is given the power to regulate trade;
- The Congress has the right to declare war;
- The Senate must give "advice and consent" to the President's cabinet including all political appointees, ambassadorships, and senior military appointments by a simple majority;
- The Senate must pass all treaties negotiated by the President by a two-thirds majority.

In addition Congress must also approve or "appropriate" all required funding of international activities undertaken by the government. This is perhaps the most important power – the power of the purse.

Appropriations and budgets

The most traditional mechanism through which Congress influences US foreign policy is the budget and appropriations process. The President's State of the Union address, given at the end of January each year, outlines his future political agenda. At the beginning of February, the President sends Congress a budget proposal that details all government spending for the implementation of the administration's programs for the next fiscal year. The appropriations committees of both houses then begin working on their estimate of the necessary and appropriate levels of spending required. Their deliberations may result in an increase or in a reduction of the amounts requested by the President.

Once the budget levels are decided, the functional committees (e.g. Armed Services, Finance) review the President's budget program and policy proposals. Within the guidelines established by the budget committee, the committees establish the language authorizing the expenditures, determining the policy purposes for which money may be spent within the guidelines of the budget committee. Often there is a substantial shortfall between the White House requests and the congressional decision that can have a significant impact on foreign policy. In recent years successive Secretaries of

State have spent considerable time on Capitol Hill testifying and lobbying to ensure an adequate budget for the State Department. Occasionally, the positions are reversed with Congress increasing amounts for specific programs. In the 1990s, Congress added to the proposed budget for democracy support in southeastern Europe, dismantling nuclear weapons in the former Soviet Union and AIDS funding for Africa.

Approval of treaties

All treaties negotiated by the President must initially pass through the SFRC. If the treaty in question involves particular areas of expertise, other committees may hold hearings and provide opinions to the SFRC. This usually applies to treaties on mutual tax recognition, maritime agreements, and military accords. As with all legislation, the SFRC chairman has the sole discretion to advance a treaty for a public hearing and passage. Only an extraordinary vote by the Senate can compel the chairman to act on a treaty he or she opposes, a move never seen in American history. The chair of the SFRC thus plays a significant role in US foreign policy and all Presidents are keen to enjoy a close relationship with the SFRC chair. At a minimum, the President will wish to avoid needlessly antagonizing the chair and search for some basis of cooperation, even in the face of deep party and ideological differences. In the second Clinton administration, for example, Secretary of State Albright engaged in a political courtship of Republican Senator Helms, the then SFRC chair, in an attempt to secure support for the administration's foreign policy agenda. The courtship was at best only partially successful. Helms was a strong supporter of one China – the capitalist republic of Taiwan – and given to colorful expressions. He described Europe as "currying favor with terrorists" after the US lost its seat on the UN human rights commission and told CNN viewers on 11 May 2001 that "if other countries retaliate against us for taking positions (NMD) to defend the United States they can go fly a kite."

Regulating trade – imposing sanctions

Congress plays an extremely important role in foreign trade policy. All trade-related bills are referred to the House committee on Ways and Means and the Senate committee on Finance, the tax-writing committees. These two committees and their specialized subcommittees have jurisdiction over all tariff adjustments for imports, and must pass the implementing language for all trade negotiations. Significantly, simple majorities in both chambers may pass all trade bills. Trade-related programs such as the Caribbean Basin Initiative, NAFTA, or the WTO, as well as the operations of the USTR, the trade agencies at the Commerce Department, the trade offices of the State Department, EXIMBANK, and the Overseas Private Investment Corporation (OPIC) are all under the purview of these two committees for their operational funding authorizations. US export controls and economic sanctions are considered foreign policy issues and do not strictly fall to the tax writing committees. Economic boycotts or limits on the sales of US goods to certain countries fall within the HIRC, and in the Senate to the Committee on Banking, Housing and Urban Affairs.

Case study: fast track/trade promotion authority

Several areas of trade legislation have developed or require special procedural elements. In the case of fast track (or trade promotion) authority for the President, this is a term that is not actually descriptive of the process. Congress must specifically authorize the President to negotiate a new trade round on its behalf. As a result of this delegation of power to regulate trade, Congress puts all trade negotiations, including NAFTA, on the "fast track." This does not necessarily result in speedy or swift consideration, but rather suspends Congress's right to amend or reopen final negotiated trade agreements. It greatly simplifies the legislative procedure and results in an up or down vote. Simple majorities are all that are required to pass the trade bills considered under fast track authority.

Foreign trade officials are reluctant to negotiate with the US, and risk political opposition within their own countries, without "fast track" arrangements in place in the US for fear that Congress could add or delete provisions in the agreement after they have been agreed with the negotiating partner. When George W. Bush took office, he stated that "fast track" authority would be a top priority in order to ensure that the US had the appropriate negotiating clout in international negotiations. The USTR in the George W. Bush administration, Robert Zoellick, changed the terminology from the politically charged "fast track authority" to the more positive and neutral term "trade promotion authority (TPA)."

On 6 December 2001 Congress voted by the tiniest of margins, 215–214, to grant the President TPA. In the run up to the vital vote, the President made an all-out effort to win over wavering members of Congress. In typical fashion some were promised various federal projects in their congressional districts in return for voting with the administration. The vote was largely on party lines with most Democrats opposing TPA because of concern about job losses or concern about insufficient attention to environmental aspects. The re-election of President Bush in 2004 and the increase in Republican congressmen would make it easier for the White House to secure an extension of TPA in 2005.

As noted above, Congress contains a mix of free traders and protectionists who cross party lines although in general it is Democrats who oppose more free trade because of their closer ties to the labor unions. Only twenty Democrats voted for the trade promotion authority bill in Congress on 6 December 2001.

An increasing trend has been for Congress to link trade policy to political and other ends: treatment of Jews in the Soviet Union (Jackson–Vanik), human rights in China (PNTR) and Cuba (Helms–Burton), support for terrorism in Iran and Libya (ILSA), protection of labor and environment in the WTO. In 2001, the US imposed more sanctions against third countries (75) than any other country in the world. The sanctions were estimated to cost American business some $19 billion annually in lost exports. This increasing congressional use of unilateral sanctions has been widely criticized but successive administrations have done little to confront Congress on individual cases.

When the Republicans took office in 2001, Secretary of State, Colin Powell, ordered a review of sanctions policies, making clear his doubts as to their effectiveness. Powell told Congress that he wanted to get rid of most sanctions. He asked Congress to "stop, look and listen, count to ten, and then call me" before imposing any new sanctions (*Washington Post*, 2 February 2001). There was considerable pressure from business (e.g. USA Engage) to drop or modify the various sanctions regimes, but there was equally a great deal of political pressure to maintain and even tighten these regimes, particularly in light of the terrorist attacks on the US. The Bush administration's review of sanctions policy was not completed before the terrorist attacks of September 2001 and it was decided to postpone any revisions until after the outcome of the initial war on terrorism. After the terrorist attacks of September 2001, President Bush sought and obtained from Congress executive authority to waive sanctions in the interest of national security. Congress meanwhile remains sharply divided on the whole sanctions issue.

Declarations of war

Declarations of war are perhaps the most serious responsibility of the Congress. While the President is the commander-in-chief of the US military, Congress is supposed to authorize his use of the armed forces in a war. The constitutional roles between Congress and the President are, however, often in conflict. The President's authority to use the military outside the US is clear, but the funding of continued operations is the responsibility of Congress. Since the founding of the republic there have been approximately 150 cases of American military involvement overseas. But Congress has only declared war on five occasions. It never declared war on North Korea or North Vietnam, nor did it authorize the sending of American troops to Grenada in 1983, nor Panama in 1989. At the height of the Kosovo conflict in 1999 the House had a tied vote on whether or not to support the bombing campaign.

The exact nature of what constitutes a war is not clear in the constitution, hence there are continuing debates about the President's right to send troops abroad and to participate in UN peacekeeping operations that do not meet the "war criteria," and thus are not technically under congressional authority. The most famous effort to clarify this situation was the Vietnam era "War Powers Act" which sought to establish a series of criteria and scenarios under which the President was required to come to Congress for authority to engage the military without a full declaration of war. The Act, however, did not succeed in bringing any clarity to a sensitive area. In recent years Presidents of both parties have refrained from asking Congress to approve sending troops abroad to fight although they have reported to Congress on their actions. For its part, Congress has never invoked the "60 days clock" that would cut funding and require the President to bring the troops home.

President George H. W. Bush did not formally seek congressional approval for the Gulf War, arguing that UN authority was sufficient. Nevertheless the Senate did narrowly vote in favor of using force in January 1991. Similarly, President Clinton argued that he possessed "executive authority" to send troops to Haiti and that NATO authority was sufficient for the Bosnian and Kosovo engagements. This angered Congress and led to passage of a resolution in 1993 stating that "the President should have sought and welcomed congressional approval before deploying US forces to Haiti." To a large extent the President's relationship with Congress and the seriousness of each situation in which the US military is involved determines the ability of the President to act. Within a few days of the terrorist attacks in September 2001, Congress passed a virtually unanimous resolution granting the President almost unlimited war powers. The vote in the Senate was 98–0 and in the House 420–1. Both Houses gave similar massive endorsements to the President's decision to invade Iraq in 2003.

Presidential nominations

Another important Senate power is to approve presidential nominations for Cabinet, senior State Department positions and ambassadorships. The SFRC oversees all such nominations and the chair of the committee has complete control over the timetable. Manipulation of the nominations process is one of the most important levers the Senate has over foreign policy issues. The nomination of former Massachusetts governor, William Weld, to be ambassador to Mexico in 1997 was blocked by Jesse Helms who reportedly considered his fellow Republican too soft on illegal drugs. Helms also blocked the nomination of James Hormel to be ambassador to Luxembourg on the grounds of his homosexuality. President Clinton eventually secured his nomination through a "recess appointment," a device that allows the President to approve a nominee while Congress is not in session. President George W. Bush used a similar device in January 2002 to nominate Otto Reich, a controversial supporter of the Contras in the 1980s, to become assistant secretary for Latin America in the State Department. Richard Holbrooke, whose nomination in 1998 to be US ambassador to the UN was held up for fourteen months, is a stern critic of the confirmation process.

> The confirmation process for ambassadors and other presidential appointments has become a nightmarish obstacle course where everyone is trying to play "gotcha" for partisan political or personal reasons, thus immobilizing the entire process. We need to call off these dogs of revenge, because the endless holds and delays on our ambassadors are having a very negative impact on our national interests.
>
> (*National Journal*, 1 September 2001)

The departure of Jesse Helms brought a significant improvement to the situation. His successor, Joe Biden, promised not to play politics with the nomination process. This promise was made good as the SFRC moved quickly to ratify most nominations of the Bush administration in the second half of 2001.

The informal process

Congress's influence over crises such as the response to the September 2001 terrorist attacks derives less from its constitutional authority than from the reputation, experience, and expertise of its politicians. In particular, it derives from their standing with fellow legislators and the executive branch as well as their experience in policy making and oversight. If the interaction between the executive and legislative branches rested solely on the formal mechanisms, little would be achieved. But there are numerous informal processes at play that help oil the wheels. To manage these informal dynamics, Congress and the executive rely on traditions and habits that have developed over the years to preserve smooth working relationships. For example, in the area of conventional arms transfers, the State Department honors a largely unwritten yet extensive notification system designed to keep members and their staffs fully apprised of expected transfers. The entire US foreign aid program is rife with such requirements, but security assistance activities stand out as there are as many as thirty-six different types of reports and notifications.

One such arrangement is the twenty-day pre-notification of prospective arms sales required by the Arms Export Control Act. These include sales of major defense equipment for $14 million or more, defense articles or services of $50 million or more, or design and construction services for $200 million or more. This requirement dates back to a 1976 agreement between the Defense Department and Congress and has remained in effect ever since. The State Department adheres to the system religiously, and a simple call from a staffer warning about congressional concern or asking for additional information is usually enough to bring the proposed transfer to a temporary halt. Such requests by members or their staffs to delay action on a given issue are commonly referred to as "holds." A "hold" by a member, especially if it is conveyed in writing, is almost never ignored even though it is not legally binding. "Holds" are used in other areas such as nominations and have become a common tool. According to one critic:

> It's gotten to the point where if a senator wants anything from the administration, they just look around for an important nomination to take hostage. The human toll this takes on honorable people ... who are left twisting in the wind for several months, should not be underestimated.
>
> (Norman Ornstein, *National Journal*, 1 September 2001)

The President and Congress

Presidents and Congress have enjoyed a love–hate relationship throughout American history. According to one authority, the President's power derives less from his formal legal authority and more from his power to persuade Congress and other parts of the machinery (Neustadt 1990). President Clinton, for example, found it much easier to gain congressional support for his priority issues such as NAFTA, WTO, and the chemical weapons convention in his early years when he was riding high in the opinion polls than he did after the Republicans took control of Congress. In his second term, as relations worsened between the White House and Capitol Hill, partly due to the Monica Lewinsky scandal, Clinton failed to obtain fast track authority, failed to secure ratification of the CTBT, and failed to obtain back payment of US dues owed to the UN. James Lindsay, however, suggests that "what lies at the heart of almost all disputes between the White House and Capitol Hill is not differences over interpretation

of the constitution but rather disagreement over the substance of foreign policy"
(Wittkopf and McCormick 1999: 175).

On entering office, Presidents usually enjoy some months' honeymoon with Congress, regardless of who controls the House and Senate. When George W. Bush took over the White House in January 2001 he was helped by the fact that the Republicans were in control of both chambers. He nevertheless enjoyed broad support for his huge tax cuts that he made his top priority. Six months into his presidency, however, the Republicans lost control of the Senate and the Democrats attempted to make life difficult for the President. Bush was saved from some embarrassing defeats in Congress by the need to respond to the terrorist attacks. The Republicans won back control of both Houses in November 2002 and further increased their ascendancy in 2004. A major crisis, such as the 11 September 2001 terrorist attacks, usually results in at least a temporary end to hostilities between the White House and Congress and a swing back to increased presidential power.

Although the bipartisan consensus supporting US foreign policy during the Cold War has sharply deteriorated, it is important to note that an inherent institutional tension between administration and Congress has characterized the foreign policy arena for most presidencies following the Second World War. While bipartisanship was the norm during the Truman and Eisenhower administrations, sharp partisan disagreements existed over policy toward China and other issues. The US involvement in Vietnam was a watershed event leading to sharpened congressional–presidential institutional rivalry and a more intensely partisan environment for the foreign policy process. Some administrations have been more skilled than others in managing their relationship with Congress, but all have been constrained in their foreign policy actions. Even Ronald Reagan, working with a Republican Senate and a Democratic House, faced intense scrutiny of his policies in Central America and dealings with Iran.

One analyst has put forward a two-president theory, namely that the President has considerable more leeway to operate in foreign compared to domestic policy (Wildavsky 1975). While this may have had some validity in the past it does not really hold true today. Although there was a tendency to grant Presidents more leeway in foreign policy during the Cold War, there was also repeated questioning of the wisdom of such presidential dominance. Critics pointed to such questionable foreign policy undertakings as the Vietnam War, Iran-Contra, covert action in Chile and elsewhere, and domestic surveillance of American citizens as evidence that presidential dominance did not lead to a successful or wise foreign policy. Accordingly Congress took steps to ensure that it was better informed, providing more resources to agencies such as the congressional budget office (CBO) and the Congressional Research Service (CRS). It also hired many more staff with backgrounds in foreign affairs and thus began to prepare itself for the role of equal player in foreign policy. Although it cannot be said to have reached this status across the board, in many areas such as policy toward international organizations and "rogue states" it is indeed an equal player.

Most administrations begin with at least the intention of creating an active dialogue with Congress but quickly lose their enthusiasm for such cooperation. In discussion with the author, Lee Hamilton, former HIRC chair, stated that in his thirty years in Congress no administration consulted enough with Congress on foreign policy. The result was that every President experienced deep trouble or failure to convince Congress of the merits of his policy. Almost all problems could have been avoided or ameliorated if the President and his team had spent more time with Congress, understanding its concerns, listening to its advice, and explaining the difficulties of the situation. Every President complains that consultation with Congress is too difficult – that there are too many members and too little time. Hamilton added that the ability of the President to work with Congress is also influenced by his perceived strength or weakness.

Other observers argue that the presidency has been weakened and Congress strengthened in the aftermath of the Watergate scandals (Woodward 1999). Others believe that a stronger Congress would have developed naturally without executive scandals (Mann 1990). The administration may also be divided on particular issues, with the State Department competing with Defense, Commerce, and other agencies to take the lead on issues that cut across departmental boundaries. This can be particularly harmful for the administration in dealing with Congress. Rival departments or units within the same department may seek out congressional allies and extend their disagreements to the Senate and House committees dealing with these issues.

Changes in Congress

As the general mood in Washington has become more partisan, the composition of Congress has undergone dramatic change. There are few senators and congressmen today with first-hand experience of the bipartisan approach during the Cold War. Over 60 percent of the 2000 Congress and 45 percent of the Senate first took office after 1992. These new members have known only the fractious politics of the new partisanship. The loss of senior legislators like Lee Hamilton, Sam Nunn, Bill Bradley, Nancy Kassebaum, who played a leading role in foreign policy debates, has also weakened the internationalist cause and marks the declining prestige of foreign policy issues. Internationalist "old hands" like Republican Senator Richard Lugar no longer have significant influence within their own parties.

Organizing political support in Congress thus presents particular problems for the remaining internationalists who consider that the US can best further its interests through multilateral fora and international institutions. It is also increasingly difficult to interest members of Congress in meeting with fellow legislators from other parliaments. The decline of the committee system and leadership roles for senior internationalists has been accompanied by the enhanced use of parliamentary procedures by individual legislators to delay or block passage of unfavorable bills. One of the most notable cases involved representative Chris Smith, supported by Senator Jesse Helms and other Republicans, and his lengthy crusade on abortion that effectively prevented the US paying its back dues to the United Nations. Similarly, in the case of the CTBT, Republican Senator Jon Kyl and a few colleagues pressed majority leader Trent Lott to hold a vote that was sure to end in defeat for the President and cast doubt on the international commitments of the US. Their promise to make Lott's life miserable if he delayed overrode the fact that twenty-four Republican Senators had publicly asked that the treaty be withdrawn from consideration.

Many foreign policy issues are now dominated by interested "issue leaders" which, in Congress, may coincide with the particular interest or ethnic background of members. Representative Ben Gilman, the former chair of the HIRC and a New York Jew, has a special interest in the Middle East. Another member of the HIRC, Tom Lantos, took an interest in EU enlargement because of his Hungarian background. Senator Ted Kennedy has a long-standing family interest in Ireland. Most other members take a particular interest in the country of their ethnic origin while the Black Caucus takes a special interest in the problems of Africa. In a few cases administration officials or representatives of non-governmental organizations may also become issue leaders, but they do not have access to the arsenal of parliamentary procedures available to members of Congress. In addition to controlling the budget, the threat of inaction or retaliation on separate issues constitutes powerful bargaining chips in dealing with the adminis-tration. Cabinet members and other administration officials take pains not only to cultivate individual legislators, but also to anticipate their objections to actions or proposals, often leading to a tacit censorship of administration activity. One writer has observed that "in the absence of public interest or a political consensus on a defining mission, large swathes of American foreign policy were essentially privatized in the 1990s by special interests in Congress, the business world, or ideological missionaries of one stripe or another" (Jackson Diehl, *Washington Post*, 1 October 2001). This trend for Congress to attempt to micro-manage foreign policy has been strongly criticized.

> For American foreign policy, ever in quest of the magic, all-purpose formula, the need for ideological subtlety and long-range strategy presents a special and as yet unresolved challenge. Unfortunately domestic politics is driving American foreign policy in the opposite direction. Congress not only legislates the tactics of foreign policy, but also seeks to impose a code of conduct on other nations by a plethora of sanctions. What is frequently presented as America's overweening quest for dom-ination is very frequently a response to domestic pressure groups. Whatever the merit of the individual action, their cumulative effect drives American foreign policy toward unilateral and occasionally bullying conduct.
>
> (Kissinger 2001: 17)

Another observer concerned about growing unilateralism and arbitrariness in US for-eign policy suggests that this trend is driven by the growing assertion of the US Con-gress that American law, religion, and family values – as defined by Congress – should prevail everywhere as the international norm (Hoagland in Boren and Perkins 2000: 21). This new-found congressional assertiveness in foreign affairs has meant that foreign governments and diplomats have had to pay increasing attention to Capitol Hill. Most embassies have sections entirely devoted to Congress. Nearly all visiting foreign min-isters and other ministers concerned with international affairs seek to spend some time with key members of Congress. Their desire to speak with American legislators, how-ever, is not always reciprocated. It is difficult to secure appointments for such visitors and even when a date is fixed, it is quite likely to be moved or canceled at the last minute. In 1995, one defense minister from a leading ally of the US turned up for a breakfast meeting on the Hill. Ten senators and congressmen said that they would be present but in the event not a single one appeared and the angry minister was left to brief half a dozen staffers.

Despite this treatment, embassies in Washington invest considerable time and energy to meet with members of Congress and their staffs, plying them with invitations to visit their countries. Such invitations are rarely accepted. Many members of Congress are reluctant to travel overseas lest they be criticized at home. A high percentage of congressmen are unencumbered by passports and House majority leader, Richard Armey, famously said that he had been to Europe once, and that was enough. One staffer on the SFRC told the author that if it came to a choice between his boss meeting a visiting foreign minister from a NATO ally and meeting the chief of his local fire brigade union, the latter would win every time.

Conclusion

Since the end of the Cold War, Congress has played an increasingly important role in the formulation and control of US foreign policy. Indeed some observers have spoken of "the 535 secretaries of state on Capitol Hill." As the lines between foreign and domestic politics become more and more blurred it is unlikely that there will be more harmonious relations between the President and Congress in future. Growing partisan differences have compounded the natural institutional tension that arises between Congress and the presidency resulting from the constitutional separation of powers. After 1994, Clinton discovered what Reagan and Bush had learned before him: foreign policy is much harder to conduct when the other party controls Congress. At the same time it can be argued that Clinton failed to build support in Congress or in the wider public for many of his actions, including Somalia, Bosnia, and the request for "fast track" authority. When he did seek to build a broad coalition, as with NATO enlargement, Congress approved his policy.

In the past there was some evidence that Congress allowed the President more of a free hand in foreign policy. Congress would make its points usually in symbolic fashion, holding hearings, issuing reports, attaching "waivers" to legislation that allowed the President to maintain ultimate control of policy. These practices allowed Congress to take a public profile on foreign policy issues while leaving the decisions in the hands of the President. Since the early 1990s, however, Congress has become more willing to take action that does interfere directly with the executive. Some examples include the Helms–Burton legislation whereby the White House effectively abdicated Cuba policy to Congress, the Iran–Libya Sanctions Act (ILSA) that was extended for five years in 2001 against the wishes of the administration, the failure to ratify the CTBT; and the failure to pay UN dues for many years. The reasons for this change are complex. On the one hand, politics have become more partisan. There was massive distrust of President Clinton amongst Republicans in Congress. At the same time, the issues have become more complex with few able to state with certainty what is best for the long-term interests of the US in any foreign policy issue. Partly as a consequence, Congress has become more irresponsible and single issue orientated.

It is impossible to understand how much of US foreign policy is made as a result of the informal process outside the legislative process. Votes, hearings, legislation only tell one part of the story. Use of the media, informal procedures, personal commitments and relationships are equally crucial to the foreign policy process. Letters, opinion pieces, talk show appearances all influence the debate. It is to the domestic environment and the power of the lobbies that we now turn.

Selected further reading

The role of Congress in foreign policy is well described in Lindsay (1994) *Congress and the Politics of US Foreign Policy*, Blechman (1990) *The Politics of National Security*, Crabb (2000) *Congress and the Foreign Policy Process*, Henehan (2000) *Foreign Policy and Congress*, Hersman (2000) *Friends and Foes* and Mann (1990) *A Question of Balance*. Hamilton's article in *The Washington Quarterly*, Spring 2001, reviews the question of bipartisanship in foreign policy. *The Congressional Quarterly* is a mine of information on the workings of Congress. Both main congressional committees have websites detailing their organization, membership, schedules, and recent testimonies and speeches: *www.senate.gov/ ~foreign* and *www.house.gov/international_relations* (accessed 11 April 2005).

5

The domestic environment

Key facts

- The US is a country divided politically. Population movements are increasing the influence of the south and southwest at the expense of the north. Changing immigration patterns could also influence foreign policy. The white population is declining relative to Hispanics, Asians, and others.
- There are thousands of lobby groups and other actors seeking to influence US foreign policy. These include ethnic groups, business interests, and NGOs. Many of these groups are well organized with considerable financial resources that they use to further their interests. They are also often involved in political campaigns as well as seeking to influence Congress directly. The rise of religious interest groups in the past decade, especially the conservative Christian coalition, has been noteworthy.
- The power of domestic lobbies has increased substantially since the end of the Cold War. As a result, it is increasingly difficult to define the national interest when there are so many vocal groups pushing their own narrow interests.
- NGOs are becoming increasingly sophisticated in influencing the policy process. Business and labor organizations have fought a number of battles over free trade and protectionism.
- The US has a very rich network of think tanks that provide regular input into the foreign policy debate and also provide a home for the "government-in-exile."

The changing body politic

In addition to the executive and legislative branches of government and the media, there are numerous other actors that seek to influence US foreign policy. These include a multitude of lobby groups, business interests, trades unions, non-governmental organizations (NGOs), think tanks, religious groups, foreign governments and international organizations. There is a long tradition of lobbies seeking to influence foreign policy in the US. The most visible, vocal, and successful lobbies are generally ethnic related with the American-Jewish lobby and the Cuban-Americans perhaps two of the best known. Other important ethnic lobbies include the Irish, Poles, Greeks, Armenians as well as the growing Hispanic and Asian communities. On any one day the Secretary of State and the national security adviser may have appointments with several different interest groups. Before turning to the growing influence of these lobbies it is useful to consider the changing domestic political environment of the US.

The US at the turn of the century appeared a nation divided. On 2 November 2004 George W. Bush won re-election by 51 percent to 48 percent for Senator John Kerry. There was a much higher turnout (60 percent) compared to 2000 (50 percent) when Bush won 47.9 percent of the vote and Al Gore 48.4 percent. Despite winning fewer votes than Al Gore in terms of the popular vote, George W. Bush won more electoral votes (based on states) and thus became the forty-third President of the US. In 2004, the Republicans also managed to increase their hold on both houses of Congress. In 1996, Clinton was re-elected President with 49.2 percent of the vote. That same year, the Republicans held the House by 48.9 percent to 48.5 percent. In 1998, the Republicans again held the House, by 48.9 percent to 47.8 percent. In 2000, the Republican winning margin was even less, 48.3 percent to 48.2 percent. This went up slightly in 2002 (51 percent to 46 percent) and again in 2004.

Apart from 2004, the last three presidential elections and congressional elections have thus resulted in neither party gaining 50 percent of the votes. Democrat support is concentrated in the large metropolitan areas (New York, Los Angeles, Chicago, San Francisco, Philadelphia, Detroit and Washington DC). The Republican strength is in the south, southwest and mountain states as well as in suburban areas. The mid-west is largely disputed territory, home to the swing states (Ohio, Pennsylvania, Michigan). The two nations follow very different lifestyles and have very different values. Most Democrats favor gay marriage, want abortion rights honored, guns controlled, the environment protected and the US to play its global role through multilateral institutions. Most Republicans believe gay marriages and abortions are immoral, guns part of a healthy way of life, land and water best protected by those who use them every day, and the US to play a limited, unilateral, and muscular role in global affairs. In many other countries there would be serious conflicts between groups with such different views. But the US is so vast that the two nations can live peaceably side by side. There were signs, however, that the bitter disputes over moral values, a central issue in the 2004 campaign, could lead to deeper social divisions.

During the 1990s, the population of the north (mid-west and northeast) grew by 7 percent, while the south grew by 17 percent and the west by 20 percent (figures based on the 2000 census). In 2000, the north accounted for 42 percent of the US population, while the south and west accounted for 35 percent and 22 percent respectively. Estimates suggest that by 2025 the north will account for only 38 percent of the population, with the south and west accounting for 37 and 22 percent. It is not clear how these trends will impact on foreign policy. On the one hand, more people are moving to traditional Republican strongholds. On the other hand, the fastest growing ethnic group is the Hispanic population that tends to vote for the Democrats. The south and southwest have traditionally been more conservative and more unilateralist in their approach to foreign policy. The south also has stronger ties to the military. It sends a disproportionate number of its population into the armed services and it is over-weighted in terms of military spending and military bases.

The growing political and regional divisions in the US could be further widened by changing patterns of immigration, the increasing role of ethnic groups, and economic changes. In the booming economy of the 1990s there was general nationwide support for free trade and globalization although a clear majority of northern Democrats voted against NAFTA in 1994 and refused to grant President Clinton "fast track authority" in the late 1990s. In the face of an economic downturn in 2001 there were increased protectionist voices to be heard around the US. The automobile, steel, and airline sectors all benefited from government support in 2001–2 as did agriculture and the textile industry. Reduced economic growth could translate into weaker congressional support for international trade agreements. The one vote margin in favor of trade promotion authority in December 2001 is evidence of such a change. In the 2004 election campaign Kerry was more protectionist in his rhetoric than Bush, reflecting Democratic concerns at losing jobs to developing countries such as India and China.

The new immigration

America is a country of immigrants from all parts of the world and in recent times the US has had Secretaries of State born in Germany (Henry Kissinger), Czechoslovakia (Madeleine Albright), and another (Colin Powell) the son of immigrants from Jamaica. Former national security adviser, Zbibniew Brzezinski, was of Polish origin, while Condoleezza Rice, the first black female to hold the same office, can trace her origins back to the slave trade. In the early part of the twentieth century about 90 percent of all immigrants came from Europe. Since the 1970s there has been a significant change in the pattern of immigration into the US and today European immigrants number only about 15 percent. This is due to the 1965 Immigration and Nationality Act that abolished the national quota system and gave preference to family reunification, a policy that favored recent immigrants rather than the traditional European ethnic base of the US. The result has been a drastic drop in immigrants from Europe. In 2000, there were 120,000 immigrants from Mexico and only 2352 from France. As the number of Europeans has declined dramatically, the number of Asians, Hispanics, and others from war-torn regions such as the Horn of Africa has risen steadily.

Current estimates suggest that by the middle of the century, white Americans will decline to just over half the population, Hispanics rising to 25 percent, Asians 8 percent, and blacks 14 percent. Will the new immigrants assimilate as the Irish, Italians, and Jews did a hundred years ago? One study notes that there were similar fears about the above minorities, yet they became good "Americans." The author suggests that one should not be concerned about today's new immigrants as they also want to be good "Americans" (Barone 2001). While these immigrants have concentrated on finding employment, often at the bottom of the economic ladder, they have gradually become more involved in issues with a foreign policy component. A prime example is the lobbying done by Mexican-Americans and Asian-Americans to ensure that changes to immigration laws and procedures did not negatively affect their interests.

It is important to note, however, that immigrants are not scattered evenly throughout the country. It is their concentration in specific regions and states that gives them influence. For example, if the central Europeans had been spread evenly throughout the US instead of being concentrated on Illinois, a key electoral state, they would not have had so much impact on the decision over NATO enlargement. Similarly the high percentage of Hispanics in California, Texas, and Florida, three states with high numbers of electoral votes, gives their voice an added influence. In California, the white population declined 9 percent from 17.3 million in 1990 to 15.8 million in 2004. The black population remained constant at around two million. The Asian population increased from 2.8 to 3.8 million. The largest increase, 6 percent, was in the Hispanic population, from 8.2 million in 1990 to 11 million in 2004. By 2025, whites will constitute only a third of California's population, with Hispanics representing over

40 percent, Asians nearly 20 percent, and blacks 7 percent. Whites will also fall well below the 50 percent mark in Texas, George W. Bush's home state.

It seems inevitable that, in future, Hispanics will continue to concentrate more on Latin America, Asians on the Pacific, and blacks on Africa. California and Texas already have their own mini-foreign policy toward Mexico as a result of the large Hispanic populations in these states. Miami has the most travel, financial, and cultural connections to Central and South America. The West Coast also hosts the most immigrant Asians, who give the universities and cities a very distinctive Chinese, Japanese, and Korean flavor. The black population is more evenly distributed and traditionally has not taken a major interest in foreign policy. Although the Black Caucus takes a close interest in Africa, there are different groups supporting Somalia, Ethiopia, and other countries. Furthermore, the Black Caucus does not rival the passionate interest other ethnic groups take in regions such as the Middle East, Cuba, Greece or Armenia. The problem for the Hispanics and Asians is their lack of unity. Mexican-Americans have a different agenda from Cuban-Americans and from Central-Americans. The Asian community is split into Chinese, Japanese, Korean, Vietnamese and other groups, each with a different agenda. The Chinese-Americans, although large in numbers, generally refrain from active lobbying, perhaps because they are less sure of their status and acceptance in American society.

It is an open question how the future generation of ethnic groups will approach foreign policy issues. It will certainly be a challenge to avoid the fragmentation of US foreign policy and ensure a broad consensus for a "national" approach to policy making. At the same time, one should also not forget that ethnic lobbies are also a useful conduit for US foreign policy and American values of democracy and the rule of law. The many East Europeans who returned to their homelands after the Cold War took with them experience of the American market economy and a vibrant political system. The Baltic states are a good example of this two-way influence. Since the 1940s, the Baltic states have enjoyed a special place in US politics stemming partly from the fact that the US never recognized their incorporation into the Soviet Union during the Second World War and partly because of their size, exposed geographical position, and desire for independence. Their fight for independence from the Soviet Union was strongly supported by ethnic groups from Estonia, Latvia, and Lithuania living in the US. Many members of these ethnic groups, often holding US citizenship, returned to the Baltic states after independence to help rebuild their countries. As a result of this history, there is considerable sympathy for the Balts and a strong lobby in Congress helped promote their membership of NATO.

Increasing power of lobbies

In the early part of the twentieth century the most active ethnic groups – German, Irish, Italian, Scandinavian – acted as a brake on US involvement in world affairs. During the Cold War, in contrast, virtually all ethnic groups were staunch internationalists, backing US containment of the Soviet Union. Since the end of the Cold War, and the lack of a consensus on guiding principles for US foreign policy, there has been more scope for ethnic groups to pursue individual aims. They have increased their access to Congress, encouraged the legislature to be more active in foreign policy, and made large contributions to finance political campaigns. As one analyst notes, "today more than ever is the ethnic group moment in the making of American foreign policy" (Smith 2000: 48). The same analyst argues that the ethnic lobbies have more power than is commonly recognized, that the negative consequences of ethnic involvement in foreign policy may outweigh the benefits and that this influence raises a serious problem for democracy. Another observer has written that "over the past three decades example after example springs to mind where ethnic groups have proven more powerful and effective as influences on congressional foreign policy decisions than the views of highly competent persons in the executive branch" (Kennan 1997: 4).

Samuel Huntington has also noted that for an understanding of American foreign policy

> it is necessary to study not only the interests of the American state in a world of competing states but rather the play of economic and ethnic interests in American domestic politics. In recent years the latter has been a superb predictor of foreign policy stands. Foreign policy in the sense of actions consciously designed to promote the interests of the US as a collective entity ... is slowly but steadily disappearing.
>
> (*Foreign Affairs*, March/April 1997)

Huntington points to the erosion of the predominant Anglo-Saxon culture and the worrying impact of immigrants who do not wish to be assimilated into the predominant culture. Economic and ethnic groups now have so much influence that "the institutions and capabilities – political, military, economic, intelligence – created to serve a grand national purpose in the Cold War are now being suborned and redirected to serve narrow sub-national, transnational and even non-national purposes." Huntington's alternative to particularism is not promulgation of any "grand design" or "new world order" but a policy of restraint. Such a policy, he argues, would win public support and enable the US to lower its involvement in the world in a manner that safeguarded its ability to act when it really needed to defend its national interests. A former Secretary of Defense, James Schlesinger, speaking in 2001, summed up the increased influence of ethnic groups:

> The United States has less of a foreign policy in a traditional sense of a great power than we have the stapling together of a series of goals put forth by domestic constituency groups ... The result is that American foreign policy is incoherent. It is scarcely what one would expect from the leading world power.

Ethnic groups tend almost exclusively to focus their interests on their "home" region. The Jewish lobby concentrates on events in Israel and the Middle East as well as the fate of Jews in other countries, such as Russia. The Irish follow the peace process in Northern Ireland. The Greeks maintain a watchful eye on the Balkans and the Aegean.

The Armenians focus on the Caucasus. East Europeans pushed for NATO enlargement. The Black Caucus seeks greater US engagement in Africa. Hispanics and Asians are active regarding hemispheric trade deals and immigration legislation. Sometimes there is a coincidence of interests between the ethnic lobbies and the US government. Clinton's call to expand democracy was taken up by many ethnic groups with ties to Africa, Latin America and the former Soviet Union. It was no coincidence that in 1996 President Clinton chose to announce his support for NATO membership for Poland (Hungary and the Czech Republic) in Detroit, a Polish stronghold that voted heavily for the Democrats in 1996 and 2000.

The US historically has been divided along the lines of race, ethnicity, national background and region. Politically a tension has endured between the individualistic and group components of US identity. But the problem is how to define the national interest when there are so many vocal groups pushing their own narrow ethnic interests. Given these traditions and trends, it may be difficult to maintain support in future for a more coherent and multilateral approach to foreign policy. It is perhaps illustrative to consider some examples of the influence of ethnic lobbies.

The Jewish-American lobby

Although representing less than 3 percent of the population, the Jewish-American lobby is arguably the most effective ethnic lobby in the US. Jews are among the most wealthy, best educated, and upwardly mobile groups in the US. They have remarkable influence in the media, cultural, and financial worlds, in addition to their entrenched positions in the political arena. The lobbying effort in support of Israel is the combined work of over a dozen organizations that have a presence in Washington. Within the pro-Israel lobbying complex, the American Israeli Public Affairs Committee (AIPAC) stands out as the most enduring and effective of all such groups with 55,000 members, a staff of over 150, and an annual operational budget of over $25 million. AIPAC's stated agenda consists of strengthening Israel's security through the expansion of US–Israeli strategic cooperation programs; changing US policy to recognize Jerusalem as Israel's undivided capital; maintaining continued US economic aid to Israel; and securing Israel's economic future by expanding US–Israel trade, investment, and research and development.

Originally established to counter the power of Arab oil money on Capitol Hill, AIPAC, and other pro-Israel organizations, have amassed an impressive record of lobbying accomplishments in the last four decades. This support has been manifested in unstinting support for Israel in the Arab–Israeli conflict: several US-sponsored UN resolutions in support of Israel and vetoes to protect Israel; the Jackson–Vanik Amendment (tying trade with the Soviet Union to Jewish emigration); and critical wartime intervention (especially during the 1967 and 1973 Arab–Israeli wars). President Bush went as far as declaring Israeli prime minister, Ariel Sharon, "a man of peace" and openly supporting Israeli views on settlements and refugees. He also accepted the Israeli argument that it was pointless to deal with Yasser Arafat, the former elected leader of the Palestinians. At the same time, US administrations have not bought into the entirety of this agenda. Washington has refused to move its embassy from Tel Aviv to Jerusalem, continues from time to time to push Israel toward the negotiating table and sells more advanced weaponry to Arab states than Israel likes.

AIPAC and other groups were particularly active following the 11 September attacks asserting that the terrorist attacks on the US were just what Israel had been facing for many years. The spate of Arab suicide bombings in Israel in the fall of 2001 and spring of 2002 gave some credence to this Israeli claim among many Americans. Israel was also a strong supporter of the US invasion of Iraq and has been active in seeking to emphasize the potential threat from Iran. Over the longer term it remains to be seen whether Americans come to question their hitherto largely uncritical support for Israel. Israel is the largest recipient of US assistance and since the establishment of the Jewish state, direct aid to Israel has exceeded $78 billion. The lobby was also instrumental in pressing the US government to pursue claims on behalf of holocaust victims against Swiss banks and German industry.

The effectiveness of the Jewish lobby in the US is a result of the utilization of the large financial resources and intellectual capabilities of the Jewish community to pursue political objectives. AIPAC has a large cadre of political activists who speak at thousands of meetings each year across America, reaching into every congressional district, especially those with little or no Jewish population. The Jewish lobby backs up its political agenda with policy papers, position reports, and background information. The political power of the Jewish-American lobby is brought to bear constantly on the media, during election campaigns and in promoting legislation that affects Israeli interests. AIPAC was the dominant organization pushing for an extension of the Iran–Libya Sanctions Act (ILSA) in the summer of 2001. Within a matter of days it was able to secure the signatures of over 70 senators and 200 congressmen to support the move.

The concentration of Jewish voters in populous states with large electoral votes, such as New York, California, Florida, Illinois, Massachusetts, Pennsylvania and New Jersey, can be decisive in close presidential and congressional elections. One example of this was the 1992 and 1996 presidential elections, where Bill Clinton received more than 80 percent of the Jewish vote. It is also worth noting that over 60 percent of the individual contributions to Bill Clinton's 1992 and 1996 campaigns came from Jewish donors. Although the Jews have had traditionally closer ties to the Democrats they also have excellent contacts and wide influence within the Republican party.

The Cuban-American lobby

The Cuban-American lobby is another highly effective lobby whose activities have resulted in Congress maintaining an economic embargo on Cuba and passing legislation, notably Helms–Burton, that affect other countries wishing to trade with Cuba. Compared to the two largest and most successful ethnic groups in the country, the Israelis and the Irish, the Cuban lobby is very small. There are only about two million Cubans in the US altogether compared to 10–12 million Jewish-American citizens and a far vaster number of Americans who claim some Irish heritage. The lobby spends considerable sums in its campaign to prevent a normalization of US relations with

Cuba under Castro. Furthermore, the Cuban émigré community is an important political bloc in Florida, the fourth largest state in the Union with twenty-five electoral votes in the presidential election process. This was to prove the decisive state in the 2000 elections when there were several recounts and ultimately the Supreme Court had to adjudicate.

US policy toward Cuba over the past forty years has been strongly influenced by the nature of the communist revolution, the perceived security threats from Cuba and deep-rooted hostility to Fidel Castro. The US–Cuban relationship virtually disintegrated during the early 1960s between the failed Bay of Pigs episode (a CIA-backed plot to invade Cuba and topple Fidel Castro) and the Cuban missile crisis in 1962 during which the current economic embargo was established. After the collapse of the Soviet Union and the termination of Moscow's economic assistance to Cuba many US observers were convinced that the collapse of Castro's government was near. However, even minor attempts at normalization in the early 1990s by the Bush and then Clinton administrations brought vociferous objections from the Cuban-American community.

The initial waves of immigrants from Cuba prior to and just after the revolution were the upper-class, wealthy Cubans of mostly Spanish descent. They came to the US with relatively high levels of education and political sophistication as well as the means to enrich themselves quickly in the US. Over the last forty years this community, largely based in southern Florida, has grown in wealth and power. There are two Republican Cuban-American members of Congress from south Florida and another, from New Jersey, is a Democrat.

Using Miami as a base, the émigré community expanded business and investments throughout the Caribbean. They also developed powerful political allies in Washington, mainly through the Cuban national foundation, an anti-Castro lobby group, which continues to raise money for the campaigns of mainly Republican congressional supporters of the economic embargo. On the issue of US–Cuban relations the émigré community leaders over the age of forty are virtually unanimous in their hostility to the regime. Younger, poorer Cuban-Americans, especially those of African descent, tend to be more sympathetic to relaxing the embargo and developing closer ties to Cuba. But they also tend to vote the same way as their parents, if they vote at all. In 2000, the Elian Gonzalez child custody battle split the Cuban-American community. Those favoring the retention of the boy in Florida were the most vocal even if they did not win the battle. It is a good example of the passions that narrow, special interest groups can bring to national politics.

Throughout 1993 and 1994, there were increasing problems with Cuban refugees fleeing the island mainly by flimsy boats and rafts. Because of the dangerous currents between Cuba and Florida, several private organizations started monitoring by air the movements of the refugees with the aim of helping them to safety once they had left Cuban national waters. One of these organizations, partially funded by the Cuban national foundation, was Brothers to the Rescue, which was mainly composed of pilots and volunteers of Cuban origin. When two of their planes were shot down in 1994 this provided Senator Helms with the opportunity to secure passage of a toughened sanctions bill (Helms-Burton) that also included anti-foreign investment clauses. By early

1995 the legislation passed through both houses of Congress by veto-proof margins and the President essentially abdicated his authority and control of US policy toward Cuba. The Helms–Burton legislation was a serious irritant to relations between the US and the EU (plus Canada and other countries) as it sought to apply sanctions to foreign firms engaged in trading with Cuban entities upon which Americans still had some legal claim.

Although most informed opinion "inside the beltway" considers that US policy toward Cuba is bankrupt, any attempt to modify the embargo will be difficult to pass through Congress. Cuba is not usually an important issue to the rest of Congress unless there is a serious incident. A few die-hard opponents of the embargo continue to seek its demise annually but most members of Congress are simply unwilling to expend the substantial political capital necessary to overturn the embargo. Outside the congressional districts and Senate seats directly involved with large Cuban communities, there has not been enough at stake for other leaders to get involved. Thus the situation will probably fester under the current circumstances until there is a significant change in Cuban leadership.

The Greek-American lobby

The activism of the Greek-American community in the American political scene is a relatively recent phenomenon. It was not until the Turkish invasion of Cyprus in 1974, that Greek-Americans began to mobilize on a national scale. The invasion spurred the various Greek lobbies to unite, at least for a period, and resulted in a lobbying campaign that led to a partial US arms embargo on Turkey. The total Greek-American population is estimated at 1.2 to 1.5 million and is concentrated in several urban settings, including New York, Massachusetts, Illinois, Florida, California and the Washington–Baltimore area. In its present configuration, the Greek lobby consists of over a dozen organizations that reflect different aims and agendas. The most influential, and the most moderate, is the American Hellenic educational progressive association (AHEPA). In 2004, AHEPA had about 25,000 members, with an additional 20,000 belonging to its auxiliary organizations. AHEPA organizes an annual banquet for congressmen and senators, while its members engage in fundraising activities for presidential candidates and pro-Greek legislators. Its publications include a semi-annual magazine, *The Ahepan*, advocacy reports, and a regular congressional report card. It is also active organizing legislative conferences, presenting testimony before congressional committees, and sponsoring legislative resolutions.

The most notable accomplishment of the Greek lobby was the 1975 partial arms ban on Turkey, a legislative victory that was due to the ability of several Greek-American congressional representatives to frame the ban as an issue of upholding the rule of law and human rights. But the victory was short-lived as the Turkish government began a counter campaign stressing the strategic importance of Turkey to the US and NATO. During the Carter administration a formula was agreed setting proportions for US arms sales to both countries. In 1995, a coalition of human rights organizations and ethnic groups succeeded in imposing a reduction in US aid to Turkey. Several Greek lobbies took the lead in forging an alliance with Armenian and Kurdish organizations to sponsor this legislation, mobilizing grassroots support, and presenting congressional testimony. Finally, a strong lobbying campaign in 1998 held up the transfer to Turkey of three US naval frigates for several months with the Greeks arguing that Turkey would use arms of this kind against civilians in the Kurdistan war or against the Greeks themselves.

A second policy initiative pursued by the Greek lobby came with the break-up of Yugoslavia in 1992, and the declaration of independence as the "Republic of Macedonia" by the Former Yugoslav Republic of Macedonia (FYROM). This triggered a wave of lobbying and demonstrations, which resulted only in a temporary delay in US recognition of the new state. In November 2004 the US decided to recognize the name Macedonia in order to help promote stability within the country. This prompted a furious reaction from Greece. As these examples show, efforts of the Greek lobbies over the past two decades have had a mixed record of success. One reason for this mixed record is the multiplicity of small Greek-American organizations with competing agendas. Another is the powerful lobbying effort mounted by the Turkish government after the initial Greek success in imposing the 1975 arms embargo. The failure to present persuasively the Greek agenda within the larger framework of American strategic interests has diminished the significance of the Greek lobby's goals in the perception of US decision-makers.

The Armenian-American lobby

The Armenian-American community, estimated at just under one million, mainly lives in California and the large urban centers of the northeast and the mid-west. The umbrella Armenian Assembly of America (AAA) was established following widespread demonstrations and other actions marking the fiftieth anniversary of the alleged genocide by Ottoman Turkey in 1915. The largest single organization within the AAA is the Armenian National Committee of America (ANCA). The Assembly's lobbying agenda is focused on supporting the Humanitarian Aid Corridor Act (the act bans US assistance to any country – mainly aimed at Turkey – that refuses to allow aid to pass through its territory to reach Armenia), providing economic assistance to Armenians in Nagorno-Karabakh, increasing US aid to Armenia (already the second highest per capita in the world, after Israel), reducing US economic and military aid to Turkey, pressing for a resolution of the Nagorno-Karabakh conflict, and seeking a reaffirmation of the Armenian genocide by the President and Congress.

The ANCA regularly endorses or opposes candidates for public office through an elaborate process which includes distributing questionnaires to all candidates seeking their party's nomination in order to determine each candidate's position on Armenian issues; writing letters to the President, the Secretary of State, and other executive branch officials; keeping congressional report cards, the results of which are summarized and distributed to Armenian constituents before each electoral cycle. ANCA has developed close lobbying coalitions with other ethnic lobbies and interest groups, particularly with the American Hellenic Institute, Kurdish American organizations, as well as human rights and religious groups. Along with the Armenian Assembly, ANCA has supported the formation of the congressional caucus on Armenian issues.

ANCA tends to take a more assertive stance than the Assembly, particularly on the genocide issue and opposition to Turkey.

Despite the relatively small size of the Armenian-American community and its limited resources, both ANCA and the Assembly have registered considerable success, not least in placing the Armenian genocide as a permanent item in the US legislative and foreign policy agendas. The lobbies have succeeded in garnering increased economic and humanitarian aid to Armenia and reducing US economic aid to Turkey. Nevertheless, their performance is inhibited by the emerging counter power of Azerbaijan's lobbies, which are supported by Turkey, and major US oil companies.

Influencing policy

The influence that a lobby can bring to bear depends very much on its size, organization, unity, commitment and resources as well as the broader political context in which it operates. The lobbies described above are not so large, but they are concentrated in key states, and are all highly motivated. The Jewish-American and Cuban lobbies are more united and better organized than the Greek and Armenian lobbies and hence achieve greater influence. It is also easier to help maintain the status quo (e.g. the embargo on Cuba) rather than to try and change long-standing policy. It also helps if there is broad political support for the aims of the lobby in question. For example, polls show that there is widespread American public sympathy for "plucky, democratic Israel." The Greeks and Armenians have more of an uphill struggle to get the US to harm Turkey's interests because there are powerful counter lobbies (oil, defense) arguing the importance of Turkey as a strategic ally.

There are three main channels for ethnic groups to bring their influence to bear on US politics – voting, financial contributions, and legislative action. In terms of demographics one could question the voting power of the ethnic lobbies. The Jews are about 3 percent of the population, Greeks barely 1 percent, Cubans and Armenians less than half a percent. However, all have real clout in Washington. Part of the reason is that the ethnic groups are concentrated in a small number of states, and, in the case of the Jews in New York, exercise their voting power mainly through the selection of candidates in the primary system. In 2000 Hillary Clinton had to court the Jewish lobby assiduously to receive its endorsement first for the Democratic nomination for the Senate, and then for their financial and organizational support in the main election. Bill Clinton also benefited hugely from ethnic electoral votes in both his presidential victories. In 1996 Clinton received only 43 percent of the white vote, compared to 46 percent for Robert Dole. But Clinton won handsomely due to chalking up 84 percent of the black vote and 72 percent of the Hispanic vote. Ethnic groups have also learned that money buys influence. Although Congress passed a mild campaign finance reform bill in spring 2002, it remains to be seen how effective it will be in practice. The 2000 presidential race cost the candidates close to $1 billion with 2004 even more expensive. Senate and House races may cost several hundred million dollars. In these circumstances candidates are loath to turn down money from any source.

Interest groups are also always ready with drafts of legislation to further their interests. In addition, the interest groups maintain close contacts with friendly congressmen and supply them, and others, with information about their case. Congressmen and their staffs are inundated with invitations to attend lunches, dinners, and visit exotic venues to hear the case of this or that interest group. These direct ties to Congress are followed up with contacts with the administration and a continuous bombardment of the media about their case.

Not all ethnic groups, however, engage in lobbying on foreign policy issues. There are many Scandinavians, British, Dutch, Italian immigrants in the US but they do not lobby like the Greeks or Armenians. Ethnic groups usually only lobby if there are large numbers of political exiles (e.g. Cubans) or if their former homeland appears threatened by neighbors (e.g. Greece, Armenia, Israel). It helps that these groups are among the most economically successful in America. Impoverished ethnic groups are more interested in bettering their own lot than worrying about their homeland. This helps to explain why most Latino lobbies such as the Mexican American Legal Defense and Educational Fund concentrate on social and economic issues. As political and economic conditions change, so too does the power and influence of ethnic lobbies. One can already witness increasing activity of the growing and affluent Indian-American community, seeking to warn the US of the dangers posed by China and Pakistan.

Business and unions

The major US corporations and financial institutions, which play an important role in financing US elections, are generally supportive of an internationalist and free trade approach. Trades unions, in contrast, are generally more protectionist in their outlook. Both sides claim to support human rights abroad but whereas business argues that engagement is a more fruitful approach, the unions argue that the US should not engage in free trade with countries that have no minimum wage and exploit workers. Some of the biggest clashes between business and unions have occurred over China and NAFTA. The large number of trade sanctions imposed by the Congress has also affected business. Another area of concern to business is the attempt to impose controls on carbon dioxide emissions.

Case study: the US and global warming (the Kyoto Protocol)

Perhaps no issue has brought so much criticism on the US than its failure to sign up to the 1997 Kyoto Protocol that sought to address the global problem of climate change. American business lobbied strongly against the protocol that set targets for industrialized countries to reduce their emissions of greenhouse gases to an average of 5 percent below 1990 levels during the years 2008 to 2012. With less than 5 percent of the world's population the US consumes over 25 percent of the world's energy resources and is responsible for around 20 percent of greenhouse gas emissions. Under the Kyoto Protocol, the US, which accounts for about a third of the world's greenhouse gas output, would have to cut its emissions by about 7 percent. The Clinton administration was sharply divided on the implications of the Kyoto targets. It signed the protocol but made clear that it would not submit it to the Senate for approval until developing countries were required to adhere to binding emission targets. The Senate expressed similar reservations in a resolution, passed 95–0 in 1999, that opposed any treaty without targets for developing countries. When the Bush administration took over in January 2001, it did not conceal its dislike for Kyoto (and its CO_2 reduction targets) and seemed to take delight in telling the rest of the world that as far as Washington was concerned the treaty was "dead." Rice later conceded that the public relations side could have been handled better.

President Bush, under strong pressure from domestic lobbies, argued that the Kyoto Protocol was "fatally flawed" because it excluded targets for developing countries; that the targets were arbitrary and not based on science; and that the targets set for the US were too high and would lead to a downturn in economic activity and job losses. With this strong statement by the President it seemed to many that the Kyoto Protocol was indeed dead. But at two conferences in Bonn and Marrakesh, the EU took the lead in rallying support to ratify the agreement. Concern about the possible scale of climate change this century, coupled with a determination to preserve the multilateral negotiating process, persuaded governments to press on with the protocol without the US. Securing Russian support was critical as to enter into force, the protocol needed to be ratified by at least fifty-five countries, representing 55 percent of industrialized countries' 1990 emissions. That meant ratification by the EU, Russia, Japan and the rest of Europe which, together, produce 58 percent of the industrialized world's emissions.

Speculation about the future intentions of the US, which is the world's largest emitter of carbon dioxide, will continue to dominate the debate about climate change. In the short term, there is little prospect of the US changing its mind on Kyoto. In a closing speech to the Morocco convention, Paula Dobriansky, the leader of the US delegation, said that the administration remained convinced that the protocol was "not sound policy." President Bush said that the administration would continue to work on alternative climate change policies, including a national energy plan, and would not seek to block the implementation of Kyoto. The events of 11 September 2001 had little direct impact on American attitudes on climate change, other than increasing concern about the security of future energy supplies from the Middle East. The heavy dependence on Persian Gulf oil means that the US has viewed the maintenance of the status quo in Saudi Arabia and other Gulf countries as a vital national interest. Some of America's closest allies, however, seized the opportunity to remind the US of the importance of multilateral cooperation. British Prime Minister, Tony Blair, stated that "the power of the international community gearing up to fight terrorism could be used to improve the environment. We will implement Kyoto and call upon all other nations to do so."

Despite the current unwillingness of the US administration to change course on Kyoto, there could be pressure from Congress to adopt tougher restrictions on the carbon dioxide emitted by public utilities, which account for about 40 percent of American carbon emissions. This could in turn prompt a rethink of US policy and US involvement in the next round of climate change negotiations. US participation would be eased if the developing countries were involved. However, winning the support of developing countries cannot be taken for granted. Under the 1992 UN Framework Convention on Climate Change, the developed countries agreed to take the lead in addressing climate change. Many developing countries doubt whether the wealthy nations have yet taken credible action on this score. The American reaction to the Kyoto Protocol demonstrated the power of the domestic energy lobby in the US.

The annual debates in Congress on granting China continuing preferential trade status always provoked a fierce dispute between US business and labor unions. In the spring of 2000 the main trade union organization, AFL-CIO, organized 15,000 people in Washington to protest against the granting of trade preferences to China and to oppose the negotiations for China to join the WTO. American labor leaders questioned the morality of granting China trade preferences on the basis of its poor record in human rights and labor standards. They also argued that it would cost thousands of jobs in the US. Meanwhile the US chamber of commerce took the opposite position, arguing that denying China trade preferences would prevent American companies, workers, and families from enjoying the benefits of lower trade barriers with China. Congress narrowly approved both the annual trade preference bills and the bill in favor of China's admission to the WTO. In the fight for Chinese trade preferences and China's WTO entry, groups such as the Business Roundtable, the chambers of commerce, and the American Farm Bureau mobilized executives, workers, and farmers around the country to lobby Congress.

Another dispute between the business and union lobbies arose over NAFTA. Although a comfortable majority in Congress approved the agreement in 1994, labor claimed, and continues to claim, that NAFTA would lead to heavy job losses in the US. Business disagreed. Although NAFTA was passed, Congress refused to grant President Clinton "fast track" authority in 1997, with many Democrats wary of the job implications for further free trade deals. The lingering resentment over China and NAFTA led the unions to oppose the WTO negotiations that were supposed to have been launched in Seattle in 1999 and the start of a new trade round in Doha. Labor has also been very active in promoting higher labor and environmental standards in international trade negotiations.

Business has also been concerned at the rising protectionist voices in the US and the growing number of economic and trade sanctions. In the mid-1990s, a broad-based coalition of nearly 700 business and agricultural groups set up USA Engage, to lobby for free trade and against the proliferation of unilateral US economic sanctions. Major companies all have their own lobbyists in Washington to defend their interests and monitor political and legislative proposals that might affect their business. In the aftermath of the September 2001 terrorist attacks, the airline companies, both individually and collectively, lobbied successfully for government assistance. In the final few days before the Christmas 2001 recess, Congress approved the purchase of a hundred Boeing military planes in order to keep the production lines busy.

Sometimes companies lobby against each other. For example, in 2000, Chiquita and Dole took opposite sides in the famous banana war between the US and EU. Companies also lobby in favor of issues that might help their business. Lockheed Martin helped finance the campaign for NATO enlargement. The same company plus other missile manufacturers such as Raytheon helped support the campaign in favor of national missile defense. Individual industries also lobby to protect their interests. In 2001, the North Carolina textile manufacturers protested against the Caribbean Trade Bill and engaged their Senator, Jesse Helms, to help them restrict textile imports. Helms held up four nominations to the Treasury Department until he secured satisfactory changes to the bill. The powerful sugar lobby also ensured limits on imports from Caribbean and other Latin American competitors. Automobile manufacturers, with support from the labor unions, have lobbied continuously to set limits on Japanese and South Korean car and truck exports to the US. American farmers are another powerful domestic lobby that manages to extract millions of dollars each year in government subsidies for their industry. When a particular industrial sector is affected by world conditions there is usually a sympathetic ear in Washington to listen and act on their concerns. For example, the steel lobby succeeded in persuading the President to impose 30 percent tariffs on imported steel in March 2002.

One of the most controversial aspects of business and government related to the awarding of contracts after the Iraq War. Initially the US stated that all reconstruction contracts would go only to the US and those allies that had supported the war. After intense lobbying by foreign companies and their governments these guidelines were modified. The substantial involvement of Haliburton, a Texas oil company in which Dick Cheney was involved, also raised political controversy.

Other non-governmental organizations (NGOs)

The rapid increase in the number of NGOs around the world has had a profound impact on US foreign policy. Not even the world's foremost power likes being subject to criticism by Amnesty International or Greenpeace. American and international NGOs are also a prime conduit for foreign aid, often in difficult circumstances but with television cameras present, and hence have a profile that Washington cannot ignore. There is also a negative side to the influence that NGOs can have on policy. A prime example was the disruption to the WTO meetings in Seattle in 1999 and to the IMF and World Bank meetings in Washington DC in 2000.

The US likes to consider itself as a staunch promoter of democracy and both major parties have foundations with substantial budgets that support democratic practices abroad (see *www.ned.org*, accessed 11 April 2005). The National Rifle Association was instrumental in securing US government support in watering down the provisions of a UN small-arms treaty in 2001. Even though the US did not sign the land mines convention, a measure successfully pushed by the international committee to ban land mines, it did agree, under pressure from the Red Cross and other humanitarian NGOs, to fund and engage in the development of de-mining technology.

There are also several important human rights and religious NGOs that seek to influence policy. Human Rights Watch is one such organization that carefully monitors US foreign policy from a human rights angle. It provides input into the annual assessments on human rights abroad produced by the State Department and seeks to restrict American exports to countries with poor human rights records. The religious lobby is also active in foreign policy. The conservative, Christian movement is particularly influential in the right wing of the Republican party and seeks to ensure religious freedom in foreign countries as well as to influence policy on abortion, at home and abroad. The Mormons are also highly active in promoting religious freedom. Their policy of sending volunteers abroad for lengthy spells has resulted in Utah, the state where most Mormons live, having the highest percentage of the population speaking a foreign language. This helps Utah attract inward foreign investment and leads to a disproportionate number of Mormons serving in the various external agencies of the US government. Women's groups are also active promoting equal rights abroad and lobbying against practices such as child prostitution and female circumcision in Africa. They achieved quite a success in securing Hillary Clinton to lead the US delegation to the 1995 UN conference on women's rights in Beijing.

Environmental groups are also heavily involved in seeking to influence American foreign policy. Despite the lack of enthusiasm in the administration for the Kyoto Protocol, the Sierra Club, an environmental NGO, is a powerful lobbying group that has chalked up a number of successes in Congress, including highlighting the damage done by logging in the Amazon rainforest. Other environmental groups make it a practice to provide congressional representatives with all expenses paid trips to the homes of certain endangered species or environmentally unique areas. Another and deceptively insignificant example is the role played by environmental institutions, such as the Orangutan Foundation and the Dian Fossey Gorilla Fund. These two foundations, which have for their goal the preservation of the endangered apes, were both awarded money from the 2000 appropriations bill ($1.5 million each). Closer inspection reveals that the Orangutan Foundation heavily contributes to the Democratic party, while the Gorilla Fund is a strong supporter of the Republican party.

Case study: think tanks

A substantial and influential network of think tanks adds considerable analytical and advocacy resources to the foreign policy establishment. There are well over 100 such public policy institutes, including over twenty dealing with foreign policy issues, ranging across the political spectrum. In addition to scholarly analysts, their ranks include high-level policymakers in exile from government positions, those on "sabbatical" between administrations or spells in Congress, or in retirement after public service. The incoming George W. Bush administration drew heavily on people working in the American Enterprise Institute, the Heritage Foundation, and other pro-Republican think tanks when it took office in January 2001. Similarly many people who had worked in the Clinton administration were hired by think tanks, e.g. James Steinberg went to head the foreign policy program at Brookings. The previous holder of this position, Richard Haass, joined the Republican administration and then later moved back to become president of the Council on Foreign Relations, a good example of the revolving door at play.

Among those concentrating on foreign policy, are the Council on Foreign Relations, www.cfr.org. The CFR is non-partisan and regards itself as the most prestigious and influential think tank. Its headquarters are in New York but it has offices in Washington DC and Chicago. The Brookings Institution, www.brookings.org pursues a liberal research agenda and hosts regular seminars and working lunches to discuss foreign policy issues. The Center for Strategic and International Studies (CSIS), www.csis.org is also non-partisan but regarded as leaning center right. RAND www.rand.org has headquarters in Santa Monica, California and offices in Washington DC. It built its reputation in defense policy research for the US air force but now covers a wide range of domestic issues in addition to national security themes. The Carnegie Endowment for International Peace, *www.ceip.org*, the US Institute of Peace, *www.usip.org* and the Woodrow Wilson Center, *www.wwics.si.edu* are leading liberal think tanks with a strong focus on conflict resolution issues. On the right of the political spectrum are the American Enterprise Institute, *www.aei.org*, the Heritage Foundation, *www.heritage.org*, the CATO Institute, *www.cato.org*, and the Nixon Center, *www.nixoncenter.org*. Other more specialist think tanks include the Atlantic Council of the US, *www.acus.org*, the Center for Defense Information, *www.cdi.org*, the Henry L. Stimson Center, *www.stimson.org*, the Institute for International Economics, *www.iie.com*, the Washington Institute for Near East Policy, *www.washingtoninstitute.org*, the Middle East Institute, *www.mideasti.org* (websites accessed 11 April 2005).

The administration and Congress rely heavily on the think tank community for a great deal of analytical input and public policy advice. The frequent personnel movement back and forth among the ranks of the administration, Congress, and the think tanks ensures that the output is policy orientated. In addition to a vast output of publications, both of an advocacy and independent scholarly nature, the think tanks stage a continuous menu of conferences, workshops, seminars, and lectures on a wide variety of foreign and security policy issues. They provide a common meeting ground for frequent interchange of views and networking among policymakers, diplomats, legislators, business, academia, media, and the NGO community. There is some evidence, however, that commercial and media pressure ensure that their focus is too short-term and not sufficiently focused on the longer-term direction of US foreign policy.

Foreign influences

Foreign governments, international organizations, including the European Commission, and foreign companies also impact on the foreign policy process. The British claim a permanent inside track due to their "special relationship" but critics doubt whether Tony Blair had much influence over Bush on any policy area, including Iraq. Israel will have an important voice in determining US policy toward the Middle East. Dublin will be heard when US policy on Ireland is being formulated. The UN will be heard when the reconstruction of Afghanistan is debated. The WTO will be heard on trade matters. Increasingly the European Commission will be heard on a range of global (environment, biotechnology) and bilateral (trade and competition) policy issues. Many foreign governments and companies employ US law or public relations firms to lobby on their behalf. China has been particularly successful in developing a lobby of American consultants and businessmen prepared to argue its case. Perhaps the most famous figure is Henry Kissinger, the chair of Kissinger Associates, who, according to one critic, has become the leading apologist for China. Beijing has also been ready to use a mixture of sticks and carrots to secure influence in policy circles. It has often awarded contracts on the basis of political as much as economic guidelines (Wittkopf and McCormick 1999: 71).

Conclusion

It is clear that the number of actors involved in the formulation of US foreign policy has steadily increased over the past two decades, thus limiting the executive's freedom of action to decide and implement policy. Diplomacy is also no longer the preserve of the East Coast Ivy League elite manning the government bureaucracies and think tanks. What happens "inside the beltway" still matters but, more than ever before, so do attitudes and decisions in Miami, Dallas, Seattle, Silicon Valley and Los Angeles. Regional interests play an increasing role in shaping US foreign policy. There used to be a broad internationalist group overlapping the parties. But increasingly Democrats are likely to be foreign policy liberals, as southern conservatives switch to the Republican party; and Republicans are likely to be foreign policy conservatives, as moderate or liberal northern Republicans vanish from the scene. The changing domestic political environment could have significant implications for the future of US foreign policy. Population movements in the short-term would seem to favor the Republican party and could lead to increasing unilateralism. In the longer-term the higher birth rates of Hispanics and blacks could help the Democrats. It will be a growing problem to integrate the demands of the various ethnic lobbies into a coherent US foreign policy.

The voices of various lobbying interests represented on Capitol Hill today enjoy the ear of many of Washington's policymaking elite. Given the decline of the importance of political parties in recent decades, this development has led these special interest groups to act as mini-political parties that act in support of certain micro-causes. In the specific cases of NATO enlargement and China's WTO entry, the outcome was heavily influenced by the lobbying efforts mounted by powerful business and ethnic organizations. Criticism of such groups comes from observers who suggest that the former manipulate to their advantage the increased power of money on Capitol Hill. These critics suggest that the very processes and institutions of democracy are undermined by such organizations. Whether or not this is true, it is indisputable that since the end of the Cold War, interest groups and their lobbying organizations have increased their influence in the formulation of US foreign policy.

Without any overarching principles to guide American foreign policy there is some truth in the claim that the promotion of domestic interests has become the default strategy of US foreign policy. Congress, domestic lobbies, and interest groups have gained in importance whilst the influence of the media and public opinion has often been a determinant factor in particular cases. It is to the media and public opinion that we now turn.

Selected further reading

Wittkopf and McCormick (1999) *The Domestic Sources of American Foreign Policy* provides a good overview of the domestic environment as does Kaplan (1998) in *An Empire Wilderness*. Smith (2000) *Foreign Attachments* gives a comprehensive overview of the growing power of ethnic lobbies. Krenn (1998) looks at the Black Caucus in *The*

African American Voice. Barone (2001) *The New Americans* examines the new patterns of immigration and considers how the newcomers will influence foreign policy. Nearly all lobbies have their own websites, e.g. AIPAC is at *www.aipac.org* (accessed 11 April 2005). Smith (1991) *The Idea Brokers* and Abelson (1996) *American Think Tanks and Their Role in US Foreign Policy* look at the influence of think tanks. A list of the leading think tanks and their websites is given in the bibliography.

6

The media and public opinion

Key facts

- Media coverage of foreign affairs in the US has declined dramatically since the end of the Cold War although there was a sudden increase after 9/11. At the same time, thanks to CNN and the internet, there has developed 24-hour news coverage that demands instant comment and analysis. The executive branch attempts to control the news by "spinning" its version of events.

- Politicians are often concerned at the "CNN effect" as television images, such as fleeing refugees in Kosovo or starving children in Somalia, can have a major impact on policymaking. Presidents often resort to public opinion polling before taking decisions.

- Presidents have had to become skillful media presenters in order to sell and secure public support for their policies. Some (Reagan, Clinton) have been better than others (Carter, Bush senior).

- Polls reveal that most Americans remain misinformed or unconcerned about international issues but are broadly internationalist in outlook. The terrorist attacks of September 2001, however, have led to greater public interest in foreign affairs and support for multilateralism.

- A clear majority of Americans consider that dealing with international terrorism should be the top foreign policy priority, followed by preventing the spread of weapons of mass destruction.

Public attitudes

Since the Vietnam War, public opinion has become a very important factor in shaping US foreign policy. Presidents pay careful attention to public attitudes before deciding on a course of action, particularly when committing US troops in circumstances where there might be fatalities. Public opinion played an important role in shaping US engagement in the Gulf War, Somalia, and Kosovo. Polls demonstrate that the public is broadly supportive of an internationalist approach but neither the executive nor legislative branches seem willing to tap this support. One recent study points out that members of Congress systematically misread, misinterpret, and distort the public's stance on foreign policy (Kull and Destler 1999).

According to the four-yearly surveys produced by the Chicago Council on Foreign Relations, the regular surveys of the Pew Research Center, the Program on International Policy Attitudes (University of Maryland) and other polling organizations such as Gallup, American public attitudes toward foreign policy are changing. While the public continues to support an internationalist approach, Americans are more likely to support US foreign policy objectives if they are related to the interests of the economy, national security and terrorism, a humanitarian crisis, immigration policy or drug trafficking. Any military intervention should preferably avoid "body bags" and must have an "exit strategy." After eighteen US soldiers were killed in 1993 in Somalia and the body of one being dragged through the streets was shown on television, the public demanded an immediate withdrawal. The President complied. According to one observer, "Somalia was a tragic example of the fickle quality of foreign policy arrived at because of images, in this case images of starving people, which can quickly be reversed by a counter image, that of a dead body being dragged through a foreign capital" (Halberstam 2001).

According to a number of opinion polls carried out after the September 2001 terrorist attacks, there was a considerable rise in the American public's support for a multilateral foreign policy. By a two-to-one margin, Americans now said that the views of allies should be taken into account by US policymakers and that a more active US role in the world would be a more effective way of avoiding terrorist attacks in the future. However, this new internationalism, driven by a nearly universal imperative for defeating terrorism, may have taken some of the steam out of what had been growing public support for solving other international issues such as drug trafficking, global warming, and the spread of infectious diseases. The polls also showed a two-thirds majority in favor of taking the war on terrorism to other "rogue states." It was partly these poll results that influenced President Bush to seek regime change in Iraq. The war on terrorism also changed attitudes on security issues. Support for increased military spending rose to 50 percent, the highest level for more than twenty years and nearly two-thirds favored the development of missile defense (ABC/Washington Post poll, 21 December 2001).

The public's general pro-internationalist outlook should not be over-emphasized. Ronald Steel has written that:

> There is a chasm between a foreign-policy establishment mesmerized by notions of American leadership and "global responsibilities" and an American public concerned by drug trafficking and addiction, jobs, illegal aliens, crime, health-care costs, and the environment. Not since the early days of the Cold War, when the establishment rallied the public to a policy of global activism under the banner of anti-communism, has there been such a gap between the perceptions of the foreign-policy elite and the realities of the world in which most Americans live.
>
> (Wittkopf and McCormick 1999)

Another observer has noted that the irony of the post-Cold War period is that:

> At the very moment that the United States has more influence than ever on international affairs, Americans have lost much of their interest in the world around them. This apathetic internationalism has led to a neglect of foreign affairs distorting policy choices to favor the noisy few over the quiet many, and making it harder for Presidents to lead.
>
> (Lindsay, *Foreign Affairs*, September/October 2000)

Declining media coverage

As politicians show less and less interest in foreign policy so has media coverage declined dramatically since the height of the Cold War. Coverage of foreign affairs in television has declined by 50 percent since the 1980s and only 2 percent of the stories carried by the mainstream press touch on foreign affairs. According to the Tyndall

Report, which monitors television news content, foreign bureaus in 2000 provided only a third of the coverage for ABC, NBC, and CBS that they provided in 1990. There are almost no television programs that cover foreign affairs on a regular basis. 9/11 and the Iraq War did lead to a slight increase in foreign coverage but much of this coverage was highly partisan. The Fox News channel, owned by Rupert Murdoch, for example, did provide regular coverage of the build-up to the Iraq War but provided a very biased view in favor of the administration. Television executives maintain that programs on foreign affairs have a limited audience and have to compete, in a commercial world, for audience ratings. News channels overwhelmingly concentrate on local news, with about 10 percent of airtime covering national news and less than 1 percent devoted to international news. The CNN shown in the US has a slot entitled "The Global Minute" in which all world news is presented in sixty seconds.

Inevitably, foreign stories are simplified and villains portrayed rather than analysis attempted. With few exceptions (*The New York Times*, *Washington Post*, *Los Angeles Times*) the coverage of foreign policy in the written media tends to be limited at best to whatever the current crisis may be. During the 2000 presidential campaign, Gore and Bush were unable to generate any interest in foreign policy, an issue that languished near the bottom of topics of concern to voters. The major foreign news story in 2000 was the fate of the young Cuban refugee, Elian Gonzalez, and whether he should be returned to his father in Cuba or stay with relatives in Miami. This story was portrayed as a soap drama in the media. Indeed, one observer has criticized the media for

> transforming foreign policy into a subdivision of public entertainment. Intense competition for ratings produces an obsession with the crisis of the moment, generally presented as a morality play between good and evil having a specific outcome, and rarely in terms of the long-range challenges of history.
>
> (Kissinger 2001: 27)

Case study: the media and Elian Gonzalez

The case of Elian Gonzalez in the summer of 2000 is an example of the powerful impact of the media and ethnic lobbies, in this case the Cuban-Americans, on the US body politic. Elian Gonzalez was a six-year-old boy who was rescued by a fisherman off the coast of Florida when he and his mother attempted to flee Cuba for the US on a raft. His mother drowned. His father, divorced from his mother and unaware of the escape attempt, had remained in Cuba. On reaching the US, Elian was placed in the care of relatives who lived in Miami, where most Cuban-Americans live.

The affair might have been resolved quickly and quietly had not the relatives in Miami sought out the media with the aim of gaining public sympathy for their case. Under US law, it was clear that the boy should return to Cuba where his father lived and wanted him back. The Cuban-American community refused to accept this state of affairs and held demonstrations and petitioned the US courts to allow Elian to stay in the US rather than return to Cuba. Not one to forego a propaganda opportunity, Fidel Castro, the

Cuban leader, organized huge counter demonstrations in Havana demanding the return of the "kidnapped" Elian. These twists and turns were followed in detail by the media which made the case the dominant news story in the summer of 2000. Mindful of the importance of Florida in the presidential elections, both George W. Bush (whose brother was Governor of Florida) and Al Gore, the Democrat candidate, found themselves in a difficult situation. Neither wanted to appear to favor breaking American law, but neither wanted to appear to favor handing the boy back to Cuba. Bush, however, appeared to be the candidate who most favored Elian staying in Florida and this stance may have led to his narrow victory in the state in November. When the court case finally went against the relatives in Miami, they refused to give Elian back to his father, who had flown from Cuba to meet him. This then led to the FBI snatching Elian at gunpoint from his relatives in the middle of the night, an event photographed and filmed by the ever-present media, and shown around the world. The child later flew back to Cuba with his father and was greeted by Fidel Castro himself and thousands of cheering Cubans, again all shown on television.

The Elian Gonzalez case was a good example of the "soap drama" tendency of American television coverage of foreign affairs. The case may also have marked a watershed in the influence of the Cuban-American lobby. A clear majority of Americans considered that the boy should be returned to his father. Younger Cuban-Americans were split on the issue, as they were on the continuation of US sanctions against Cuba. It was the older generation of Cuban-Americans who raised the banner for Elian and turned it into a cause célèbre. There was some evidence that their defiance of the law had a negative impact on most Americans who considered that their influence was already too strong on US–Cuban relations.

Despite the declining coverage of foreign policy in the media, one cannot ignore its presence. Nearly all government and congressional offices have a television screen, usually tuned to CNN, and thus have instant access to news from around the world as well as the political spinning that never stops in Washington. There is also blanket coverage of congressional affairs on C-Span (a specialist TV channel) and endless talk shows, particularly on Sundays, for political junkies. But these stations and shows are watched only by a tiny fraction of the population. In the aftermath of the September 2001 attacks, there was an increased interest in foreign news coverage relating to terrorism. The major networks increased their budgets for foreign news but this was largely spent on coverage of the build-up to and the fighting in the Iraq War.

The media and warfare

The media have always taken a close interest in and often tried to influence attitudes toward warfare. One of the first examples of an attempt by the press to influence US foreign policy preceded the Spanish–American War over Cuba at the end of the nineteenth century. The bellicose headlines printed by the American newspaper tycoons, William Randolph Hearst (*New York Journal*) and Joseph Pulitzer (*New York World*) clearly helped to push the US into the conflict by influencing public opinion. This event demonstrated to politicians and newspaper owners the enormous impact that journalism could have upon foreign policy. As noted earlier President Wilson failed to rally public support in his unsuccessful campaign to have the US join the League of Nations in 1919. Learning from his mistakes, President Roosevelt ran a much better prepared public campaign to persuade Americans that the US should join the United Nations in 1945. But Roosevelt also found it difficult in the period between September 1939 and December 1941 to persuade Americans to join the allied war effort in the face of media skepticism and even hostility. This changed overnight as a result of the Japanese attack on Pearl Harbor.

During the Cold War there was overwhelming public support for the tough line adopted by successive administrations against the Soviet Union and communism. This public support, however, began to wane as a result of the Vietnam War. When US troops first went ashore in Vietnam in 1963–4, to protect the South from "northern aggression," a clear majority of Americans approved of the intervention. A plurality continued to support the war, albeit in decreasing numbers, until October 1967, when for the first time more Americans opposed the distant war (46 percent) than approved of it (44 percent). Students were particularly vociferous in the anti-war protests. It was the Tet offensive in January 1968 that marked the turning point in the war. The Vietcong launched several attacks on American and South Vietnam targets, demonstrating that they had the capacity to fight on several fronts at the same time. Although they suffered substantial losses, the Tet offensive was widely regarded as a victory for the Vietcong. In addition, for the first time in history the unspeakable horrors of war were brought into the living rooms of all Americans (Arlen 1982). The infamous photographs of the execution of a crying Vietcong guerrilla by a South Vietnamese officer and a young, naked, Vietnamese girl running in terror along the road after a napalm bomb attack were burned into the collective memory of that generation. Although the Pentagon insisted otherwise, from that point on it was widely believed that the war was not winnable. Within days of the Tet offensive, American campuses were in uproar again. Within weeks, a clear majority of Americans turned against the war, some advocating a negotiated peace and some an immediate US withdrawal. Within two months, President Johnson shocked the nation by stating that he would not seek re-election in 1968.

For the first time in US history, public opinion on events from abroad, shaped by the media, toppled a President. After the Tet offensive, there was no possibility of the administration achieving its objectives within a timeframe or with force levels politically acceptable to the American people. The waves of protest and societal discord led Congress to pass the War Powers Act in 1973 that sought to limit the President's unfettered ability to engage the country in war. The term "Vietnam Syndrome" was born and taken to mean that henceforth foreign policy should have public approval and that US forces should only intervene abroad to protect clear national interests with minimal or zero loss of life. The Vietnam War not only galvanized Congress into a more forceful assertion of its constitutional rights but also gave the media a new role as a watchdog for public interests. The anti-war movement and media coverage "played an important role in presenting credible information on the war, slowly undermining the official version of events" (Dumbrell 1997: 154).

The example of the Vietnam War served to advance the learning curve first established by Hearst and Pulitzer's efforts in 1898. Subsequent Presidents and the Pentagon seem to have learned from the experiences of the Vietnam War and have sought to maintain control over the media when US forces invaded Grenada and operated in the Gulf, Kosovo, and Afghanistan (Rosenblum 1993; P. M. Smith 1991). In 2000, the Pentagon spokesman during the Kosovo campaign told a seminar audience that he had no regrets about claiming 150 Serb tanks had been destroyed by the American bombing – although the real figure was less than twenty. Despite attempts to muzzle the media, journalists have continued to publicize foreign policy missions that failed and revealed the government's secret use of covert operations (e.g. Iran-Contra), which further undermined presidential and congressional credibility in the eyes of the public. At the same time some Presidents became proficient at using the media for their own purposes. President Reagan was a masterful manipulator of the media and used it to gain support for his robust policy toward the Soviet Union, or "the evil empire" as he called it. President George W. Bush continued this theme in January 2002 when he described Iraq, Iran and North Korea as an "axis of evil."

Following 9/11 the neocons launched a propaganda blitz to prepare the nation for war against Iraq. In countless articles, op eds, speeches and radio and TV talk shows they propagated the view that Iraq had WMD and Saddam Hussein was in cahoots with Osama bin Laden. The President and his chief advisers, particularly Cheney and Rumsfeld, supported this line. Congress also went along with the plot and not surprisingly the media followed with Fox News in the vanguard. Even traditional liberal papers such as *The New York Times* and the *Washington Post* supported the war. According to some observers there was a war hysteria in America (Halper and Clarke 2004). Only several months after the war, when it was clear that no WMD were to be found, did some newspapers, including the two mentioned above, publicly apologize for their coverage of the war.

The CNN effect

In recent years there has been much talk of the "CNN effect," implying that no crisis will receive attention unless the television cameras are present to relay pictures into voters' homes. The "CNN effect" most frequently refers to the potentially debilitating impact that a round-the-clock news network with global reach can have on a government's ability to control foreign policy. Some media analysts have suggested that the "CNN effect" threatens to wrench diplomatic control from experienced statesmen only to place this power in the hands of journalists, photographers, and editors. Television reporting and images (often of human suffering) can generate public awareness that is often translated into pressures upon the government. Continual television coverage of the terrorist attacks on the World Trade Center in New York ensured that there would be massive public support for retaliatory action.

During the last decade, the speed at which troops are deployed or withdrawn is a matter over which public opinion has had some impact. In particular, television images, such as starvation and warfare in Somalia, ethnic cleansing in Bosnia, bloody repression in Haiti, and the flight of refugees escaping slaughter in Rwanda, touched the sensibilities of viewing audiences and forced policymakers to explain situations on which they otherwise may have chosen to remain silent. Arguably, therefore, the "CNN effect" has taken the foreign policy formation process out of the back rooms of the policy elite and into the living rooms of American citizens (for a more limited view of the CNN effect see Strobel, *The CNN Effect: Myth or Reality?* in Wittkopf and McCormick 1999).

From conversations with American officials, it is clear that newspapers such as *The New York Times* and *Washington Post* have a distinct impact on the policymaking elite themselves, while television affects opinion formation on a more mass level. This fact, in turn, has shaped the form of reporting that is found in newspapers today. In particular, television coverage has had an interesting effect on the style of print coverage: while the networks provide the superficial, round-the-clock reporting, newspaper editors and columnists, at least in the quality press, are left with more time for comment and analysis. The quality press often benefits from leaks from officials in the administration seeking to promote their own viewpoints and denigrate those of their opponents. But even in the quality press there is little foreign policy reporting or analysis unless American interests are involved. The launch of the euro on 1 January 2002 was hardly covered in the American media. Arab countries complain about the very limited and entirely negative coverage they receive. Coverage of many other regions and countries is conspicuous by its absence.

Clearly, the manner in which television and print journalists cover news stories influences public perception of events, and, subsequently, their political attitudes. The importance of Fox News during the run-up to the Iraq War has already been mentioned. This, in turn, influences the actions of the policymakers themselves. Two developments over the last decade have significantly increased the ability of news agencies to shape policy: recent advances in communications technology and the end of the Cold War. The coincidental appearance of the internet and 24-hour cable and satellite networks against the backdrop of the small-scale conflicts that have flared up in countless areas of the globe after the fall of the Soviet Union has added an important new dimension to the making of foreign policy today. Administration spokesmen, congressmen, think tank specialists and other pundits are rarely absent from the screens, usually offering instant comment and analysis on the latest developments in a crisis. A central issue is always what should the US do in the situation? Presidents also use the media to inform and educate the public on matters of foreign policy. In recent years, however, there has been a decline in Presidents addressing the nation on foreign policy issues with the exception of terrorism.

Polling results

Presidents want to be liked by the public because the level of their popularity with the American people affects their ability to work with Congress and achieve policy goals. The more popular Presidents are domestically, the more they are free of constraints to do as they wish abroad. But concern at what the public thinks on any issues has meant that public opinion polling has become a multimillion-dollar industry. President Clinton was often criticized for using focus groups (a representative selection of voters) to determine what course of action to take. The end of the Cold War made it more difficult for American Presidents to explain to the public the nature of the new security threats and to seek their support for political, military, or humanitarian interventions. Neither Bush senior nor Clinton, however, really tried to explain to Americans the nature of the new post-Cold War world. In this sense, George W. Bush had an easier task rallying the public to support "the war on terrorism" after 9/11.

Yet, though often misinformed or unconcerned about international affairs, Americans support internationalism and guarded engagement. Surveys show that most Americans consider that the main foreign policy priorities should be to maintain economic prosperity and to ensure national security. Although for some time after 9/11, terrorism became the dominant priority. Americans demonstrate overwhelming support for foreign aid in principle but are ignorant about the size and scope of current US external assistance programs. These overlying trends lay the foundation for a more in-depth analysis of the American public's foreign policy priorities.

US public opinion

According to the 2004 Chicago Council on Foreign Relations polling data, three years after 9/11, terrorism and other security threats still loom large in the minds of most Americans. However, the polls reveal a lowered sense of threat overall compared to 2002, and the domestic concern of protecting American jobs was the most commonly cited goal of US foreign policy. Support for foreign policy goals overall was down, as were the numbers of Americans who want to increase spending on homeland security and defense. There was lower support for stationing US troops abroad, particularly in Middle Eastern or Islamic countries. Yet Americans are still committed to playing an engaged role in the world and support taking action when clearly threatened, especially against terrorism. Unlike the neocons, they do not want to play a dominant role, supporting diplomatic and multilateral approaches to international problems in even greater numbers than in 2002. The highlights of the 2004 poll, the most authoritative study on the US public's attitude toward foreign policy, were as follows:

- International terrorism, chemical and biological weapons, and unfriendly countries becoming nuclear powers remain the most commonly cited critical threats, but the percentages who view them as critical have dropped significantly since 2002. Virtually all other threats were regarded as less important, with majorities no longer considering critical the threats of Islamic fundamentalism, the development of China as a world power, and military conflict between Israel and its Arab neighbors.
- Similarly, while the ranking of US foreign policy goals has remained largely constant, there is an overall drop in the numbers believing they are very important. The major exception is for protecting the jobs of American workers, which now ranks first, followed by preventing the spread of nuclear weapons and combating international terrorism.

- While the American public favor having bases overseas, support for stationing troops in specific countries – especially those in the Middle East – has dropped substantially since 2002.

- Strong majorities still believe the United States should take an active part in world affairs. Despite majority support among the American public for taking active steps to ensure no other country becomes a superpower, Americans strongly believe that the United States should work together with other nations to solve international problems. Additionally, a large majority of the public rejects the idea that the United States has the responsibility to play the role of world policeman and think the most important lesson of September 11 is that the United States needs to work more closely with other countries to fight terrorism.

- Americans are still willing to use force in a variety of contexts when critical interests are threatened, especially in responding to terrorism. Many diplomatic means to combat terrorism, such as helping countries to develop their economies and trying suspected terrorists in the International Criminal Court, score as high as military options, and a plurality believes more emphasis should be placed on diplomatic and economic methods compared to military ones in the fight against terrorism.

International norms and the use of force

Following September 11, there has been substantial discussion regarding the international norms governing the use of force and whether they need to become less restrictive to respond to the new threat posed by terrorists and the spread of weapons of mass destruction. The American public strongly endorses the traditional constraints on the use of force by individual states and resists new ideas for making them looser. They also indicate readiness to give wide-ranging powers to states acting collectively through the United Nations to address various potential threats.

- A majority of the public does not support states taking unilateral action to prevent other states from acquiring weapons of mass destruction, but does support this action if it has UN Security Council approval. They also reject preventive unilateral war, but endorse a country's right to go to war on its own if there is strong evidence of an imminent threat. A clear majority also believes the United States would need UN Security Council approval before using military force to destroy North Korea's nuclear capability.

- The public strongly endorses the UN having the right to authorize the use of force to stop a country from supporting terrorist groups. Although a majority of the public says a country should have this right without UN approval, a clear majority only supports the right of the United States to overthrow a government supporting terrorist groups when the threat is imminent.

- There is strong support for a state acting on its own or the UN Security Council having the right to authorize force against genocide and favor using US troops for this purpose. A majority agrees that the UN, but not an individual state, has the right to intervene to restore a democratic government that has been overthrown. The public even more forcefully rejects the use of US troops to install democratic governments in states where dictators rule.

- There is strong endorsement of the right of a country to defend another country that has been attacked even without UN approval. However, support for this measure increases with UN authorization. While the public opposes using US troops to defend South Korea from a North Korean attack, a majority favors the US contributing forces to a UN-sponsored effort to defend South Korea.
- The American public supports the use of nuclear weapons only in response to a nuclear attack and rejects using torture to extract information from suspected terrorists.

Multilateralism and international institutions

Some have argued that in a globalized world it is necessary for countries to participate in a rules-based international system that constrains decision-making by the United States and other individual countries so that consensus can be reached on critical issues. Others argue that the United States, as the world's most powerful nation, should not accept these constraints. The survey results indicate there is substantial US public support for collective decision-making and for strengthening international organizations. The public also support US participation in a wide range of international treaties and agreements.

- A strong majority agrees that the US should be more willing to make decisions within the UN even if this means the United States will have to go along with a policy that is not its first choice. Significantly, a clear majority of the public favors changing UN Security Council rules so that no single member could veto a decision favored by all other members.
- A similar strong majority says decisions in international economic organizations should always be made by a majority of members without the possibility of a US veto and favor US compliance with unfavorable WTO rulings. The public also roundly endorses giving the World Health Organization the authority to intervene in a country in response to a world health crisis even if the country disagrees.
- Similarly, the public favors US participation in the nuclear test ban treaty, the treaty banning the use of land mines, the Kyoto agreement to reduce global warming, and the International Criminal Court (ICC). They additionally support the trial of international terrorists in the ICC and the United States making a general commitment to accept World Court decisions.
- The American public has a positive feeling toward the UN and believes it should have a stronger role than the United States in helping Iraqis write a new constitution and build a democratic government. It supports US participation in UN peacekeeping activities, and favors strengthening the organization through creating a standing UN peacekeeping force and giving the UN the power to regulate the international arms trade. A plurality of the public even supports giving the UN the power to fund its activities by taxing the international sale of arms or oil.

- The public believes the United States should withdraw its forces from Iraq and other countries in the Middle East if the local population so wishes.

International norms and economic relations

The survey also touched on the debate on the equity of the international trading system and the degree to which trade should be free. Related to this are questions about the structure and role of the World Trade Organization and the growth of regional trade agreements. The survey findings indicate Americans want to pursue free trade provided displaced American workers are assisted and the environment is protected. They strongly support an international trading system regulated through multilateral institutions and requiring compliance with decisions that have majority support.

- A majority of the public thinks globalization is mostly good for the United States. The public, however, clearly sees positives and negatives in international trade, with the US economy and American consumers considered winners, while job security and job creation in the United States suffer.
- A majority of the public thinks bilateral trade with Japan, the countries of the EU, and Canada is fair, and economic competition from Europe scores very low as a critical threat. A majority of the public believes that rich countries are not playing fair in trade negotiations with poor countries. There is, however, concern about developing countries, with a notable number of the public citing competition from low-wage countries as a critical threat, a majority seeing China as practicing unfair trade, and a large majority believing that outsourcing is mostly bad.
- Americans support lowering trade barriers such as tariffs, but want government programs to help displaced workers. Overwhelming majorities of the public also favor including minimum standards for working conditions and the protection of the environment in international trade agreements.
- While Americans support giving subsidies to small farmers, this support is predicated on need. Only very small percentages of the public and leaders favor regular annual subsidies.
- Americans favor aid to help needy countries develop their economies as a measure to fight terrorism and to achieve numerous humanitarian goals.
- There is support for extending free trade agreements, although there is mixed feelings about NAFTA, seeing it as benefiting Mexico more than the United States and providing fewer advantages than international trade overall.
- The public opposes increasing legal immigration levels and also opposes unilateral reform measures such as giving undocumented workers temporary worker status. Yet they are willing to endorse a bilateral agreement with Mexico that would increase legal immigration levels in the United States in exchange for Mexican efforts to reduce illegal immigration and drug trafficking.

The results of the Chicago survey are very interesting, notably in the consistent support from the American public for a more multilateral approach to foreign affairs. Yet, from the outcome of the 2004 elections, when foreign policy was center stage, a clear majority of Americans would appear to be broadly satisfied with the current position of the US on the international stage and believe that President Bush is properly handling foreign policy matters. At the same time, the results show that the number of people "very interested" in international news has been on the decline since 1990, dropping from 36 percent in 1990 to 29 percent in 1998. There was a sudden upward blip in these figures after September 2001 but by 2002 the numbers had fallen again.

A comparison of the 1999 and 2004 surveys does not reveal major differences. A large majority of Americans believe preventing the spread of nuclear weapons should be a "very important goal" of the US, along with stopping the flow of illegal drugs into the country, protecting American jobs, combating international terrorism, and securing adequate supplies of energy. In contrast, barely one-quarter of the public believes the US should consider helping to improve the living standards in less developed countries and help bring a democratic form of government to other nations as "very important" goals. The ranking of these goals shows a strong emphasis on self-interest and preserving America's economic and social well-being, as well as the physical security of the US and American property.

In the era of increasing globalization, two-thirds of the public believe a country's economic power is more important than military strength when considering influence in the world. Americans cite the global economy as the second greatest foreign policy problem facing the US and therefore 60 percent of the public agree that making the world economic and financial system more stable should be a top priority for the US government. The increased interest in US global economic performance over the last decade corresponds to reduced concerns about direct military threats, as well as economic competition from Japan and Europe. Despite an overall lessening of concerns about economic competition, the historic trend of protectionism remains prevalent among the American public. To protect American jobs and maintain national economic prosperity nearly half the population believes tariffs and quotas are necessary to reduce foreign imports.

One of the greatest misconceptions Americans have about US foreign policy regards the size and scope of US aid spending. The majority of Americans think the US is spending up to twenty times more than it actually is on foreign aid. Despite these misperceptions, public opposition to aid has shown a marked decrease over the past decade, with strong support for alleviating hunger and disease, and improving development aid – particularly programs that emphasize education and those that help women and children. The public, however, remains skeptical about the effectiveness of US aid programs, somewhat in contradiction to the above. Eighty-four percent also agree that "taking care of domestic problems is more important than giving aid to foreign countries."

Americans are generally supportive of aid programs that help developing countries to strengthen their economies, as long as American jobs are protected and it helps the US economy. Sixty-four percent of Americans feel that promoting economic growth in developing nations helps to create more markets for US exports. Americans feel that helping developing countries strengthen their economies will have a positive impact on

American jobs because of an increased demand for American products and the decline of wage competition as developing countries grow. Even though direct US bilateral assistance to countries has its benefits, most Americans prefer to give aid through multilateral institutions or private organizations.

Regions and countries of vital interest

Americans continue to look favorably on countries in the western hemisphere and in Europe with a clear majority believing Europe is more important to the US than Asia (42 percent v. 28 percent). Americans consider Canada to be their closest ally and friend, followed by Britain, Israel, Australia, Mexico, France and Germany. Both France and Germany suffered a drop in esteem as a result of their opposition to the Iraq War. On the other hand, a majority of Americans continue to consider China and Russia "not friendly." Regarding the conflict in the Middle East, 69 percent of Americans are sympathetic to the Israelis, while only 11 percent are sympathetic toward the Palestinians. This is the area of greatest difference between the US and Europe. Europeans are far more sympathetic to the Palestinian cause.

Sixty-nine percent of Americans expect China to play a greater role on the international stage over the next ten years. At the same time, 52 percent of Americans also express a willingness to impose economic sanctions against China because of human rights issues and trade issues. Sixty-seven percent of Americans feel China does a "mostly bad" or "very bad" job in respecting the human rights of its citizens. Regarding trade with China, Americans are split evenly on whether this is of benefit to American workers.

Assessment

These results show that Americans are generally satisfied with the US position as the world's economic, political, and military leader. Americans want the US to remain internationally active and support guarded engagement and multilateral cooperation when addressing international issues. Americans want the US to stop nuclear proliferation, combat terrorism and illegal drug trafficking, and protect American jobs. The public feels less threatened by Japan and Europe as economic heavyweights, but is instead more focused on China's emergence as a world power. Americans also favor increasing military and intelligence spending to counter the activities of terrorist organizations and to aid efforts to combat nuclear proliferation. Americans are largely ignorant about US foreign aid spending levels but overwhelmingly support aid to Africa and to programs that work to eliminate hunger, poverty, disease and social injustice within developing countries. Americans continue to look favorably upon their immediate neighbors and European nations, but unfavorably toward China, Russia, Iran, and North Korea, which are considered threats to US vital interests.

These views also reflect the diverging opinion of Americans away from the Cold War mentality whereby all US actions abroad were of strategic significance to combat and contain the "communist threat." Though not always informed or concerned with the direction of US foreign policy or international events, Americans are slowly but surely becoming more aware of the global environment and all of its facets, as well as the important role the US needs to play in it. Yet despite these positive attitudes, few Americans are prepared to do anything to change congressional views. Americans may have wanted to pay their UN debt but few wrote to demand action. Similarly, most Americans supported the CTBT but they did not descend on Washington in busloads to save it. As James Lindsay notes, "Americans approach foreign policy the way they approach physical fitness – they understand the benefits of being in good shape, but they still avoid exercise." Most Americans, while proud of their global leadership role, are also profoundly uninterested in the details of its implementation.

Conclusion

Clearly, the American media has a significant influence on modern day foreign policy making. Despite increasing foreign travel and Americans studying and working abroad, most Americans still get their views on foreign policy from the media. Given the limited coverage of foreign affairs in the media this means that most Americans are only informed about foreign policy when there is a major event, such as the fall of the Berlin Wall, or when the President travels overseas, or when the media decide that there is a strong human interest story. Gory images such as the victims of terrorist attacks or refugees fleeing persecution in Rwanda, Somalia, Kosovo and Dafur quickly lead to inflamed emotions that are often channeled into battle cries for increased action from the government. Advances in technology and 24-hour political reporting, commentary, and analysis usually mean that the administration is struggling to keep up and respond. The White House dislikes these kinds of situations where it cannot "control" the news agenda. The President then has to make a calculation taking into account the strength of these calls for action, the American interests involved, and the likely consequences if things were to go wrong – usually interpreted as American casualties. As a result of such assessments, including consulting focus groups, President Clinton came to the conclusion in both the Bosnian and Kosovo campaigns that the US would only use air power and not ground troops. As regards the genocide perpetrated in Rwanda, Clinton decided not to become involved. President Bush successfully manipulated the media to secure overwhelming endorsement for the war on Iraq. Only much later were serious questions asked about the preparations and conduct of the operation.

Public opinion can thus set limits on US action. There were hawks in the Pentagon who argued for nuclear strikes both in Vietnam and against Cuba but different Presidents came to the conclusion that public opinion would not accept such a move. Public opinion also tends to be more vocal when direct economic interests are threatened. The opposition of most Democrats to NAFTA and later the granting of "fast track" authority to begin new trade negotiations was a result of heavy pressure from their constituents and organized labor. Some interest groups can also be highly vocal in getting their message across and bringing pressure to bear on the White House. It helps if these groups also coincide with the personal preferences of Presidents and Secretaries of State. For example, Madeleine Albright, born in Czechoslovakia, was an ardent supporter of NATO expansion and spent considerable time persuading the public of the merits of this policy. President George W. Bush, coming from Texas, initially gave priority to Mexico. The administration also leaks stories to the media to test the water before officially announcing a policy change or to damage political opponents or even to damage proposals from some branch of the executive. The debate on whether to invade Iraq after finishing the war against the Taliban in Afghanistan was carried out in the media largely as a result of leaks from the Pentagon and State Department. Given the public's assessment of the importance of international economic and financial stability, it is timely to look at US trade policy and the impact of globalization.

Selected further reading

The role of the media is covered in Arlen (1982) *Living-Room War*, Berry (1990) *Foreign Policy and the Press*, Gruff (1999) *The Kosovo News and the Propaganda War*, Sefarty (1991) *The Media and Foreign Policy*, Seib (1997) *Headline Diplomacy*. Kull and Destler (1999) *Misreading the Public*, Holsti (1996) *Public Opinion and American Foreign Policy* and Shapiro and Page (1992) *The Rational Public* examine public attitudes toward foreign policy. Gergen (2002) *Eyewitness to Power* provides some fascinating glimpses of how Presidents seek to manipulate the media. P. M. Smith (1991) *How CNN Fought the War* looks at the impact of television. Reilly (1999) "Americans and the world" is a survey of the Chicago study. The Program on International Policy Attitudes has an excellent website with polling data on a broad range of international policy issues, see *www.americans-world.org* (accessed 11 April 2005). Other polling organizations include the Congressional Institute, Gallup, Harris Interactive, Howard W. Odum Institute Poll Database, Marist Institute for Public Opinion (MIPO), Pew People and the Press, Polling Report, Public Agenda, Washington Post Poll Vault and Zogby International. Nearly all the major media organizations such as CNN, *New York Times*, *Washington Post* have their own websites.

7

Foreign trade, the economy and globalization

Key facts

- For much of its history the US pursued protectionist policies but since 1945 it generally has been a champion of free trade and supportive of all the major international economic and financial organizations. The promotion of free trade and open markets became a central plank of US foreign policy in the 1990s.
- Priority has been given to the western hemisphere (NAFTA, FTAA) but the US also played an important role in the Uruguay Round, and in negotiations to establish a new round of international trade negotiations (Doha). There are many actors involved in the formulation of trade policy.
- The US economy is the largest and most productive in the world. Any change to its economic performance has significant consequences around the world. The downturn after the terrorist attacks of September 2001 led to major job losses not only in the US but across the world. The US is increasingly dependent on the import of oil, a development that colors US foreign policy.
- The US is the key player in the process of globalization, often seemingly synonymous with "Americanization" of the world. The US has a huge lead in most areas of high tech computers, information technology, and software. At the same time it usually runs a huge trade deficit and the budget surplus of the Clinton era was transformed into a huge fiscal deficit during the 2001–2004 Bush administration. The dollar depreciated over 25 percent against the euro between 2000 and 2004.
- Globalization has also led to a backlash as protestors point to increasing inequality and a world divided into "haves" and "have nots." This could have far-reaching foreign policy implications.

From protectionism to free trade

US foreign trade policy has changed dramatically since the founding of the republic when Alexander Hamilton advocated a protective tariff to encourage American industrial development, advice the country largely followed throughout the nineteenth century. Government and business mostly concentrated on developing the domestic economy regardless of what went on abroad and showed a marked reluctance to embrace free trade. American protectionism peaked in 1930 with the enactment of the Smoot–Hawley Act, which sharply increased US tariffs. The Act, which quickly led to foreign retaliation, contributed significantly to the Great Depression that gripped the US and much of the world during the 1930s. In 1934, Congress seemed to recognize that it had gone too far down the protectionist road and passed the Reciprocal Trade Agreement Act that granted the President authority to negotiate mutual reductions in tariffs.

After 1945, with the US the undisputed, strongest nation in the world, Washington recognized that the domestic stability and continuing loyalty of its allies would depend on their economic recovery. US aid was important to this recovery (a prime example being the Marshall Plan), but these nations also needed export markets, particularly the huge American market, in order to regain economic independence and achieve economic growth. The US took the lead in pressing for trade liberalization and was instrumental in the creation of the general agreement on tariffs and trade (GATT), the IMF, and the World Bank. These bodies, which helped regulate international trade, finance, and development assistance, became known as the Bretton Woods institutions after the small town in New Hampshire where the negotiations were carried out.

Since the Second World War, the US has increasingly come to see free trade as a means not only of advancing its own economic interests but also as a key to building peace in the world. This was a theme that Presidents Kennedy and Johnson proclaimed in the 1960s. President George H. W. Bush also highlighted the point before the Gulf War when he talked of a "new world order." It was a central plank in Clinton's foreign policy, with the President and other leading figures in his administration constantly referring to the links between free trade and democracy. George W. Bush maintained this commitment when he took office in 2001, stating that "free trade was a top priority." This did not prevent him, however, from imposing a 30 percent tariff on imported steel in March 2002.

As a result of its inherent economic strengths, the fact that its industrial machine was untouched by war and American advances in technology and manufacturing techniques, the US dominated most export markets for much of the postwar period. By the 1970s, though, the gap between the US and other countries' export competitiveness was narrowing. Furthermore, oil price shocks, worldwide recession, and increases in the foreign exchange value of the dollar, all combined during the 1970s to produce trade deficits. These deficits grew larger still in the 1980s and 1990s as the American appetite for foreign goods consistently outstripped demand for American goods in other countries. This reflected both the tendency of Americans to consume more and save less than people in Europe and Japan and the fact that the American economy was growing much faster during this period than Europe or economically troubled Japan.

Mounting trade deficits reduced political support in Congress for trade liberalization, first in the early 1980s and again in the late 1990s. Congress considered a wide range of protectionist proposals during these years, many of them from American industries that faced increasingly effective competition from other countries, but few measures were actually passed. In the 1990s, Congress also grew reluctant to give the President a free hand to negotiate new trade liberalization agreements with other countries. Despite these setbacks to free trade, the US continued to advance trade liberalization in the 1990s, ratifying NAFTA, completing the Uruguay Round of multilateral trade negotiations, and joining in multilateral agreements that established international rules for protecting intellectual property and for trade in financial and basic telecommunications services. At the same time, the federal government operated a "Buy America" policy that ensured federal agencies should give preference to American goods and services and American officials had to fly on American carriers.

With the change of administration from Clinton to George W. Bush, US trade policy became more overtly political. Although the Bush administration remained committed to free trade, political support for such policies was finely balanced, as was seen from the narrow vote in Congress in favor of TPA in December 2002. Bush showed that he was prepared to buy votes in key states by slapping on steel tariffs to protect American producers and granting farmers huge subsidies. But despite these protectionist measures, there was little prospect of the US seeking to withdraw from the global economy. Its growing prosperity was linked to increased trade and several financial crises, especially the one that rocked Asia in the late 1990s, demonstrated the increased interdependence of global financial markets. As the US and other nations worked to develop tools for addressing or preventing such crises, they found themselves looking at reform ideas that would require increased international coordination and cooperation.

The Clinton administration added another dimension to US trade policy by contending that countries should adhere to minimum labor and environmental standards. In part, the US took this stance because of concern, particularly on the union side, that America's own relatively high labor and environmental standards could drive up the cost of American-made goods, making it difficult for domestic industries to compete with less-regulated companies from other countries. The Clinton administration raised these issues in the early 1990s when it insisted that Canada and Mexico sign side agreements pledging to enforce environmental laws and labor standards in return for American ratification of NAFTA. Efforts by the Clinton administration to link trade agreements to environmental protection and labor-standards measures became controversial in many countries and even within the US. There are substantial differences between the Democrats and Republicans on these issues.

Despite general adherence to the principles of non-discrimination, the US has created certain preferential trade arrangements. The generalized system of preferences (GSP) program, for instance, seeks to promote economic development in poorer countries by providing duty-free treatment for certain goods that these countries export to the US; the preferences cease when producers of a product no longer need assistance to compete in the US market. Another preferential program, the Caribbean Basin Initiative, seeks to help an economically struggling region that is considered politically important to the US; it gives duty-free treatment to all imports to the US from the Caribbean area except some textiles, leather goods, and sugar. This initiative is not as generous as it sounds because it is largely sugar and textiles that these countries have to sell, and they have to be content with powerful sugar and textile lobbies protecting domestic production in the US. A 1997 program called the Partnership for Economic Growth and Opportunity for Africa, which has similar protectionist exceptions, aims to increase US market access for imports from sub-Saharan countries. It also provides US backing to private sector development in Africa, supports regional economic integration within the continent, and institutionalizes government-to-government dialogue on trade via an annual US–Africa forum.

Multilateral, regional, and bilateral approaches

The US has traditionally been a supporter of multilateralism in the trade arena and has played an important leadership role in successive rounds of international trade negotiations. The Trade Expansion Act of 1962, which authorized the so-called Kennedy Round of trade negotiations, culminated with an agreement by fifty-three nations accounting for 80 percent of international trade to cut tariffs by an average of 35 percent. In 1979, as a result of the success of the Tokyo Round, the US and approximately one hundred other nations agreed to further tariff reductions and to the reduction of such non-tariff barriers to trade as quotas and licensing requirements.

A further set of multilateral negotiations, the Uruguay Round, was launched in September 1986 and concluded eight years later with an agreement to reduce industrial tariff and non-tariff barriers further, cut some agricultural tariffs and subsidies, and provide new protections to intellectual property. Perhaps most significantly, the Uruguay Round led to the creation of the World Trade Organization (WTO), which included a new, binding mechanism for settling international trade disputes. By the end of 2001, the US itself had filed over fifty complaints about unfair trade practices with the WTO, but numerous other countries had filed more than one hundred complaints against the US. In January 2002, the EU won the largest ever case in the history of the WTO when the US practice of granting tax breaks to companies on their foreign earnings was declared illegal.

In addition to its multilateral commitments, the US in recent years has also pursued a number of regional and bilateral trade agreements. This is partly because such agreements are easier to negotiate and can often lay the groundwork for larger accords as well as serve wider foreign policy goals. The first free trade agreement between the US and Israel took effect in 1985, and the second, between the US and Canada, took effect in 1989. There have since been further agreements, largely for political reasons, with Jordan, Singapore and Morocco. In the run up to the Iraq War in March 2003, the US administration used trade negotiations as a weapon to try and gain support in the UN. For example, Australia and Singapore were rewarded with swift negotiations while negotiations with Chile and Mexico were delayed. These special deals have been criticized by Joe Stiglitz, the former chief economist of the World Bank (*International Herald Tribune*, 12 July 2004), as having created more ill will than good will.

The pact with Canada led to the NAFTA 1994, which brought the US, Canada, and Mexico together in a trade accord that covered nearly 400 million people who collectively produce some $9.5 trillion in goods and services. Geographic proximity has greatly boosted trade and investment between the NAFTA partners. As a result of the NAFTA, the average Mexican tariff on American goods dropped from 10 percent to 1.68 percent, and the average US tariff on Mexican goods fell from 4 percent to 0.46 percent. Of particular importance to the US, the agreement included some protection for US owners of patents, copyrights, trademarks, and trade secrets. Americans in recent years have grown increasingly concerned about piracy and counterfeiting of US products ranging from computer software and motion pictures to pharmaceutical and chemical products (see *Business Week*, 9 July 2001 for an assessment of the impact of NAFTA).

Despite these successes, there are still formidable obstacles to further trade liberalization. The Uruguay Round addressed some service-trade issues, but it left trade barriers involving roughly twenty segments of the service sector for subsequent negotiations. Meanwhile, rapid changes in science and technology are giving rise to new trade issues. US agricultural exporters are increasingly frustrated, for instance, by European rules against the use of genetically modified organisms (GMOs) in food that are increasingly prevalent in the US.

Case study: the US and a new trade round

The 142 nations that gathered in Doha, Qatar, in November 2001 to launch a new trade round, met in quite different circumstances to the meeting in Seattle two years previously. In 1999 there were major differences between the US and the EU, the two main players in international trade, and differences between the US, EU, and developing countries. These differences centered on issues such as labor and the environment, agricultural subsidies and the level of tariffs to protect industries. American labor unions were opposed to a new round and came to demonstrate along with thousands of anti-globalization protestors. As the "Battle of Seattle" took place in the barricaded streets, the hundreds of official delegates attending the meeting were unable even to agree on the agenda.

Two years later, the meeting in Doha took place against the background of the global economic downturn following the 11 September terrorist attacks; and there were few protestors as it was difficult to reach Doha in the Persian Gulf. A failure to launch a new round would have weakened the WTO's authority and endangered the rules-based multilateral system. It would also have led to the possible fragmentation of the world economy into hostile regional trade blocs and increased protectionism. Although fear was probably the biggest driving force behind the deal, several positive factors also contributed. They included better preparation than before Seattle, close cooperation between the US and the EU, and greater involvement of developing countries, many of which had previously been indifferent or hostile toward a round. All the major players at Doha made some concessions to get the negotiations started. The US agreed to a wider agenda than it originally envisaged; the EU agreed to consider reductions in its agriculture subsidies, and the developing world agreed to place the environment on the agenda. The close ties and friendship between the USTR, Robert Zoellick, and the EU's chief negotiator, Pascal Lamy, were also important factors in securing the Doha agreement. The meeting also endorsed the inclusion of China into the WTO. This had been a major policy aim of the US for several years.

At Doha, ministers agreed a three-year timetable for the negotiations, which was always going to be an ambitious target given that the climax would coincide with the 2004 US presidential elections. As it transpired negotiations were to continue into 2005. A 2001 World Bank study estimated that elimination of trade barriers could add as much as $2800 billion to global economic income by 2015. However, for every group pushing for liberalization, there is another interest group determined to resist it – and even the positions of countries supposedly preaching open markets are not always clear cut. Liberalization efforts in the new round will focus on three main areas:

- Agriculture: this is the most protected sector and the one where liberalization would most benefit exports by developing countries, which dominate WTO membership. Despite cuts mandated by the Uruguay Round, tariffs are on average three times higher than on industrial goods and, in some cases, exceed 500 percent. The EU, Japan, and Korea are likely to resist further reductions, and even some ostensible free traders, such as the US and Canada, protect certain imports. Washington is torn between seeking more open world markets and responding to US farmers' demands for ever larger domestic subsidies.
- Industrial tariffs: although these have been reduced, on average, to about 4 percent in rich countries and 15 percent in poor ones, rates for many individual items are

much higher. The US imposes duties of more than 20 percent on truck imports, while duties on sports footwear are more than 48 percent. Arguably an even bigger barrier are anti-dumping measures, which have proliferated and spread to developing countries since the 1997 Asian financial crisis. Although WTO negotiations are due to be held on curbing anti-dumping, strong lobbies in the US will resist rapid change.

• Services: as the fastest-growing activity in most economies, these appear to offer the greatest scope for liberalization. However, after 11 September the US and some other countries may be reluctant to lower barriers in areas such as air transport and free movement of skilled workers.

Despite protests by anti-globalization campaigners, there is little sign that enthusiasm for market-based reforms has diminished around the world – and recent studies suggest that open economies have prospered more than closed ones. According to Robert Zoellick, the agreement at Doha made up for the debacle at Seattle and was an important sign, after 11 September 2001, that the international community was prepared to move forward. The Doha negotiations, however, are likely to be long and arduous. A ministerial review meeting at Cancun in September 2003 ended in failure and there was only limited progress, e.g. on agriculture in 2004, due to the imminence of elections in the US and a new European Commission in Brussels.

The emergence of electronic commerce is also opening a whole new set of trade issues. In 1998, WTO ministers issued a declaration that countries should not interfere with electronic commerce by imposing duties on electronic transmissions, but many issues remain unresolved. The US would like to make the internet a tax-free zone, ensure competitive telecommunications markets around the world, and establish global protection for intellectual property in digital products.

President Bush has said that there is no incompatibility between moving ahead on global, regional, and bilateral trade fronts. In a letter of November 2001 to Congress, he stated that apart from the Doha global trade agenda, the US aimed to move forward on the negotiations to establish a free trade agreement of the Americas (FTAA), which essentially would make the entire western hemisphere (except for Cuba) a free-trade zone. Negotiations for such a pact began in 1994, with a goal of completing talks by 2005, generally believed to be an unrealistic goal. The US also was seeking trade liberalization agreements with Asian countries through the Asia-Pacific economic cooperation (APEC) forum. There are some who consider that the insistence on regional blocs is a kind of insurance strategy lest the globalization backlash gets out of hand.

The making of trade policy

One of the problems facing any President is the sheer number of players involved in the trade policy process. The executive and legislative branches have roughly equal roles to play but there is also an increasingly wide array of private sector interest groups involved. The need to achieve a consensus within a decentralized policymaking process often leads to inconsistencies in trade policy. Even within the executive branch there are many players which means that there are often lengthy inter-agency coordination meetings. In Congress, there are also several committees claiming some jurisdiction over different aspects of trade policy. The two principal committees, however, are the House Ways and Means and the Senate Finance committees. The various executive agencies and congressional committees represent different constituencies which makes the definition of the "national interest" in trade policy difficult to determine. When private companies clash over an issue such as bananas (Chiquita and Dole) it is again difficult to define the "national interest." Personalities also play a role. Those closest to the President and those skilled in bureaucratic infighting can often play a role greater than their office would suggest.

The USTR is *primus inter pares* among executive branch agencies dealing with trade policy but it is so small (around 150 staff) that it has to rely on the greater personnel resources of other departments. Partly because of its size, and other constraints, the USTR has never been able to take the leadership role on all trade issues. The NEC seeks to develop a consensus among the ten or more members of the Cabinet and senior presidential advisers having jurisdiction in trade and international economic policy. These would include the departments of State, Treasury, Commerce, Agriculture, Labor and involve bodies such as the international trade commission, which provides analysis on trade policy issues, the council of economic advisers, and the office of management and budget. The NSC also has an economic role overseen by the deputy for international economic policy.

The private sector seeks to influence trade policy by operating mainly through Congress and through its own lobbying efforts in Washington. There are thirty-eight advisory committees, created by Congress, representing all parts of the private sector. In addition, no interest group worth its salt is without representation in Washington. The private sector can bring first-hand knowledge of business conditions to the table and its lobbying efforts usually encompass former government officials who often have detailed knowledge and institutional memory of programs and legislation exceeding that of incumbent officials. For example, former USTRs, Carla Hills and Mickey Kantor, have consulting contracts while Sandy Berger and Madeleine Albright have established their own consulting firms. Tom Pickering, a leading State Department official with considerable foreign policy experience, moved to a senior post at Boeing on his retirement from State.

Trade deficits

In the late 1990s, rapidly growing trade deficits contributed to American ambivalence about trade liberalization. As other countries became more successful, American workers in exporting industries worried that other countries were flooding the US with their goods while keeping their own markets closed. American labor unions also charged that foreign countries were unfairly helping their exporters win markets in third countries by subsidizing select industries such as steel and by designing trade policies that unduly promoted exports over imports. Adding to American labor's anxiety, many

US-based multinational firms began moving production facilities overseas during this period. Technological advances made such moves more practical, and some firms sought to take advantage of lower foreign wages, fewer regulatory hurdles, and other conditions such as proximity to markets, that would reduce production costs.

An even bigger factor leading to the ballooning US trade deficit, however, was a sharp rise in the value of the dollar. Between 1990 and 2000, the dollar's value rose some 50 percent in relation to the currencies of America's major trading partners which made US exports relatively more expensive and foreign imports into the US relatively cheaper. The reason for the appreciation of the dollar can be found in the strength of the US economy and in the huge federal budget deficits, which acted together to create a significant demand in the US for foreign capital. This, in turn, drove up US interest rates and led to the rise of the dollar (Quinlan and Chandler, *Foreign Affairs*, May/June 2001). But floating currencies mean just that. After 9/11 the dollar began a steady descent against other major countries, especially the euro. Whereas the exchange rate in 2000 was roughly 90 cents to the euro, in November 2004 it was $1.30 to the euro.

In 1975, US exports had exceeded foreign imports by $12.4 billion, but that would be the last trade surplus the US would see in the twentieth century. By 1987, the American trade deficit had swollen to $153.3 billion. The trade gap began sinking in subsequent years as the dollar depreciated and economic growth in other countries led to increased demand for US exports. But the American trade deficit rose sharply again in the late 1990s as the US economy grew faster than the economies of its major trading partners. Two Asian countries, Japan and China, have caused the US considerable concern due to rising trade deficits. US–Japan trade relations have been troubled since at least the 1970s, and in 2001, the US continued to be concerned about Japanese barriers to a variety of US exports, including agricultural goods, automobiles, and auto parts. Americans also complained that Japan was exporting steel into the US at below-market prices (a practice known as dumping), and Washington continued to press Japan to deregulate various sectors of its economy, including telecommunications, housing, financial services, medical devices, and pharmaceutical products. There was little evidence that the Japanese took kindly to this advice and pressure.

In the 1990s, the US trade deficit with China grew to exceed even the American trade gap with Japan. From the American perspective, China represents an enormous potential export market but one that is particularly difficult to penetrate. In November 1999, the two countries took a major step toward closer trade relations when they reached a trade agreement that would help bring China formally into the WTO. As part of the deal, which was negotiated over thirteen years, China accepted a series of reforms and market-opening measures. It agreed, for example, to let American companies finance car purchases in China, own up to 50 percent of the shares of Chinese telecommunications companies, and sell insurance policies. China also agreed to reduce agricultural tariffs, move to end state export subsidies, and take steps to prevent piracy of intellectual property such as computer software and movies. The US subsequently agreed, in 2000, to normalize trade relations with China, ending a politically charged requirement that Congress vote annually on whether to allow favorable trade terms with Beijing. China formally joined the WTO at Doha in November 2001.

By 2004, the American trade deficit was nearly $700 billion, a figure larger than the economies of all but thirteen of the world's 206 countries. US trade with three countries – China, Japan, and Mexico – is responsible for two-thirds of the trade deficit. Congress shouts loudly about the unfair trading practices of the Asian countries but if one looks at the per capita figures then it is clear that Canada is the leading culprit.

Americans viewed the trade balance with mixed feelings. Inexpensive foreign imports helped prevent inflation and helped keep US firms competitive. At the same time, however, some Americans worried that a new surge of imports would damage domestic industries. The American steel industry, for instance, fretted about a rise in imports of low-priced steel as foreign producers turned to the US after Asian demand shriveled. And although foreign lenders were generally more than happy to provide the funds Americans needed to finance their trade deficit, US officials worried that at some point they might grow wary. This, in turn, could drive the value of the dollar down, force US interest rates higher, and consequently stifle economic activity. In the early 1980s the US was a net creditor relative to the rest of the world by about $150 billion. At the end of 2004 the US was a net debtor to the rest of the world to the tune of $3 trillion, or 25 percent of US GDP. The US current account deficit in 2004 was over $500 billion, or almost 5 percent of GDP.

Dollar diplomacy

When the international financial institutions were established at the end of the Second World War, the US played a dominant role. Because the US at the time accounted for over half of the world's manufacturing capacity and held most of the world's gold, the leaders decided to tie world currencies to the dollar, which, in turn, they agreed should be convertible into gold at $35 per ounce. Under the Bretton Woods system, central banks of countries other than the US were given the task of maintaining fixed exchange rates between their currencies and the dollar. They did this by intervening in foreign exchange markets. If a country's currency was too high relative to the dollar, its central bank would sell its currency in exchange for dollars, driving down the value of its currency. Conversely, if the value of a country's money was too low, the country would buy its own currency, thereby driving up the price. The Bretton Woods system lasted until 1971. During its lifetime it brought a certain stability to international finance and trade, most of which was invoiced in dollars. By the early 1970s, however, partly due to the Vietnam War, inflation in the US and a growing American trade deficit were

Table 7.1. US cumulative trade deficits 1993–2003

	China	EU	Mexico	Japan	Canada
Trade deficit	$241bn	$123bn	$83bn	$425bn	$129bn
Population	1.3bn	450m	100m	126m	31m
Per capita trade deficit	$35	$329	$829	$3375	$4184

Source: OECD

undermining the value of the dollar. Finally, the US abandoned the fixed value of the dollar and allowed it to "float" – that is, to fluctuate against other currencies.

The IMF, to which the US contributed the largest amount, 25 percent of an initial $8800 million in capital, often requires chronic debtor nations to undertake economic reforms as a condition for receiving its short-term assistance. Traditionally, countries that turned to the IMF had run into trouble because of large government budget deficits and excessive monetary growth. In short, they were trying to consume more than they could afford based on their income from exports. The standard IMF remedy, often perceived as US imposed, was to require strong macroeconomic medicine, including tighter fiscal and monetary policies, in exchange for short-term credits. But in the 1990s, a new problem emerged. As international financial markets grew more robust and interconnected, some countries ran into severe problems paying their foreign debts, not because of general economic mismanagement but because of abrupt changes in flows of private investment dollars. Often, such problems arose not because of their overall economic management but because of narrower "structural" deficiencies in their economies. This became especially apparent with the financial crisis that gripped Asia beginning in 1997 and Argentina in 2001.

In the early 1990s, countries like Thailand, Indonesia, and South Korea astounded the world by growing at rates as high as 9 percent after inflation – far faster than the US and other advanced economies. Foreign investors noticed, and soon flooded the Asian economies with funds. Capital flows into the Asia-Pacific region surged from just $25,000 million in 1990 to $110,000 million by 1996. In retrospect, that was more than the countries could handle. Belatedly, economists realized that much of the capital had gone into unproductive enterprises. The problem was compounded by the fact that in many of the Asian countries, banks were poorly supervised and often subject to pressures to lend to politically favored projects rather than to projects that held economic merit. When growth started to falter, many of these projects went bankrupt.

The US was widely criticized for being slow to help the Asian countries surmount the financial crisis and it led some to suggest that there was declining respect for its international economic leadership. According to one economist, the inability for many years to secure fast track authority for trade negotiations, the delay in augmenting IMF funds, and the initial refusal in 1997 to contribute to the IMF rescue package for Thailand caused widespread concern. "The US is increasingly seen as wanting to call the shots without putting up much of its own money or making changes in its own laws and practices" (Bergsten, *Foreign Affairs*, March/April 2001).

The US response was to press for an increase in capital available to the IMF to handle the crisis and to require countries borrowing from the IMF to adopt structural reforms. These requirements led to rapidly rising unemployment in countries such as Indonesia and as a consequence, an anti-American backlash. The US thus lost on two fronts. It was criticized by Asian leaders for being slow to respond to the crisis, and by the local population for imposing harsh austerity measures through the IMF. The crisis led to massive protests at IMF meetings and contributed to a review of IMF policies. The fund acknowledged that its traditional prescription for countries with acute balance-of-payments problems, namely, austere fiscal and monetary policies, might not always be appropriate for countries facing financial crises. In some cases, the fund eased its demands for deficit reduction so that countries could increase spending on programs designed to alleviate poverty and protect the unemployed.

The US has also been widely criticized for alleged interference in the policies of the World Bank, or, to give it its full name, the International Bank for Reconstruction and Development. In an unwritten deal between America and Europe, the President of the World Bank has always been an American while the Managing Director of the IMF has always been a European. The US contributed approximately 35 percent of the World Bank's original $9100 million capitalization and remains the largest single contributor. In its early days, the World Bank was often associated with large projects, such as mining and dam building. In the 1980s and 1990s, however, it took a broader approach to encouraging economic development, devoting a growing portion of its funds to education and training projects designed to build "human capital" and to efforts by countries to develop institutions that would support market economies. Despite these changes, the World Bank was also a target of anti-globalization protestors.

The US also provides unilateral foreign aid to many countries, a policy that can be traced back to the US decision to help Europe recover after the Second World War. The assistance program is administered through the US Agency for International Development (USAID). In the 1990s, USAID was still providing assistance in varying amounts to fifty-six nations. Like the World Bank, USAID in recent years has moved away from grand development schemes such as building huge dams, highway systems, and basic industries. Increasingly, it emphasizes food and nutrition, population planning and health, education and human resources, specific economic development problems, famine and disaster relief assistance, and Food for Peace, a program that benefits American farmers while selling food and fiber on favorable credit terms to the poorest nations. Congress has not been a supporter of USAID and has consistently cut appropriations for the program. In 2001, USAID accounted for less than one-half of 1 percent of federal spending. In fact, after adjusting for inflation, the US foreign aid budget in 2001 was almost 50 percent less than it had been in 1946.

The US and globalization

Globalization may be defined as the interaction of information, financial capital, commerce, technology and labor at exponentially greater speeds and volume than previously thought possible. It is a process where decisions are taken on a global basis and the constraints of geography on economic, political, social and cultural arrangements gradually become less important. Although globalization is usually defined in economic terms, other aspects are equally important such as the environment (climate change), migration (illegal immigration), biological (infectious diseases such as smallpox, AIDS), military (conquests), religion (spread of Islam) and communications (internet and satellite television).

Without doubt the US is the leading player in the process of globalization. The US economy is not only the largest in the world but it is the engine of global growth and technological change. It is often said that when the US sneezes, the rest of the world catches a cold. Between 1992 and 2002 the US economy grew by 36 percent in real terms compared to only 19 percent for the EU and 7 percent for Japan. This remarkable growth helped other nations, particularly in Asia, recover from the financial crisis of 1997–8. A strong dollar and stock market boom during the 1990s ensured continued investment into the US economy. Furthermore, with a well-educated and skilled workforce the US has been able to reach new heights in high-tech and services areas. Globalization allows US multinationals to penetrate to every corner of the planet. The decisions taken in the information technology centers in Seattle or northern Virginia have a global impact. The US has more than two-thirds of the top five hundred companies in the world and imports more than any other country. Americans own more than half the world's computers and more than half of all the royalties and licensing fees paid in the world are to Americans. Inevitably such global economic dominance has an impact, both positive and negative, on foreign policy. The global use of the dollar and the size of the American economy also give the US decisive weight in international economic issues.

Contemporary globalization is often equated with Americanization. The first target of anti-American protestors, whether students in Korea or farmers in France, is usually McDonald's restaurants. Several dimensions of globalization are indeed dominated by activities based in the US whether on Wall Street, in the Pentagon, in Cambridge, in Silicon Valley, or in Hollywood. Books written in America have a 32 percent share of the world market. Music recorded in America has a 60 percent share of the world market, and prepackaged software 75 percent of the world market. These are impressive statistics from a country with less than 5 percent of the world's population. More than 25 percent of Americans use the internet compared to less than one hundredth of 1 percent of the population of South Asia. The central position of the US in global networks also creates "soft power," sometimes defined as the ability to get others to do what Americans want. Most of the world is fascinated by American culture, whether Big Macs or Madonna, but an increasing number are clearly opposed to American values and culture. The terrorists involved in the New York and Washington attacks may have detested American culture and values but they benefited enormously from the open features of globalization in planning their attacks.

American domination of the globalization process, however, has led to a backlash at home and abroad. The protestors in the streets of Seattle, Prague, Genoa and Washington were a demonstration of the anger many people feel about globalization and America's leading role in the process. Many see the US as pulling the strings of the various international financial organizations. The protestors' demands include more transparency for WTO, IMF, and World Bank meetings, cancellation of debts owed by the poorest countries, an end to "structural adjustment" programs that lead to economic austerity, and an end to World Bank support for socially and environmentally destructive projects, such as oil, mining and gas activities, and large dams (see World Bank report on "Globalization, Growth and Poverty," 2001). American financial power is another target. In a reference to the American agency that rates the financial stability of foreign countries, Thomas Friedman wrote in *The New York Times* on 22 February 1995:

you could almost say that we live again in a two superpower world. There is the US and there is Moody's. The US can destroy a country by leveling it with bombs. Moody's can destroy a country by downgrading its bonds.

Although the protestors in Seattle and elsewhere view globalization as an unmitigated disaster, with devastating consequences for the developing world, successive US administrations have portrayed globalization as an important and largely positive force for global economic growth and integration. The phenomenon of globalization is of course not entirely new. The first wave of closer economic cooperation between states and movement toward free trade occurred in the late nineteenth and early twentieth centuries but was brought to a shuddering halt by the First World War. The levels of economic "openness" in this period, as measured through free flow of goods, capital, and labor, were remarkably similar to international indicators in the 1970s. Since then, there has been an acceleration in the process of globalization as ever increasing flows of trade, labor, and capital are now complemented by astonishingly high flows of capital and information.

Although, partly thanks to globalization, Americans are enjoying lasting levels of prosperity never before achieved, the rapid change and harsh competition associated with globalization mean that increasing numbers of Americans are worried about its impact on their lives. Although polls show a majority of Americans in favor of globalization, there are also concerns at the implications for American jobs and, after the September 2001 terrorist attacks, for their own security. At times of crisis economic slowdown is just as contagious as growth during economic booms. Whereas in the 1960s and 1970s, American workers could be confident of being able to remain in the same industry for the whole of their lifetime, today, investments are often rapidly shifted to countries with lower labor costs and few workers are shielded from the devastating effects of capital flight. Job insecurity and uncertainty about the future are commonplace, particularly in traditionally industrial and rural communities. This situation gives rise to painful social tensions prompted by income differences between those working in high-tech and financial services industries and those making a living in low-wage occupations (Kaplan 1998). Politicians such as Ross Perot and Pat Buchanan have been tapped into these anxieties with mixed success. As globalization has led to rising inequalities around the world, inequalities have also been growing rapidly within the US. The top 1 percent of equity owners hold about 50 percent of all corporate stock. The top 5 percent own about 80 percent of all stock.

The 11 September 2001 terrorist attacks had a considerable impact on a US economy that was already sliding into recession. Apart from the huge damage inflicted on New York's financial district, the attacks led to a dramatic drop in aircraft passenger traffic, which in turn led to greatly reduced revenues and substantial job losses amongst US airlines. The recession was felt in many other sectors. Amongst the hardest hit were telecommunications, auto manufacturing, and the travel sector. It was not clear how long the downturn in consumer confidence would last. The rosy picture of future budget surpluses was also punctured by 11 September. When Bush took office in January 2001 there was a predicted budget surplus of $236 billion. Four years later the country was running an annual budget deficit of over $400 billion partly due to the impact of 9/11 and partly due to Bush's tax cuts. Inevitably this reduced fiscal situation will have an impact on expenditure for foreign and security policy (see Congressional Budget Office reports).

Politically, there is broad cross-party support for globalization, although many Democrats and some Republicans from industrial areas affected by job losses clamor for protectionist policies. Others, such as Senator Jesse Helms, raise concerns at the alleged loss of American sovereignty by joining the WTO. A majority, however, argue that US support for globalization is inherently good and view the US as a world power akin to Britain in the nineteenth century, bringing economic prosperity to the world by opening up new markets and by spreading the values of democracy and free trade. Some go on to argue that it follows that the US is justified and also widely expected to engage in unilateral decision-making (Mosler and Catley 2000). However, in today's shrinking world, unilateral action is not always an option even for the US. The strength of the post-industrial state lies more in its ability to build alliances and to navigate complex international systems rather than attempt to go it alone.

Case study: the US and oil

American dependence on the rest of the world is well illustrated by the energy sector, especially demand for oil. Over the next twenty years, to 2025, US energy demands will increase by 62 percent for natural gas, 33 percent for oil, and 45 percent for electricity. Yet as consumption soars, domestic production declines. The US is now importing 54 percent of its oil requirements (cf. 36 percent in 1973) and no new refineries have been built in more than twenty-five years. As the demand for oil in America continues to increase, it makes the US more and more dependent on the vast oil resources controlled by non-democratic regimes in the Persian Gulf. In 1974, the US imported one million barrels of oil per day from the Persian Gulf. In 2004, the figure had increased to 2.9 million barrels per day. Saudi Arabia supplies around one sixth of American oil imports (1.2 million barrels a day) and purchases $6 to $10 billion of American goods each year. Other main suppliers include Venezuela and Nigeria.

American gasoline prices are about one third of the price consumers pay in Europe. About half of all new vehicles licensed on American roads are sports utility vehicles (SUVs) that have very high gas consumption. It is estimated that increasing the average fuel economy in the US by a single mpg would save 300,000 barrels of oil each day. If fuel economy were improved by 5 mpg, the US would save 1.5 million barrels a day. Some critics argue that the high fuel consumption and corresponding necessity for large-scale oil imports into the US is a security threat. They argue that a national fuel efficiency program would reduce dependence on foreign imports from highly dangerous regions. Many of these critics, however, are doubtful whether a Texas President and Vice President, both with an oil background and elected partly by oil money, would do anything that might harm the interests of the oil lobby.

A 2001 National Defense University (NDU) sponsored study on globalization and security pointed to the downside of globalization, predicting that the growing disparities between rich and poor countries would lead to more chaos. The threats most commonly associated with globalization are inequality, instability, and unsustainable economic growth. The statistics regarding inequality are sobering. Ten percent of the world's population receives 75 percent of its income and produces 70 percent of its goods and services. Half of the world's population lives on less than two dollars a day, and these three billion people produce just 6 percent of world output. Meanwhile the three richest men in the world have combined assets equaling the output of the world's forty-eight poorest nations.

Most analysts agree that to tackle instability there will need to be better management of the global financial system. The Asian crisis was prompted in part by lack of transparency as well as poor administration and corruption. There would appear to be a strong case for a more inclusive form of global economic governance rather than relying on traditional G8 and IMF mechanisms which are widely seen as "rich men's clubs" dominated by the US. Sustainability also requires a full commitment from the developed countries to tackle both environmental concerns and to ensure that minimum targets for development assistance are met. There was greater interest in these subjects after the September 2001 terrorist attacks but little concrete action by governments. The NDU study called for closer cooperation between those studying traditional security issues and those in other disciplines such as economics. Despite recognition of globalization as a major factor in the international system most parts of the US government have been very slow to adapt structures and processes accordingly (Kugler and Frost 2001). According to one of the authors, only a few senior figures in the Bush administration, including Condoleezza Rice and Robert Zoellick, seem aware of the threats posed by globalization.

The high priest of globalization is *The New York Times* columnist, Thomas Friedman, whose bestseller, *The Lexus and the Olive Tree*, vividly describes the process of globalization. An ardent advocate of globalization, Friedman divides US policymakers into two categories: those still thinking within the constraints of the Cold War system and those working outside constraints in the interconnected world – the "walls" guys and the "web" guys. Friedman notes with satisfaction that "web" guys are becoming more common and the "walls" guys are slowly dying out. Friedman identifies three waves of democratization, all concerned with removal of barriers and with opening up to the world, that each country has to manage: first, introduction of the internet and acceptance of the communications revolution, the "democratization of technology"; second, opening of markets to smaller players and relative simplification of investment procedures or "democratization of finance"; third, spreading and reducing cost of obtaining information, the "democratization of information." Once a country has experienced these three waves of democratization it is ready to engage with other players in the global world.

In this system it is in America's interest to ensure that as many countries as possible experience this process of democratization. In the yearly debates on granting China trade preferences, the administration argued that opening up the Chinese market would inevitably lead to a more democratic system. This huge task, however, cannot be accomplished without international cooperation. No matter how powerful a country, it cannot spread the message of globalization if it considers itself above the international community. The international world order as it is expressed through international organizations is the essence of the globalizing world. A unilateral attempt to open up markets and to encourage states to drink from the golden cup of free trade is meaningless outside an international framework. A major power such as the US can lead in the international arena, but it cannot proceed on its own. Just as America has needed allies to deal with security issues, it now needs allies to guide and support the globalization process. As the country that has benefited most from globalization, the US has a special responsibility to deal with the backlash from opponents of globalization at home and abroad. This must involve support for a stable international system, and ensuring that the benefits of globalization reach as many people as possible in as many countries as possible.

Friedman's analysis would suggest that if the US wishes to maintain and to improve on the current levels of prosperity, it has little choice but to maintain the process of globalization at a cost of losing some sovereignty to international organizations and multilateral agreements. Others, however, argue that although economic arguments carry a lot of weight, they are not the only ones to be considered. The traditional concerns with national pride, sovereignty, questions of culture and religion remain very potent.

> Events following the Cold War dramatically demonstrate the political weakness of economic forces ... governments and people sacrifice welfare and even security in pursuit of national, ethnic and religious ends. The nation state, although waning, still has enough potential to prompt a complete reversal of globalizing tendencies. Furthermore the globalization process itself is not sufficiently advanced to be considered irreversible.
>
> (Waltz, *The National Interest*, 23 June 2000)

This thesis would seem to be borne out by the dramatic measures imposed by the US after 9/11. In passing the Patriot Act and establishing the Department of Homeland Defense security trumped economics. The federal government spent huge sums in seeking to protect transportation systems, US borders and US facilities overseas. The administration argued that lower economic growth was a price that had to be paid to make the US secure. But by 2004 there were more and more business voices complaining about the negative side effects. Employers criticized the difficulties foreign skilled workers encountered in getting visas to come to the US. Delays at borders resulted in higher production costs. There was no indication, however, that the administration was prepared to relax controls. Indeed it moved to establish a mandatory requirement for all foreigners entering the US to have a biometric passport and undergo fingerprint examination.

Conclusion

After a long period of protectionism, from the founding of the republic until the Second World War, the US since then has played a major part as the engine of world growth and as a pillar of international financial, economic, and trade organizations. The internationalism of the 1990s was fueled by the greatest economic expansion in US history. During the 1990s, trade as a share of the gross domestic product rose by almost 5 percent and American prosperity is linked to the international economy more than ever before. The US has benefited enormously from globalization but also has had to adapt its economy to deal with global challenges. This has led to increased voices calling for protectionism.

The US remains well placed to maintain its leadership role in globalization and thus its international political and economic leadership role. It enjoys political stability through a federal system of government and strong legal culture, sophisticated financial markets, a talented, inventive, multicultural population and a flexible workforce. A slowing economy following the 2001 terrorist attacks did lead to some increased protectionism but these measures were only of a temporary nature. After a pause there was a further increase in American FDI outflows, particularly to Europe and Asia. There was also little sign of the Bush administration willing to consider seriously the issues raised by the anti-globalization protestors and others arguing for a more equitable distribution of global wealth. As some commentators sought to establish a link between rising inequalities and the 11 September terrorist attacks, it is timely to consider the impact of terrorism on US foreign policy.

Selected further reading

Dryden (1995) *Trade Warriors* and Low (1993) *Trading Free* provide a good review of US trade policy. Friedman (2001) *The Lexus and the Olive Tree* is a lively read packed full of interesting data. Brewer (2000) *Globalizing America* considers the interaction between the US and the rest of the world. Hirst and Thompson (1999) *Globalization in Question* examines the international governance issue. Bhagwati (2001) *The Wind of the Hundred Days* is a critique of America and globalization. Giddens (2000) *Runaway World* provides a European perspective. Kugler and Frost's (2001) report *The Global Century* examines the impact of globalization on US security. For an extended inquiry into the dynamics that have obscured the boundaries between national and international affairs, see Rosenau (1997) *Along the Domestic–Foreign Frontier*. Larson (2001) *The Race to the Top* also covers the US role in globalization. The articles by Talbott (1997) and Haass (1998) look respectively at the diplomatic implications of globalization and the malcontents. The Program on International Policy Attitudes (University of Maryland) published a survey on American attitudes toward globalization on 16 November 1999. For the role of the IMF see Boughton (2001) *The Silent Revolution*. The environmental impact on global trade is covered in Weinstein and Charnowitz (2001) "The greening of the WTO." The World Bank Report (2001) on "Globalization, Growth and Poverty" looks at the inequality of the globalization process.

8

Terrorism and the Iraq War

Key facts

- The world changed for the US as a result of the 11 September 2001 terrorist attacks. Previously the US had been relatively sheltered from the impact of international terrorism, although there had been an increasing number of attacks on US targets abroad.
- President Bush declared war on all terrorist groups with an international reach. The first priority was to overthrow the Taliban regime in Afghanistan and capture Osama bin Laden. The US undertook a massive reorganization of its homeland defense with Bush nominating a new coordinator of all domestic agencies dealing with terrorism. The rapid passage of the USA Patriot Act tightened laws on terrorism.
- The US lifted many restrictions on intelligence and law enforcement agencies, including the CIA ban on recruiting unsavory individuals with a criminal past. There was also speculation as to whether the ban on assassination had been lifted.
- The debate on why the US aroused so much hatred abroad focused on US policies toward the Middle East and Gulf. There was an acknowledgement that the US needed to improve its image abroad and engage in a public relations battle with the terrorists.
- The US assembled an unprecedented coalition to tackle the terrorist threat. This involved Russia, China, Pakistan, Central Asian and most Arab countries as well as NATO and other European nations. But only a few members of the coalition supported the US-led war on Iraq. There was a fierce debate as to whether the war helped or hindered the fight against terrorism.

The response to 11 September

On 11 September 2001, the world changed for the US. Within the space of sixty minutes two hijacked planes crashed into each of New York's World Trade Center Towers and toppled them, causing a huge loss of life. A third hijacked airliner ploughed into the Pentagon causing extensive damage and further loss of life, and a fourth hijacked plane crashed near Pittsburgh as passengers fought with the hijackers to prevent another attack that would have cost many more lives. Estimates of total casualties vary up to 2,600 dead which would rank as the biggest loss of lives in one day in American history (with the possible exception of the battle of Antietem in the American Civil War for which there are no accurate casualty figures). There had been a number of voices predicting such a terrorist attack on the US. In 1999 the Hart–Rudman US Commission on National Security in the Twenty-First Century stated:

> America will become increasingly vulnerable to hostile attack on our homeland, and our military superiority will not protect us ... States, terrorists, and other disaffected groups will acquire weapons of mass destruction, and some will use them. Americans will likely die on American soil, possibly in large numbers.

The Clinton administration had already highlighted the terrorist threat and devoted considerable resources to tackling terrorism. The President stated in 1998 that the US

aged "in a long, ongoing struggle between freedom and fanaticism, between
of law and terrorism" and later told the UN that "terrorism was at the top of
a's agenda – and should be top of the world's agenda." Despite the warnings of
vernment and commissions, no one had predicted that the terrorists would hijack
and use commercial planes as cruise missiles. The intelligence agencies were accused of
massive failures while lax airport security and lack of coordination between the various
executive agencies that facilitated the terrorists' movements were also blamed on the
government. The official 9/11 Commission report stated that the attacks were a shock
but should not have been a surprise. Islamic extremists had given several warnings that
they intended to attack the US. The Commission further criticized the Clinton and
Bush administrations for a failure of imagination and not giving sufficient priority to
the terrorist threat.

> We do not believe leaders understood the gravity of the threat. The terrorist dan-
> ger from Bin Laden and Al Qaeda was not a major topic for policy debate among
> the public, the media or in Congress. Before 9/11 the US tried to solve the Al
> Qaeda problem with the capabilities it had used in the Cold War. These cap-
> abilities were insufficient and little was done to expand or reform them. The
> intelligence community struggled to come to terms with the new threat. Between
> 1995 and 9/11 there was no national intelligence assessment on terrorism.

Americans responded to the 9/11 attacks with a mixture of fear, determination, and
an outpouring of patriotism. The author recalls visiting Washington suburbs a week
after the attacks and finding almost every house displaying the Stars and Stripes.
Speaking to Congress on 20 September 2001, President Bush stressed that the US, in
responding to the attacks, would make no distinction between the terrorists who committed these "acts of war" and those who harbor them. He promised a "crusade" against
terrorism. The use of the terms "war" and "crusade" was perhaps unfortunate. Some argued
that to declare war on terrorists dignified them with a status that they sought but did
not deserve. To declare that one is at war also tends to create a war psychosis that may
be totally counterproductive for the objective being sought. "It arouses an immediate
expectation, and demand, for spectacular military action against some easily identifiable
adversary, preferably a hostile state" (Michael Howard, *Foreign Affairs*, January/February
2002). It also helped create the perception that terrorism was an evil that could be eradi-
cated rather than a more complex phenomenon with different aspects to be considered.

The US swiftly accepted that the Saudi dissident, Osama bin Laden and the Al Qaeda
network were responsible for the attacks. The President said that there would be a
lengthy campaign to defeat terrorism that could include dramatic strikes, covert operations, starving terrorists of funding and pursuing nations that provide aid or safe
haven to terrorists. Although the initial American reaction to the attacks involved calls
for revenge, the administration swiftly recognized that there were no quick or easy
solutions to dealing with the terrorist issue. At a press briefing on 25 September,
Defense Secretary Rumsfeld remarked that "terrorism is by its very nature something
that cannot be dealt with by some form of massive attack or invasion. It is a much more

subtle, nuanced, difficult, shadowy set of problems." As the President himself commented the following day, "what is the point of sending two million dollar missiles to hit a ten dollar tent that's empty?" These statements sit oddly with the later decision to invade Iraq.

In the weeks following the attacks, the US assembled an impressive and unprecedented international coalition whose members were asked to perform different tasks (military, political, intelligence) in the fight against terrorism. Overnight the reticence about working through multilateral institutions vanished – at least in dealing with terrorism. The Bush administration sought to maintain that there was an identity of interests between the US and the international community in preventing terrorism. The UN, NATO, the EU, the Organization of American States (OAS) and the Organization of Islamic States were quick to condemn the attacks and offer the US support. Russia, China, Pakistan and India were also brought on board as were some strange bedfellows, particularly the authoritarian regimes of Central Asia and the Arab world. Bush, who stated that there were "interesting opportunities" for diplomatic changes, apparently was working on the old Cold War maxim "my enemy's enemy is my friend."

Despite the large number of countries expressing support for the US, the only country to offer significant military assistance was Britain. One of the most important diplomatic changes was in US–Pakistan relations. Islamabad, a previous supporter of the Taliban regime in Afghanistan, came under enormous pressure to allow the US over-flying rights and base facilities. In return Washington lifted many of the sanctions against Pakistan (introduced as a result of its nuclear testing) and provided substantial economic assistance. The US also took advantage of the attacks to strengthen ties with Russia, China, Turkey and other countries, including those adjacent to Afghanistan in Central Asia. Relations with Sudan and Libya also improved as those countries offered to share intelligence on Osama bin Laden with the US.

In a speech a week after the terrorist attacks, Powell condemned terrorism but made no reference to any changes in policy. He said that terrorism eroded international stability, a major foreign and economic policy objective for the US. Terrorist groups often sought to destabilize or overthrow democratically elected – or friendly (to the US) – governments. Powell recognized that such groups often drew their support from public discontent in the Arab world over the perceived inability of governments to deliver peace, security, and economic prosperity. He concluded that because of their avowed goals to overthrow secular regimes in countries with large Muslim populations, extremist Islamic fundamentalist groups were seen as a particular threat to US foreign policy goals and objectives. But he offered no prescriptions to tackle the problem.

Why do they hate us?

Few Americans seem able to comprehend why anyone should hate them and even fewer seem willing to understand the extent and depth of resentment toward the US in some parts of the world, especially the Middle East. A New York Times journalist, reporting from Yemen after the attack on USS Cole, wrote that he saw "a halting, half-expressed sense of astonishment, sometimes of satisfaction and even pleasure, that a mighty power, the United States, should have its navy humbled by two Arab men in a motorized skiff." Another analyst noted that

> today, you cannot find a single political group in the Middle East that is pro-America. Anti-Americanism has poisoned the political culture. People are suspicious of US interests, goals and even its culture. Although the US dominates the world it does so in a way that inevitably arouses anger or opposition.
>
> (F. Zakaria, *Newsweek*, 15 October 2001)

After the initial and understandable calls for revenge, there were some Americans who began to question why the US aroused such hatred that could lead to the devastating terrorist attacks of September 2001. Retired air force general, Chuck Boyd, the staff director of the Hart–Rudman Commission, told the author that during his visits to more than twenty-eight countries with the Commission, one of the principal recurring themes was the resentment felt toward the US. He considered that there were several reasons for this resentment: first, a lingering hatred in some parts of the world as a result of anti-American propaganda during the Cold War; second, US support for corrupt and/or anti-democratic regimes; third, the leading American role in international institutions that "dominated the globalized world" such as the IMF, WTO, and World Bank; fourth, antipathy to the global influence of American culture. Boyd noted a dichotomy between elite hostility to US values and culture in Europe, and the popular embrace of them.

Significantly, in many Arab countries, the dichotomy is reversed. The educated elites welcome "Americanization" while the increasingly fundamentalist masses tend to despise US values and culture. Radical Islamic hatred of the US would appear to be based on perceived US policy toward the Middle East, American troops being stationed in Saudi Arabia, and a general messianic interpretation of the Koran. But one should not assume that all Islamic nations are anti-American. From Turkey to Bangladesh, Nigeria to Indonesia, the US has good relations with many Muslim countries, including Pakistan. Indeed, if one were to poll the world's Muslims about what they would want from America, the preferred response would almost surely be "a green card," allowing the holder to enter and work in the US.

In the wake of the September attacks, some experts called for the US to review its policies. According to two former national security advisers, Scowcroft and Bzrezinski, the US needed to re-examine its policies in the Middle East and Gulf. Scowcroft suggested the US needs to be more even-handed in its approach. Bzrezinski argued that the US should not withdraw its support for Israel but he saw no justification "for Israel's indefinite suppression of the Palestinians." Bzrezinski further questioned US support for the sanctions that "had inflicted grave damage on the Iraqi people over the past decade" and the uncritical US support for a Saudi regime "that had grown increasingly corrupt and become the object of resentment in the region" (*National Journal*, 22 September 2001). Another commentator, equally critical of US support for the Saudi and Egyptian regimes, argued that "the region won't be stable, the oil fields won't be secure, and America won't be free of the fear of terrorism, unless we identify with the aspirations of the Arab people to live under legitimate governments" (J. Beatty, *Atlantic Monthly*, December 2001).

Despite acknowledging that these factors may have played a role in fueling American resentment, neither Bush nor Powell showed any inclination to change US policy in the months after 11 September 2001 beyond lukewarm efforts to kick-start the Middle East peace process. The US did, however, step up its efforts in the public relations war with the terrorists. For a country with the biggest marketing industry in the world, the US has made a surprisingly poor job of managing its own image abroad. President Bush acknowledged at a press conference that "we are not doing a very good job at getting our message across to the Arab and Muslim worlds." This was a major under-statement. Although the US recognized that the media is a powerful force in con-frontations between terrorists and governments as each side seeks to appeal to and influence public opinion, initially the US was on the defensive in the public relations war with Osama bin Laden. It made a mistake in describing the campaign against terrorism as a "crusade" and sought to close the independent Al-Jazeera Arab news station that had broadcast video statements by Osama bin Laden. In the aftermath of 11 September, Osama bin Laden, regarded by some as the Che Guevara of the Islamic world, initially avoided taking any credit for the attacks and sought to link US reprisal bombings with Israeli aggression in the West Bank, sanctions against Iraq, and the continuing presence of American troops in Saudi Arabia. Many Arabs apparently believed that the US orchestrated the attacks itself in order to unleash a crusade against Muslims and when the US produced a video of Osama bin Laden gloating over the success of the attacks they dismissed it as a forgery.

To try and improve America's image abroad, Powell chose Charlotte Beers, a former head of the leading public relations company, J. Walter Thompson, as the State Department under-secretary for public affairs and diplomacy. Her job, selling the US, its values and foreign policy to the rest of the world, was described as "possibly the biggest brand assignment in history" (Tomkins, *Financial Times*, 19 November 2001). The administration also enlisted the help of several PR companies and Hollywood producers to advise on promoting the American message to the outside world and to produce some patriotic films. One problem was that the US message focused more on appealing to Arab leaders rather than to the average citizen. Osama bin Laden, speaking from a cave and portraying himself as an underdog, was able to communicate much more effectively with the wider Arab population. Some have suggested that America needs to train more intercultural specialists. But according to one analyst, no amount of communications training and no amount of spin from Washington will compensate for its perceived aggression against the Muslim world and its one-sided support for Israel (Zaharna, *FPIF report*, November 2001).

Three years later the Pentagon set up a study which came to a similar conclusion. The Defense Science Board report of November 2004 stated that "America's image in world opinion and diminished ability to persuade are consequences of factors other than the fail-ure to implement communications strategies." The report also criticized the adminis-tration for casting the new threat of Islamic terrorism in a way that offends a large part of those living in the Muslim world (*International Herald Tribune*, 25 November 2004).

Rogue states and the terrorist list

The concept of "rogue states" is peculiarly American. In 1998, Madeleine Albright, sensitive to the fact that no other country used the term "rogue states," tried to use another name, "countries of concern." But this did not have the same snappy ring and the expression did not stick. The "rogues" are usually defined as Cuba, Iraq (under Saddam Hussein), Libya, North Korea and Iran – all states on the State Department's terrorist list. Iraq and Libya have since been removed from the list. President George W. Bush went a stage further in referring to Iraq, Iran and North Korea as an "axis of evil" in his January 2002 state of the union address. Some of his advisers went further in advocating US support for "regime change" in the "rogue states." Although the "rogues" are all authoritarian states, there are substantial differences between their political systems and their degree of hostility toward the US. Yet Washington maintains a single policy toward the "rogues" based on a mix of political and economic sanctions, international non-proliferation regimes, and punitive military action. With the exception of Libya, the policy mix has not been particularly effective. Even close allies of the US, like the EU, do not share the policy of trying to isolate the "rogues." Europeans argue that a policy of "constructive engagement" is more likely to bring about change than isolation and sanctions. Furthermore, there is little evidence that sanctions regimes work, given the many loopholes in their application (Litwak 2000; Chomsky 2000).

Sanctions are something of a blunt instrument, especially when applied unilaterally and not through a multilateral regime. They may include a total or partial trade embargo, a ban on financial transactions, suspension of foreign aid, restrictions on transport, or abrogation of treaties. Sanctions usually require the cooperation of other countries to make them effective and, wherever possible, the US seeks to gather international support for sanctions. The UN's role in mandating sanctions against Libya for its responsibility in the 1988 Pan Am bombing (and the shooting down of a French plane over Chad) was significant as the first instance when the world community imposed sanctions against a country in response to its complicity in an act of terrorism. Several factors made the action possible. First, terrorism has touched many more countries in recent years, forcing governments to put aside parochial interests. Citizens from over thirty countries have reportedly died as a result of Libyan-sponsored terrorism. Second, the end of the Cold War has contributed to increased international cooperation against terrorism. Russia in particular has been ready to engage in a new cooperative relationship with the US in fighting terrorism. Third, US determination to punish terrorist countries, by military force in some instances, once their complicity was established, was a major factor spurring other countries to join UN-sponsored action.

But international cooperation on sanctions is not always forthcoming. Iran, Iraq, and Libya, for example, are major oil producers, producing, in 2001, 35 percent of the EU's oil imports, and 11 percent of Japan's imports. Such dependence on oil complicates universal support for sanctions against these nations. Some Americans have been critical of the EU policy of "constructive engagement" with these countries. Senator

Schumer, speaking to a group of members of the European Parliament on 12 September 2001, was very clear on US expectations:

> We have to let our European allies know that the finger is not just pointed at us, but at them. And this idea that for temporary economic advantage they can continue to have strong trading relations with countries that help, abet and harbor terrorists must go out the window.

US officials, however, sometimes use European channels to the "rogues" to pass messages or warnings.

Although the US had no prior warning of the 11 September attacks, there had been a steady increase in terrorists targeting US citizens and property. In the Middle East alone, the US had suffered two bombings in Saudi Arabia in 1995 and 1996, the bombings of its embassies in Tanzania and Kenya in 1998, and the bombing of the navy ship USS *Cole* in 2000. In that year, approximately 47 percent of all terrorist incidents worldwide were committed against American citizens or property according to the State Department – the vast majority of those acts took place on foreign soil. Already before the 11 September attacks on the US, the State Department, in its annual "Patterns of Global Terrorism" report (30 April 2001), had noted that casualties associated with terrorism worldwide increased from 233 in 1999 to 405 dead in 2000. It also drew attention to the fact that a decline in state sponsorship of terrorism had moved terrorism eastward from Libya, Syria, and Lebanon to an alliance of radical Islamic groups operating out of Afghanistan with the acquiescence of the Taliban.

In 2001, five of the seven countries on the "terrorism list" were predominantly Muslim. According to one American diplomat "the list was compiled as much due to political factors as objective criteria about terrorist activities." It certainly appeared strange that neither Pakistan nor Afghanistan figured on the list. It can also be argued that by precluding non-state groups from the list it provides a false impression of terrorist activity.

The State Department is mandated by Congress to report annually on international bribery, human rights practices, narcotics control, religious freedom and global terrorism. The 2003 *Patterns of Global Terrorism* report aroused considerable controversy as it contained many errors and was considered to have been released for political purposes, i.e. to demonstrate that the Bush administration was winning the war on terrorism. In actual fact the true figures revealed a substantial increase in the number of "significant terrorist incidents," up from 124 to 175. It is important, however, to see things in perspective. In 2003, a total of 625 people – including 25 Americans – were killed in international terrorist incidents worldwide. Meanwhile, over 43,000 Americans died from automobile accidents in the US alone, and 3 million people died of AIDS around the world.

Policy dilemmas

In June 2000 the National Commission on Terrorism issued its report which stated that there was a growing threat from terrorism and that increased efforts were required to meet this danger. It listed a number of steps that the government should undertake, including "firmly targeting" all states that support terrorism (report available at *www.access.gpo.gov/nct*, accessed 11 April 2005). It left unmentioned, however, the foreign complications of executing counter-terrorist policy. The foreign policy consequences of countering the terrorist threat received equally short attention during the debate on the 1996 Anti-terrorism and Effective Death Penalty Act. Essentially US counter-terrorist policy is based on four tenets:

- bring terrorists to justice for their crimes
- pressure on state sponsors of terrorism
- no concessions to terrorists and no deals
- seek support and assist allies in fighting terrorism.

The first three of these tenets reflect a confrontational approach that is very much in the mainstream of American thinking. Not all principles, however, have been applied evenly. The fourth tenet recognizes the international dimension of terrorism and that most progress in the fight against terrorism ultimately depends on the perspectives and behavior of foreign governments, groups, publics and individuals. But it begs a number of important questions. How much does a state have to cooperate with the US to be deemed a partner? What if that state is engaged in suppressing its own citizens? There has also been little debate in the US about the political roots of terrorism and how Washington might fashion new or modify old policies to deal with these underlying political issues.

There is no universally accepted definition of international terrorism but one definition widely used in US government circles defines international terrorism as terrorism involving the citizens or property of more than one country. Terrorism itself is broadly defined as politically motivated violence perpetrated against non-combatant targets by sub-national groups or clandestine agents. A "terrorist group" is defined as a group which practices or which has significant sub-groups that practice terrorism. One potential shortfall of this traditional definition is its focus on groups and group members and exclusion of individual (non-group organized) terrorist activity that has recently risen in frequency and visibility. Another weakness of these definitions is the criteria of violence in a traditional form and the neglect of, for example, cyber attacks on national infrastructure. Furthermore, the bombing of an American naval ship raises issues of whether the standard definition would categorize this attack as terrorist, as the USS *Cole* may not qualify as a "non-combatant."

In its fight against terrorism, the US, like other governments confronted with the problem, often faces conflicting goals and courses of action. In the past, some governments have preferred to handle terrorism as a national problem without outside interference. Some governments have also been wary of getting involved in others' battles and possibly attracting additional terrorism in the form of reprisals. Others have been reluctant to join in sanctions if their own trade interests might be damaged or if they sympathized with the perpetrators' cause. Finally, there is the persistent problem of extraditing terrorists without abandoning the long-held principle of asylum for persons fleeing persecution for legitimate political or other activity. To the consternation of the British government, for many years the US authorities turned a blind eye to American financial contributions to IRA front organizations. It was also a very slow and difficult process to extradite suspected Irish terrorists from the US to the UK.

One obvious dilemma is providing security from terrorist acts, i.e. limiting the freedom of individual terrorists, terrorist groups, and support networks to operate unimpeded in a relatively unregulated environment versus maximizing individual freedoms, democracy, and human rights. Efforts to combat terrorism are complicated by a global trend toward deregulation, open borders, and expanded commerce. The September 2001 attacks provide a good example of how the Al Qaeda network took advantage of globalization. Before hijacking the planes, the terrorists studied in Hamburg, took flying lessons in Florida, used cellular phones and e-mail to communicate with each other and accessed the internet to make hotel and plane reservations.

Although the US maintains a public stance of no concessions to terrorists, practice has not always been so pure. The Reagan administration dealt with Iran in order to finance the Contras in Nicaragua. President Clinton invited Sinn Fein leader, Gerry Adams, to the White House, although the British government argued that Adams had been a leading member of the IRA. Successive Presidents have dealt with Yasser Arafat, the former PLO leader, although many Israelis have dubbed him a terrorist. A perennial problem is differing perspectives on terrorists and terrorist activities. One person's terrorist is another person's freedom fighter. Americans fighting for independence were dubbed "terrorists" by the British. Menachim Begin, a former Israeli Prime Minister, was at one stage wanted by the British for terrorist acts. The US was slow to recognize Nelson Mandela as a black South African freedom fighter instead of a terrorist. To many Arabs, Osama bin Laden is a heroic freedom fighter against the American, Saudi, and Egyptian governments.

Another dilemma for policymakers is the need to identify the perpetrators of particular terrorist acts and those who train, fund, or otherwise support or sponsor them. The majority of those involved in the September 2001 attacks were Saudi citizens but the US struck back at Afghanistan not Saudi Arabia. A further complicating factor is that many terrorists seem to be individuals who do not work for any state and who may have no or only loose links to a known terrorist organization. The worldwide threat of such individual terrorism, or spontaneous terrorist activity, is likely to increase. This will pose problems for the US which has traditionally sought to pin responsibility for terrorism on states. A desire to punish a state for supporting international terrorism may also be subject to conflicting foreign policy objectives. Another problem in the wake of the number of incidents associated with Islamic fundamentalist groups is how to condemn and combat such terrorist activity, and the extreme and violent ideology of specific radical groups, without appearing to be anti-Islamic in general. President Bush seemed to recognize this dilemma as one of his first acts after 11 September was to visit a mosque in an attempt to reassure the four million Muslims living in the US that they were not tainted with the brush of the terrorists.

Policy options

The US has employed a range of options to combat international terrorism, from diplomacy and international cooperation to economic sanctions, covert action, protective security measures and military force. The use of force after the 11 September 2001 attacks was almost inevitable given the number of casualties and the strong desire for revenge. In fighting the Taliban and Osama bin Laden the US was not a reluctant but a very willing sheriff. Although not without problems, military force, particularly when wielded by a superpower such as the US, can have a decisive impact. The 1986 decision to bomb Libya for its alleged role in the bombing of a German discotheque was one example of the use of military force. Other examples include the 1993 bombing of Iraq's military intelligence headquarters in response to Iraqi efforts to assassinate former President George Bush during a visit to Kuwait and the 1998 missile attacks against bases in Afghanistan and an alleged chemical production facility in Sudan following the attacks on US embassies in East Africa.

The two prime examples of the use of force are the military campaign against the Taliban regime and the Al Qaeda network in Afghanistan in 2001 and the 2003 invasion of Iraq. The swift military victory over the Taliban, accomplished with the Afghan Northern Alliance, was unforeseen and gave rise to a new confident spirit in the Pentagon and White House. Military force, especially the precision bombing and the use of special units, was seen to have played a crucial role in bringing about a change of government in Afghanistan. Many argued that it should be employed for similar purposes elsewhere, particularly an attack on Iraq. Yet the military was also criticized for failing to capture Osama bin Laden in the Afghanistan campaign.

Although the war on terrorism was being fought by bankers, police, customs agents and IT specialists, it was the military that captured the headlines. Washington made it abundantly clear that it was not only ready to use force in retaliation for terrorist acts but that it had the best military capabilities in the world for such tasks. The administration also hoped that proof of US military success and its willingness to act overseas might deter other groups or states harboring terrorist groups. Not everyone was pleased at the emphasis on a military response. Strobe Talbott, the Deputy Secretary of State during the Clinton administration, held that "encouraging stable political development is the key to reducing our greatest security threat. We have no option but to get back into the nation-building business" (*Foreign Policy in Focus*, November/December 2001). Apart from the President's commitment to assist in the reconstruction of Afghanistan, there was little sign of the US wishing to become more engaged in dealing with "failed states." This could be a shortsighted attitude as, sooner or later, the US is invariably drawn into the problems resulting from "failed states" as witness the involvement in Haiti, Somalia, and Kosovo.

The military campaign in Afghanistan was allied to an unprecedented diplomatic coalition pulled together by President Bush and Secretary of State Powell. Some argue that diplomacy holds little hope of success against determined terrorists or the countries that support them. However, diplomatic measures are least likely to widen the conflict and therefore are usually tried first. In incidents of international terrorism by sub-national groups, a diplomatic response is complicated by the lack of channels to communicate. In some instances, as was the case at one time with the PLO, legislation may specifically prohibit official contact with a terrorist organization or its members. The US had no known channels to Osama bin Laden or the Al Qaeda network.

The use of economic sanctions only makes sense when a state is identified as an active supporter or sponsor of international terrorism. In dealing with sub-groups or individuals, other measures have to be taken. Two weeks after the September attacks, President Bush signed an executive order freezing assets of twenty-seven organizations known to be associated with Osama bin Laden's network. He also gave the Treasury Secretary broad powers to impose sanctions on banks around the world that provide these organizations with access to the international financial system. Previously, in 1998, President Clinton signed an executive order freezing assets owned by Osama bin Laden and his associates, and prohibiting US individuals and firms from doing business with them. The US has also been active in securing international support, through the G8 and other bodies, to block financing of terrorist networks. In setting sanctions, the President has a variety of laws at his disposal, particularly the International Emergency Economic Powers Act. The Act permits imposition of sanctions once the President has declared a national emergency because of a threat to US national security, foreign policy, or its economy. Under the sweeping powers of the Act, the President can regulate imports, exports, and all types of financial transactions, such as the transfer of funds, foreign exchange, credit, and securities, between the US and the country in question.

Experts agree that the most effective way to fight terrorism is to gather as much intelligence as possible, disrupt terrorist plans and organizations before they act, and organize multinational cooperation against terrorists and countries that support them. Intelligence gathering, infiltration of terrorist groups, and disruption of their operations involve a variety of clandestine or so-called "covert" activities. It has been very difficult for the CIA to penetrate terrorist networks, not least because of tight restrictions on who the agency may recruit as agents. There were indications that these restrictions had been eased in the aftermath of 11 September. Much intelligence activity is of a passive monitoring nature but it may also involve seizing and transporting a wanted terrorist to stand trial for assassination or murder. American officials have argued that such activity might be justified as preemptive self-defense under Article 51 of the UN charter.

Assassination is specifically prohibited by US executive order but bringing of wanted criminals to the US for trial is not. There was some speculation that President Bush may have lifted the executive order after 11 September but the administration made clear that such a move was unnecessary as the US was engaged in a war of self-defense. Regarding abduction, there exists an established US legal doctrine that allows an individual's trial to proceed regardless of whether he is forcefully abducted from another country, or from international waters or airspace. For example, Fawaz Yunis, a Lebanese who participated in the 1985 hijacking of a Jordanian airliner with two Americans among its seventy passengers, was lured aboard a yacht in international waters off the coast of Cyprus in 1987 by federal agents, flown to the US for trial, and convicted.

The abduction of persons residing abroad to face US justice, however, can vastly complicate US foreign relations, perhaps jeopardizing interests far more important than "justice," deterrence, and the prosecution of a single individual. For example, the abduction of a Mexican national in 1990 to stand trial in Los Angeles on charges relating to torture and death of a DEA official led to vehement protests from the government of Mexico, a government subsequently plagued with evidence of high-level drug-related corruption. Such conduct, moreover, raises prospects of other nations using similar tactics against US citizens.

The State Department also has a rewards program for those helping to prevent terrorist acts. This program was at least partly responsible for the arrest of Ramzi Ahmed Yousef, the man accused of masterminding the 1995 World Trade Center bombing. The program was established by the 1984 Act to combat international terrorism and is administered by the State Department's diplomatic security service. The program can pay to relocate informants and immediate family who fear for their safety. A twenty-five million dollar reward was put on the head of Osama bin Laden. The State Department and FBI run a number of other programs to combat terrorism, including specialized assistance and training to foreign countries to help them improve their anti-terrorism capabilities. International cooperation in such areas as law enforcement, customs control, and intelligence activities was another essential part of the Bush administration's response to the 11 September attacks.

The US has signed all of the major, international anti-terrorism conventions. These conventions impose on their signatories an obligation either to prosecute offenders or extradite them to permit prosecution for a host of terrorism-related crimes including hijacking vessels and aircraft, taking hostages, and harming diplomats. Extradition, however, has traditionally been subject to several limitations, including the refusal to extradite for political or extra-territorial offenses and the refusal of some countries to extradite their nationals. Given that much terrorism involves politically motivated violence, the State Department has sought to curtail the availability of the political offense exception, found in many extradition treaties, to avoid extradition.

There have been calls to attack "the root causes of terrorism" but there is no agreement on what are the root causes. There is little evidence, for example, that poverty plays a role in motivating the Al Qaeda network. Osama bin Laden has stated his wish to destroy America is based on the poisonous nature of its flagrantly secular and sexualized popular culture which is contrary to Islamic morals. There is no doubt that Al Qaeda wishes to impose an Islamic theocracy wherever possible. Under these conditions it is difficult to imagine any compromise solution.

There were some who hoped that the US opposition to the International Criminal Court (ICC) would mellow following the 11 September attacks. The US opposition to the new court was all the more difficult to fathom in the light of its potential to deal with war criminals and terrorists such as Slobodan Milosevic. But the administration and Congress continued to assert that the US would not join if it meant that American soldiers could be arraigned before the ICC. To many, this was a case of one law for the rest of the world – another for the US.

Homeland defense

The US response to 11 September was felt in many policy areas, including more resources for homeland defense, law enforcement agencies, and foreign and security policy. On the domestic front, there was a thorough reorganization of "homeland defense." The chain of command on anti-terrorism planning runs from the President through the NSC and involves several parts of the administration including State, Justice, Treasury and Commerce. To try and impose some overall coordination, Bush established a new cabinet level post for Homeland Defense, and named Governor Tom Ridge as the first occupant of the office. The massive new bureaucracy, however, struggled to impose itself against the vested interests of the traditional federal departments of government.

In the wake of the September 2001 terrorist attacks, Congress passed the 2001 USA Patriot Act that gave the government significant new powers in dealing with the terrorist threat. Building on anti-terrorist laws passed after the 1995 Oklahoma City bombing, the new act gave the federal government increased powers for wire-tapping, seizing telephone and e-mail records, medical, banking, educational and business files, and even secret searches of suspects' homes. Defending the bill, John Ashcroft, the attorney general, stated, "we are at war and we have to do things differently." Civil rights groups were concerned that some of these powers, particularly relating to domestic surveillance by law-enforcement agencies, could infringe basic rights to privacy. Another controversy was the proposal to establish military courts to try foreigners residing in the US for terrorist acts. Former Secretary of Defense, William Cohen, drew attention to the conflict between individual privacy and protection from terrorism in a lecture on 2 October 2001. "I believe that we as a democratic society have yet to come to grips with the tension that exists between our constitutional protection of the right to privacy and the demand that we make to protect us." Congress reacted to these concerns by insisting on "sunset clauses" (an expiry date after five years) for many provisions in the Patriot Act.

As the World Trade Center towers crumbled many thought that American unilateralism crumbled with it. The US rushed to assemble a broad international coalition, encompassing some dubious regimes, to fight the Taliban in Afghanistan. As in fighting communism during the Cold War, the US considered it immoral for countries not to take a stance against terrorism. But it was not clear what the longer-term implications of embracing previous pariah countries such as Sudan, Pakistan, and Uzbekistan would be. If it meant turning a blind eye to Chinese suppression of human rights in Tibet or Russian abuses in Chechnya, then many human rights organizations felt it was too high a price. The State Department will also have to face this dilemma. Testifying before Congress on 18 July 2001, a senior official, Michael Parmley, said that the Central Asian republics "had performed abysmally since gaining their independence and democracy in the region was almost non-existent." Three months later, these concerns were quietly forgotten as the US rushed to establish military bases in Central Asia.

Case study: The Iraq War

Following the first Gulf War successive US administrations pursued a policy of containment toward Saddam Hussein's Iraq. This involved support for UN inspectors searching for WMD and sanctions against Saddam which inevitably meant great suffering for the ordinary people of Iraq. For the neo-conservatives this was too weak a policy and several, including Donald Rumsfeld, Paul Wolfowitz and Richard Perle, signed a letter to President Clinton in 1998 calling for military action to ensure regime change in Iraq. They wrote:

> The only acceptable strategy is one that eliminates the possibility that Iraq will be able to use or threaten to use WMD. In the near term, this means a willingness to undertake military action as diplomacy is clearly failing. In the longer term, it means removing Saddam Hussein and his regime from power. That now needs to become the aim of American foreign policy.

Clinton, however, stuck to the containment policy, as did President Bush during his first year in office. But 9/11 gave the neocons their opportunity to make the case that Saddam Hussein was stockpiling WMD either to use himself against the US, or to provide terrorists with WMD material. In his address to the nation on 9 September 2001 Bush stated that the US "will make no distinction between the terrorists who committed these acts and those who harbor them." In his address to Congress just a week later Bush went a step further:

> We will pursue nations that provide aid or safe haven to terrorists. Every nation, in every region, now has a decision to make. Either you are with us, or you are with the terrorists. From this day forward, any nation that continues to harbor or support terrorism will be regarded by the US as a hostile regime.

The President also went on to outline his vision for a strong American leadership in the world, a leadership that would project America's power and influence.

> The advance of human freedom ... now depends on us. Our nation – this generation – will lift a dark threat of violence from our people and our future. We will rally the world to this cause by our efforts, by our courage. We will not tire, we will not falter, and we will not fail.

In his state of the union address in January 2002 Bush introduced the idea of an "axis of evil" that included Iraq, Iran and North Korea, and signaled that the US was prepared to act pre-emptively to deal with such nations. To the neocons this was a green light to start war preparations against Iraq. During the summer of 2002 Bush hardened his position against states that support terrorism and in a speech in June stated that the US must be ready for "pre-emptive action" when necessary to defend the US. He also said that "America has, and intends to keep, military strengths beyond challenge." America was now – officially – a hegemonic power.

Vice President Cheney played a key role in mobilizing support within the administration and public for the war on Iraq. Without any proof, he alleged that Saddam Hussein not only had links to Al Qaeda and was involved in the 9/11 attacks but also insisted that "he possessed WMD." Cheney also argued that regime change in Iraq would have a domino effect on the Middle East. Colin Powell fought a rearguard action on Iraq with some support from disaffected Republicans. Brent Scowcroft, a former NSC adviser, wrote an op ed in the *Wall Street Journal* on 15 August 2002 arguing that Bush was moving too fast on Iraq and that the UN inspectors should be allowed back to finish their job. Powell won a small victory when, with the support of Tony Blair, he persuaded Bush to take his case against Iraq to the UN. In a speech in New York on 12 September the President said:

> The purposes of the United States should not be doubted. The Security Council resolutions will be enforced – the just demands of peace and security will be met – or action will be unavoidable. And a regime that has lost its legitimacy will also lose its power.

A week after his UN speech the White House released the administration's National Security Strategy (NSS). This 33-page document presented a bold reformulation of US foreign policy. It outlined a new, muscular American posture in the world, a posture that would rely on pre-emption to deal with rogue states and terrorists harboring WMD. It restated that America would never allow its military power to be challenged as it was during the Cold War.

The neocons were delighted at the publication of the NSS and maintained their pressure on the President to start military preparations for an invasion of Iraq. In February 2003 Colin Powell went before the UNSC to argue the case for military action as Saddam Hussein had failed to cooperate with the demands of the UN weapons inspectors. He attempted to bolster his case with photographs allegedly showing Iraqi WMD sites. Later the Secretary of State admitted that his presentation had been based on "faulty intelligence." The UNSC was not impressed by Colin Powell's evidence and refused the US/UK request for approval of military action against Iraq.

Despite this refusal, and against strong opposition from several of its allies, the US went ahead in early March 2003 with the invasion of Iraq. It was a one-sided fight and within a few weeks the US forces had captured Baghdad. A few weeks later Saddam Hussein was captured and President Bush was photographed aboard a US aircraft carrier proclaiming "mission accomplished." The failure to find any WMD was a major embarrassment to Bush (and Blair). Both leaders then changed the rationale for the war to emphasize human rights and promotion of democracy. Contrary to the expectations of the neocons there was no peace and harmony. There was a strong Iraqi resistance movement to the US occupation, bolstered by the arrival of many fighters from other Muslim countries to engage in a Jihad against the American infidels. Both Bush and Rumsfeld were heavily criticized for not sending sufficient troops to Iraq to ensure stability after the conquest of Baghdad. General Franks, commander of the attack on Iraq, said that the Pentagon hoped to reduce the 140,000 troops involved in the invasion of Iraq to 30,000 by the end of 2003. The aim was wildly optimistic. Another top US army official, General Eric Shinseki, stated in February 2003 that "something of the order of several hundred thousand soldiers" would be required to stabilize postwar Iraq. He was brusquely dismissed by Wolfowitz as "wildly off the mark." The Deputy Defense Secretary went on to say that he was reasonably certain that the Iraqi people would "greet us as liberators." The fights between the commanders on the ground and the Pentagon were constant. General

Franks commented on Douglas Feith, the under-secretary for policy: "I have to deal with the fxxxing stupidest guy on the face of the earth almost every day" (Woodward 2004: 281).

Evidently the Pentagon's grandiose plans for Iraq did not foresee the extent of the Iraqi insurgency. The Iraq case was also the first since the Second World War where the Pentagon and not the State Department had led responsibility for the post-conflict situation. The careful, detailed plans of the State Department were ignored as the hawks in the Pentagon assumed that the US would be greeted as liberators, power could be swiftly handed over to "their man" Ahmed Chalabi, and the US could go home. The Bush administration, however, failed to take into account deep suspicion about US motives, the legacy of Western colonialism and the resentment at the US stance in the Israel–Palestine conflict.

The US had established Paul Brenner, a senior State Department official, as pro-Consul for Iraq. One of his first decisions, to disband the Iraqi army, proved hugely controversial. According to many critics, it turned the US instantly from an army of liberation to an army of occupation and helped fuel the insurgency. As American casualties mounted, the US arranged to hand over political responsibility in May 2004 to an Iraqi interim government. Elections for a provisional government were held in January 2005 but US forces were still mainly responsible for the security situation, which showed little improvement in the first half of 2005. American prestige suffered a huge blow with the publication of photographs showing American service men and women torturing Iraqi captives in the notorious Abu Ghraib prison. There were also revelations of similar torture at Guantanamo Bay where America kept several hundred "enemy combatants" without recourse to the Geneva Conventions. By the summer of 2004, America had suffered a thousand deaths in Iraq; no one knew exactly how many Iraqis had died but some estimates put the figures at tens of thousands. The US, despite talk of an international coalition, provided 90 percent of all the forces in Iraq – at an annual cost to the American taxpayer of $50 billion.

The war in Iraq was initially supported by huge majorities in Congress, the media and public opinion. But as the campaign began to turn sour so was there a backlash in the US that fed into the 2004 election campaign. Senator Kerry, although voting for the war, charged the President with taking the US into "the wrong war, at the wrong time, in the wrong place." Perhaps the most damaging critique came from Richard Clarke, the long-time head of the anti-terror campaign under both Democrat and Republican administrations. In his book (*Against All Enemies*) published in the spring of 2004 he charged the Bush team with "taking their eye off the ball" in pursuing Saddam Hussein. The Iraqi leader may have been evil but he had nothing to do with 9/11 or supporting international terrorism. He described the war in Iraq "an avaricious, premeditated, unprovoked war against a foe who posed no immediate threat but whose defeat did offer economic advantages. For Osama bin Laden the American invasion and occupation of Iraq was like a Christmas present – and would be a magnet for anti-US terrorists." Other critics charged Bush with lying over the costs of the war. A group of some 300 American professors of international relations published an open letter to the President on 13 October 2004 alleging that the war on Iraq "was the most misguided policy since the Vietnam period." Another group of 27 retired senior diplomats and officers also published a letter critical of the President for "failing to ensure national security and provide world leadership." Bush shrugged off these critics, keeping to his message that Iraq was an essential part of the wider war on terrorism.

Conclusion

The terrorist attacks on 11 September 2001 were a defining moment for the US. The America that emerged from the attacks was a different country, more united, yet more fearful of the future. President Bush sought to reassure Americans that the war would be fought largely outside the US and would not involve any tax increases. He envisaged the military playing the major role and earmarked far greater budget increases for the Pentagon than homeland security. It was by no means clear, however, whether terrorism would become a lasting or ephemeral preoccupation for the US. Contrary to the fighting words of the President, this was not a war for existence or for the survival of western civilization. The terrorists were largely a rag bag of misfits who could not even seize control in their own countries. It was also not clear whether it would mean a new emphasis on getting to the political roots of the problem. Would it lead, as many European governments hoped, to a new approach toward the Middle East? Much will depend on whether there are further terrorist outrages against the US but in the short-term one can safely predict that terrorism will remain the top priority for the US and that it will continue to seek allies to fight against terrorism wherever it can find them. In the long-term the US is too powerful compared to the rest of the world not to return to some degree of complacency, albeit not to the same extent as prevailed before 11 September 2001.

At the same time, by undertaking an open-ended war on terrorism, the US will undoubtedly make itself a continued target for terrorists and criticism, such as its treatment of Al Qaeda suspects at the Guantanamo military base in Cuba. It will also be very difficult to decide on the President's "non-negotiable demands" on values. These include respect for human rights, the rule of law, religious freedom and equality for women. These values are not always shared by many of America's allies, including many that now play host to US bases. Many hope that the US will also recognize the importance of tackling some of the major imbalances in the world and provide a lead in seeking to redress the huge gulf between the "haves" and "have nots."

A further open question is whether the US will follow Bzrezinski's advice and seek to modify the policies that have brought it so much resentment in the Arab world. The Iraq War has not led to the spread of democracy in the Middle East and continuing American support for the autocratic regimes in Saudi Arabia and elsewhere leave it open to charges of hypocrisy. Its seemingly uncritical support for Israel gives it guilt by association in Arab eyes. Its financial support for Egypt, designed originally to reward Cairo's peace with Israel, merely associates the US with another authoritarian regime that allows anti-American propaganda to pour from the state-controlled media. There is no doubt that all these policies cause widespread resentment in the Arab world. Given that terrorism is likely to remain a top American concern for some time, it is timely to consider other foreign policy priorities of the US.

Selected further reading

Piller (2001) *Terrorism and US Foreign Policy*, Simon (2001) *The Terrorist Trap*, Tucker (1997) *Skirmishes at the Edge*, Lessor (1999) *Countering the New Terrorism* provide good overviews of American reactions to terrorism. Perry (2001) "Preparing for the next attack" offers a menu of responses. US policy toward rogue states is treated in Tanter (1999) *Rogue Regimes*, Litwak (2000) *Rogue States and US Foreign Policy*, Klare (1995) *Rogue States and Nuclear Outlaws*, and Chomsky (2000) *Rogue States*. The two books by Bob Woodward *The Agenda: Inside the Clinton White House* and *Shadow: Five Presidents and the Legacy of Watergate* are among the best in covering the war on terrorism from an administration perspective.

US government websites, including State, the CIA, and FBI, all provide much useful information. See *state.gov*, *www.cia.gov*, and *www.fbi.gov* (accessed 11 April 2005). A number of think tanks and major newspapers also have special pages on their websites devoted to terrorism (see bibliography).

9

US foreign policy priorities

Key facts

- The US has had to re-assess its foreign policy priorities after the end of the Cold War and 11 September 2001. Until 9/11 there was little consensus as Presidents placed different emphasis on various regions and issues. The US spends vast sums on its military apparatus but relatively little on diplomacy, technical, or development assistance.
- In contrast to Bill Clinton, George W. Bush emphasized the importance of missile defense and pre-emptive strikes, especially after 9/11. In the face of a growing global agenda, the US was reluctant to embrace the UN and other international institutions.
- Europe and Asia have strongest ties to the US in terms of military commitments and economic and financial links. Transatlantic relations are changing as Europe unites and the US pursues a more assertive and unilateral foreign policy. US–Asian ties are also in a state of flux as a result of changes in China and Korea. The US is worried at instability in Central and South Asia.
- The US enjoys traditional close ties to its neighbors, Canada and Mexico, further cemented by NAFTA. But relations with Mexico are troubled by the economic divide and consequent large-scale illegal immigration. Colombia is a huge problem as it is the main supplier of cocaine to the US. There is considerable doubt as to future plans for the FTAA.
- For many years the US has been involved in the search for a Middle East peace agreement. Clinton made it a top priority while Bush was reluctant to become too closely involved. But in 2004 Bush launched ambitious plans for bringing democracy to the wider Middle East. The Persian Gulf remains a vital region for the US. Despite an increasing number of high-profile visits to Africa, especially during the Clinton administration, the continent is a low priority for the US although there is growing recognition of the importance of combating HIV/AIDS.

Spending priorities

Although there was some basic agreement on foreign policy between the mainstream forces in the Democratic and Republican parties, the Clinton and Bush administrations placed different emphasis at different times on various countries, regions, international organizations, global issues as well as missile defense. The Republicans criticized Clinton for paying too much attention to Russia and China at the expense of traditional allies such as Japan and South Korea. But after several months in office, largely neglecting Russia and China, Bush (especially after 9/11) came to see the importance of good relations with both countries. There was little difference in importance attached to the G8. Both Clinton and Bush seemed to enjoy this annual restricted session of the world's leading industrial countries.

A review of how the US spends its money on foreign and security policy gives a good sense of its priorities. In 2003, the US spent about 17 percent of the federal budget on national security and international activities, with the military consuming 94 percent of the total external expenditure. The Pentagon is a massive enterprise issuing over half of all government pay checks. It makes about two-thirds of all government purchases of goods and services. It sponsors over 53 percent of all government research and development. It is also the largest source of waste, fraud, and abuse in the federal government. In 2004, the General Accounting office reported that the Pentagon was unable to account for $250 billion of more than $1.3 trillion worth of property, equipment, and supplies. Congress is a prime reason for the waste. Senator John McCain estimated that $5 billion in pork-barrel special interest projects (that the Pentagon did not ask for) were added on to the 2001 defense budget. Congress has also consistently blocked Pentagon proposals to close military bases, fearing the impact on employment in members' constituencies.

In sharp contrast to its military spending, the US devotes comparatively few dollars to diplomacy, development assistance, international organizations and the promotion of democracy (often equated with the opening of markets). The total outlay in 2003 was $15 billion, less than 1 percent of the federal budget. In the opinion of many critics, it would not be too difficult for the wealthiest nation in the world to increase its spending in these areas. Between 1992 and 2002, US GDP grew from $7.3 trillion to $10 trillion in 2002 prices, an increase of some 36 percent. The US claims to be the "indispensable nation," yet complains about the cost of policing the world. Of the funding that does exist, the largest proportion is consumed by military concerns and support for international security programs. Grants and loans to foreign governments to purchase American weapons are the largest single component of this assistance.

Reductions in the defense budget or reform of the Pentagon are very difficult to achieve due to bureaucratic inertia and vested interests. Perhaps burdened by his anti-Vietnam War past and the controversy over gays in the military, Clinton never really attempted to open a national debate on the role of the military or defense spending. Nor has there been much pressure to increase non-military expenditure. In 1997, the Brookings Institute and the Council on Foreign Relations, in a joint report "Financing America's Leadership," made the case for increasing resources to diplomacy and development assistance. But their very modest proposals recommended an increase of one tenth of 1 percent.

Missile defense

One of the most controversial security policy issues in the US is whether it should unilaterally develop and deploy a missile defense system. Initially the term was national missile defense but the "national" was quietly dropped in early 2001 as a result of protests from America's allies who pointed to the negative connotations for alliance members. Missile defense has its origins in President Reagan's "star wars" policy of attempting to put satellites in space to shoot down incoming missiles. For financial and technological reasons "star wars" was not given priority during the 1990s. Research continued but President Clinton postponed a decision on any deployment of missile defense for his successor. The Republicans had always been more in favor of missile defense than most Democrats and George W. Bush came into office determined to give top priority to missile defense.

The Bush administration's arguments in favor of missile defense were buttressed by the 1998 Rumsfeld Commission report assessing the current and potential threat to the US from missile attack and the capability of the US intelligence community to provide timely warning. It reported that widespread foreign assistance and extensive efforts to hide missile development programs from Western intelligence had created conditions under which North Korea, Iran, and Iraq could, with very little warning, eventually deploy ballistic missiles with ranges long enough to strike parts of the US (see "Commission to Assess the Ballistic Missile Threat to the United States," 15 July 1998, available at *www.fas.org/irp/threat/bm-threat.htm*, accessed 11 April 2005).

Bush and his team also argued that the world had changed fundamentally since 1972 when the ABM treaty was signed which provided for a strategic balance with the Soviet Union. The US wanted to move on from a strategic policy of mutual assured destruction with Moscow. Speaking at the National Press Club on 12 July 2001, Condoleezza Rice argued that Russia was no longer an enemy and the US had to move away from a policy resting on a "balance of terror." The US needed to be released from the confines of the ABM treaty which explicitly prohibits a nationwide defense of territory from missile attack; and prohibits the development, testing, and deployment of ABM systems and components which are sea-based, air-based, space-based, or mobile land-based. Release from ABM treaty obligations would allow the US to pursue the most promising technologies for defense.

Many Democrats were concerned at the speed at which the new administration wished to move on missile defense. Speaking on 10 September 2001, Senator Joe Biden, the chair of the SFRC and one of the strongest critics of missile defense, said that the administration was risking a new arms race and draining money from other domestic and military programs for a porous system that would never add to US security. America should not be a "go-it-alone bully nation but should remain at the table, because walking away comes at a price." The US should not abandon arms control treaties as relics of the Cold War ("most of the administration were relics of the Cold War"). There were more important priorities for military expenditure than missile defense. Speaking a day before the terrorist attacks on New York and Washington, Biden said that the real threats were likely to come from "the hold of a ship, or the belly of a plane, or a backpack filled with chemical weapons." Sandy Berger also cast doubt on the wisdom of missile defense. "After twenty years and tens of billions of dollars, missile defense is still a question-ridden response to the least likely threat" (*Washington Post*, 13 February 2001). Many of America's allies were also concerned at the possible implications of missile defense for existing arms control regimes, especially the ABM treaty, the impact on Russia, China, India and Pakistan, the enormous cost and technological feasibility. Europeans also differed from the US on the likely intent of any "rogue state" to actually use a missile against the US.

The September 2001 terrorist attacks simply hardened the position of both sides in the missile defense debate. Those in favor, bolstered by opinion polls showing a sharp increase in support for NMD, argued that the attacks demonstrated the terrorists' willingness to resort to all measures, including the use of WMD. The opponents argued that a missile defense system could not have prevented the planes flying into the

World Trade Center and the money would be better spent on more productive and effective security policies. Former Defense Secretary, William Perry, suggested that missile defense should be one element of national policy, but warned that "if the single minded pursuit of it conflicts with programs designed to curb proliferation and strengthen deterrence, it could decrease our own security rather than enhance it" (*Foreign Affairs*, November/December 2001). President Bush, however, was not prepared to listen to any critics. He argued that 11 September had demonstrated more than ever the need for a missile defense and shortly after his meeting with Russian President Putin in Texas in November 2001, the President announced that the US intended to withdraw from the ABM treaty within a six-month period. Given the costs, required testing, and time for development, it would be some years, however, before any missile defense system, whether national- or theater-based, could actually be deployed. The issue resurfaced briefly in the 2004 election campaign when John Kerry cast doubt on the wisdom of spending so much money on a missile defense system.

The United Nations

Although the US was a founding member of the UN and is a permanent member of the UN Security Council it has had a mixed relationship with the New York-based organization. Although often ignored, except for propaganda purposes, during the Cold War, the UN served US purposes well during the Korean and Gulf Wars. But in the 1980s there was a growing resentment at the UN perhaps best described by Jeanne Kirkpatrick whom Reagan appointed as the US ambassador to the UN. She famously denounced the UN as "a socialist bastion of anti-Americanism." A decade later some Republican members of Congress openly questioned the value of US membership of the UN. Relations between the US and UN deteriorated sharply when President Clinton sought to blame the UN for the debacle that led to American troops being killed in Somalia in 1993. Although the operation had been carried out by American troops under sole US command, and without the UN's knowledge or involvement, President Clinton and Congress placed the blame firmly on New York and the UN Secretary General, Boutros Boutros-Ghali. As a result, the Clinton administration helped turn the UN from an instrument of global salvation into the new international bogeyman.

The UN was also held responsible for some of the disasters that occurred in the Balkans, including the failure to save Muslim enclaves such as Srebrenica in Bosnia. In 1994, the Republicans gained control of Congress and Jesse Helms became chair of the SFRC. An ideological opponent of international organizations, Helms was one of the main supporters of a policy that aimed to reduce US contributions to the UN and to impose reforms as a condition of payment. Helms was a strong opponent of any limitations on American sovereignty and believed, as did many other Republicans, that the UN was an anti-American, anti-Israeli, over-staffed organization (Helms 2001). Other conditions that individual members of Congress sought to impose included a veto on funding of birth control programs by UN agencies. Eventually a compromise was reached in 2000 when it was agreed to reduce the US contribution to the regular UN budget from 25 to 22 percent and to the peacekeeping budget from 31 to 27 percent.

The refusal to pay US dues and the conditions Washington attached to the payments infuriated the rest of the world and certainly contributed to the loss in 2001 of the US seat on the Human Rights Commission. Partly as a result of that vote, Congress was still reluctant to approve the back payments and did not do so in full until after the 11 September attacks and the swift condemnation of such by the United Nations. Speaking at the UN on 10 November 2001, President Bush thanked the organization for its support and promised that the US would work closely with the UN in the reconstruction of Afghanistan. With the deal on reduced payments, some of the hostility toward the UN appeared to lessen only to resurface in early 2003 when the UNSC refused to back the US-led invasion of Iraq. It is important to note that contrary to the views of many right-wing Americans, the UN has not been a bastion of anti-Americanism. Indeed the US has often found it both a useful and supportive organization in helping to achieve US foreign policy goals. As one congressional staffer told the author, "the problem is that the US gets its way with the UN most of the time, but not all of the time – and this can often be frustrating to many congressmen."

In September 2002, pressed by Tony Blair and Colin Powell but against the wishes of the neocons, President Bush went to the UN to argue his case against Iraq. He believed that he could persuade the world body of the need for regime change in Baghdad. Five months later, in February 2003, Colin Powell purported to show that Iraq possessed WMD in a dramatic slide presentation at the UNSC. Despite much arm-twisting, the US still failed to convince a majority of members of the UNSC that a military intervention was necessary. After the end of the Iraq War the US soon realized that it was unable alone to deal with the myriad problems of reconstruction in Iraq. Bush made an about turn and sought the assistance of the UN but their readiness to help was severely undermined with the terrorist attack on UN headquarters in Baghdad in August 2003.

In December 2004, a high-level panel set up by UN Secretary General Kofi Annan published a far-reaching report aimed at strengthening the United Nations (*www.un.org/secureworld*, accessed 11 April 2005). The US administration was cautious in its response, concerned at proposals to expand the five permanent members of the UNSC. The Congress also remained hostile to the UN, alleging structural deficiencies and corruption in the 'oil for food' program for Iraq. There was widespread concern at the nomination of a leading neo-conservative, John Bolton, to the US ambassador to the UN in May 2005.

Another issue of concern to the US was the proposed International Criminal Court (ICC) that would try individuals accused of committing genocide, war crimes, and crimes against humanity. Although the US participated in negotiations to establish the ICC and won some concessions concerning its jurisdiction, it was one of only seven countries that failed to sign the treaty (the others being Iraq, Libya, China, Israel, Yemen and Qatar). Many members of Congress, led by Jesse Helms and Henry Hyde, were concerned that American military personnel could be brought before the court for political reasons. Not content with US non-participation in the ICC, Congress passed legislation aimed at inhibiting US military assistance to countries that did sign up to the ICC. The US also lobbied hard to prevent third countries signing the ICC without first agreeing a separate bilateral deal exempting US soldiers. More than the required sixty countries have ratified the accord and the ICC has started its work in The Hague.

The American attitude toward the ICC has been strongly criticized by many of its allies, including Britain.

Europe

The US relationship with Europe is its most important global relationship, yet some analysts increasingly doubt whether the two partners share a common view of the world. In a widely-read essay "Power and Weakness" (*Policy Review*, June 2002), a leading neo-conservative, Robert Kagan, stated that on all the important questions of power – the efficacy of power, the desirability of power, the morality of power – American and European perspectives are diverging. Europe was entering a post-historical Kantian paradise of peace while the US remained mired in an anarchical Hobbesian world where might was right. "That is why on major strategic and international issues today, Americans are from Mars and Europeans are from Venus." Kagan went on to assert that the transatlantic rift on setting priorities, determining threats and defining challenges "was deep, long in development and likely to endure." Kagan's thesis struck a raw nerve in Europe. There was a barrage of articles in response. Some argued that it was an over-simplification of the rift while others accepted the premise and suggested that it was a "wake up call" for Europe. The US invasion of Iraq, and the disputes over the legality of the move, subsequently led to the greatest transatlantic rift in modern history.

America and Europe have always had a complicated relationship, partly due to the huge numbers of immigrants from Europe in the US. Throughout its history the US has consistently pursued three interconnected interests with regard to Europe: not to get involved in the conflicts of European powers; to prevent European powers intervening in the western hemisphere; and to maintain, or if need be to restore, the balance of power in Europe. With the formation of NATO in 1949, the US has been firmly committed to the defense of Western Europe for over half a century, stationing upwards of 200,000 soldiers there during the Cold War. Since the end of the Cold War, however, some of the glue that held the transatlantic relationship together has weakened and there have been a number of disputes in the political, trade, and global arenas. It was inevitable that the fundamental geopolitical changes that affected Europe during the 1990s – the collapse of the Soviet Union, the reunification of Germany, the growing integration of the EU, particularly the development of a single currency – would have an impact on transatlantic relations. The question was whether these changes would lead to a drifting apart or whether they would lead to a new partnership. A related issue was whether the US was mature enough to really want a partnership. After fifty years as the dominant actor in European security issues, and often interfering in European politics, there were doubts as to whether the US, psychologically, could adjust to a partnership with the EU, assuming the EU itself could prepare itself institutionally for this role.

Even before Kagan's essay, a spate of articles in 2001 attempted to analyze the problems facing the EU and US. One European argued that there is "a growing divergence between America's perception of its moral leadership and European perceptions of a military-minded America obsessed with rogue states and weapons of mass destruction" (Moisi, *Financial Times*, 27 August 2001). The former Europe Director in the NSC, however, argued that "what is striking is the extent to which the US and Europe are converging with respect to both values and interests. The crisis in transatlantic relations is largely a myth" (Blinken, *Foreign Affairs*, May/June 2001). Another American observer argued that the advent of a new administration and the historic changes in Europe (advent of the euro and enlargement) should pave the way for a new partnership of equals (Daalder, *International Affairs*, Summer 2001). Few American officials, however, talk about partnership in any meaningful way. Indeed, one senior American diplomat told the author bluntly that the prime American interest in the EU was having access to EU funds to support American foreign policy outside of Europe.

In terms of public presentation, the US was always supportive of European integration. Speaking in Frankfurt on 24 June 1963, President Kennedy stated that

> it is only a fully cohesive Europe that can protect us all against fragmentation of the alliance. With only such a Europe can we have a full give-and-take between equal partners, an equal sharing of responsibilities, and an equal level of sacrifice.

Some American officials have gone further, drawing parallels between European integration and American experience. Deputy Secretary of State, Strobe Talbott, speaking at the Aspen Institute on 24 August 1999, stated that the European experiment in sharing sovereignty and constructing a federal system of government "coincides with our own political and civic values and therefore with our own vital strategic interests." Former national security adviser, Bzrezinski, agreed, stating that "the transatlantic alliance is America's most important global relationship" while regretting that Europe was a mere "de facto military protectorate of the US" and unable to provide any policy leadership (*National Interest*, Summer 2000). This ruffled some European feathers as leaders such as Tony Blair, French President Chirac, and EU High Representative, Javier Solana, have been keen to secure US support for EU defense cooperation efforts. President Bush, in a joint statement with German Chancellor Schroeder, on 29 March 2001, underlined the traditional American position that "a Europe that is strong and capable – including in the defense field – lies in the interest of the United States."

The process of European integration, although supported by the US, has not meant that transatlantic relations have been trouble free. The Suez crisis of 1956, the French withdrawal from NATO's integrated military command, the disputes over Germany's Ostpolitik, the installation of short- and intermediate-range nuclear weapons in the 1980s, and the imposition of US sanctions against Poland and the Soviet Union were just a few major issues where Europe and the US did not see eye to eye even during the Cold War. As the European Union (then Community) developed in the 1970s and 1980s it became clear that the US and EU had different attitudes toward power and power projection. While the US tended to view the world in black and white and was ready to use military power as an early option in crisis situations, Europeans were more ambivalent about security issues and the use of military power. The US of course had global responsibilities and wanted to try and solve problems. The Europeans, perhaps because of their historical experience, were more prepared to live with difficult situations. These differences were most apparent in policy toward the Middle East and their respective attitudes toward "rogue states." The US preferred to operate a policy of sanctions and isolation, whereas the Europeans preferred a policy of constructive engagement. These different approaches often led to transatlantic disputes as US extra-territorial legislation, e.g. on Cuba (Helms–Burton) and Iran/Libya (ILSA), affected European companies.

Despite the rhetoric, American support for European integration remains somewhat ambivalent. There were concerns about the advent of both the EU's single market and the euro. The US worried, needlessly, about a "Fortress Europe" while the sub-text of the euro–dollar debate (after much skepticism about whether the euro would ever see the light of day) was do not tamper with US primacy in international monetary affairs. Some officials also considered that the EU should scale back its representation in international monetary institutions and do more to restore global growth and stability. Although the US supported EU enlargement on geopolitical grounds it also complained about EU trade preferences for Eastern Europe and the Balkans. The US has strongly pushed Turkey's candidacy for the EU while turning a blind eye to that country's poor record on democracy and human rights. Likewise, the US supports European efforts to forge closer defense integration, but complains when the EU begins to put together its own structures.

The Clinton administration was staunchly pro-European and a number of officials have told the author that Europe was the great success story of the 1990s. Washington had helped transform and revitalize NATO through the new strategic concept and Partnership for Peace. It had established a new relationship with the EU to tackle an increasing array of problems that demonstrated shared common values and interests. In less than a decade the EU–US relationship had moved from exclusively trade issues to discussing regional problems such as the Middle East, Russia, Africa as well as global issues like proliferation, terrorism, drugs, crime, cyber warfare, epidemics, climate change and the trafficking of women. For some critics this was not enough.

> Today the very definition of common security, and, indeed, of common purpose is being challenged. For much of the 1990s, America's Atlantic policies oscillated between imperiousness and indifference, between treating Europe as an auxiliary or as a photo opportunity. Overbearing American triumphalism bears its own share of responsibility.
>
> (Kissinger 2001: 33)

President Clinton was highly popular in Europe. President George W. Bush was not. European media described him as "the Toxic Texan" and the "Hangman", references to his governorship of Texas where he had a poor record on protecting the environment and refused to intervene to commute death sentences. Bush's unilateralism grated on Europeans and his popularity slumped to record lows in 2004. According to several polls, Europeans would have voted for Kerry as opposed to Bush by a margin of eight to one. More than 70 percent of Europeans disapproved of Bush's foreign policies and over 85 percent were opposed to the US invasion of Iraq. With such massive distrust amongst public opinion in Europe many predicted that it would be difficult for European leaders to engage with the President during his second term. Very predictably it was Tony Blair who was the first European leader to visit Washington just a week after the presidential election. Blair's relationship with Bush has been strongly criticized in the UK and also abroad. For example, former national security adviser, Brzezinski, in conversation with the author, argued that American policy blunders in Iraq were compounded by Britain's slavish following of Washington. "Had the UK spoken firmly as the stalwart of Europe, instead of acting as the supine follower, it could have made its voice felt. The US would have had no choice but to listen." The US may have listened but whether it would have had much of an impact is doubtful. To some Europeans the re-election of Bush heralded a new opportunity for the EU to unite on foreign policy and provide a strategic partner the US could not ignore. Much would depend on whether the EU could demonstrate the necessary political will to move forward in this sensitive area.

Case study: the US and the EU

During the 1990s, relations between the US and the EU steadily assumed greater importance. In 1990 both sides signed the Transatlantic Partnership agreement that committed the US and EU to regular political consultations at all levels. In 1995 the US and EU moved a stage further in signing the New Transatlantic Agenda (NTA) that outlined the main areas for cooperation in the political, economic, trade, human and cultural spheres. The NTA spawned a huge number of meetings and working groups involving ministers, officials, businessmen, consumers and many others in "people to people" dialogues.

Europeans had great empathy for Bill Clinton whereas his successor, George W. Bush, entered the White House to a chorus of European criticism. At his first summit with Europeans in Gothenburg, Sweden, Bush emphasized the many areas of transatlantic agreement, including the Balkans, Russia, Korea, Africa, as well as admitting a number of policy differences including climate change and missile defense. Secretary of State Powell also gave an upbeat review of the summit in testimony to the US Congress on 20 June: "when America and Europe are partners, there is no limit to our horizons."

The good news tended to be drowned out by the bad. Although there was and is a sound economic base for cooperation between the US and EU there are also a growing number of disputes. In addition to climate change and missile defense, the irritants to the transatlantic relationship include the US rejection of the draft verification protocol to the biological and toxic weapons convention and its continued refusal to sign up to the ICC, the CTBT, the UN small-arms treaty, the Ottawa land mines convention and other arms control instruments. There are also differences in approach toward the regulation of biotechnology and genetically modified organisms (GMOs) in foodstuffs. There have also been disputes over payments to the UN and respective contributions to other international bodies and to aid programs. The US was also doubtful about the usefulness of the twice-yearly summits and proposed to reduce their frequency.

Trade relations between the EU and US have always had some degree of tension, going back to the "chicken wars" of the 1960s. Today, the transatlantic economic and trade relationship is the most important in the world. In 2004 the value of trade and investment flows between the EU and US was $850 billion. Ninety-nine percent of these trade flows occur without any problem but it is the remaining 1 percent that receives all the negative press attention. It is inevitable that there are some problems given the size of the trading relationship and the fact that the EU and US are economic competitors in the world. In recent years, the two sides have sparred over bananas, data privacy, aircraft subsidies and noise levels, company taxation, steel and many more issues, some of which have been resolved bilaterally and some of which have been sent to the WTO for dispute settlement. Some Americans have predicted that these growing disputes, plus the prospect of the euro challenging the dollar, could escalate into serious transatlantic conflict (Bergsten, *Foreign Affairs*, March/April 1999). This is highly unlikely as even during the worst days of the crisis over Iraq, France and other European countries continued to pour investment into the US. Indeed there is more European investment in Texas than total US investment in Japan and China combined. Europe is also by far the most attractive overseas destination for American foreign direct investment with more than 60 percent of all such outflows going across the Atlantic in the decade to 2004. In this period Americans invested ten times as much in the Netherlands as in China.

Even taking into account that disputes get attention while cooperation does not, the rising number of political and economic disputes points to some fundamental differences in approach both to societal and global problems. The EU is becoming a more cohesive global player as befits a power with a larger population than the US, a larger percentage of world trade, a roughly similar GDP, and which contributes more to the UN budget and to development assistance than the US. For Washington, accustomed to receiving or if necessary demanding obeisance from its European allies, this change has proved hard to accommodate. Since the NTA was adopted in 1995, Washington has begun to take the EU more seriously as a political partner as well as a trade competitor, although there is a long way to go before the EU is treated as a foreign policy equal. Congress, in particular, tends to take a dismissive view of the EU with many members critical of the common agricultural policy (CAP), the lack of defense spending, and the tendency of Europeans to preach about the ills of American society. It is difficult to attract congressmen to meet visiting members of the European Parliament. In contrast, European Commissioners dealing with trade, agriculture or competition (areas where they have real clout) have no difficulty securing an audience on Capitol Hill.

An additional factor is the attitude of many US policymakers, particularly in the Bush administration, toward the EU. The vast majority have been schooled in NATO affairs, which the US has traditionally dominated, bilateral relations with EU member states, or the established international monetary and economic institutions. Those in the American policy machine (including the White House) with personal experience of the EU are considerably outnumbered by those with little understanding of the complexities of EU policymaking. Frustration, impatience, and tensions often ensue as a consequence. This was shown in the aftermath of the September 2001 terrorist attacks. The EU response was an immediate affirmation of support for the US and a special meeting of the European Council was held that agreed to extend cooperation in several areas to the US. For example, it was agreed to establish closer ties between Europol and the FBI, to work together on money laundering, extradition, and sharing intelligence. But despite these unprecedented moves, the US preferred to work primarily through its bilateral relationships with the major member states of the EU. Whatever the rhetoric, it seems likely that the US will continue in future with its ambivalent attitude toward closer European integration.

It was the Iraq War, however, that led to the biggest split in transatlantic relations since the end of the Cold War. France and Germany opposed the war while Britain, Spain, Italy and Poland supported the US-led invasion. There was considerable mutual recrimination with Paris and Berlin arguing that the Bush administration had failed to prove that there was an imminent threat from Iraq and that there was no legal base for war. The US retaliated by decrying "old Europe" (France and Germany) and praising "new Europe" (Britain, Italy, Spain and the countries of central Europe). Americans went a step further in calling the French "cheese-eating surrender monkeys" and renamed French fries "freedom fries." Condoleezza Rice was widely quoted as saying that the US "should punish France, ignore Germany and isolate Russia." This political mud-slinging severely damaged political relations but did not affect trade relations. Indeed in 2003 there was a record flow of goods and services between Europe and the US.

Russia, Ukraine and Central Asia

The US was unprepared for the end of the Cold War and struggled to find a policy toward Russia, Ukraine, and other successor states to the Soviet Union. Clinton attempted to support a rapid political and economic reform program in Russia and was sharply criticized by his domestic opponents for too close a personal relationship with President Yeltsin and for turning a blind eye to evidence of corruption, money laundering, and abuse of human rights. Faced with a rapidly declining superpower with 30,000 aging nuclear warheads, the US could not ignore Russia. The main US policy instruments are the Cooperative Threat Reduction Initiative (CTRI), otherwise known as the Nunn–Lugar program, and the strategic arms reduction negotiations, which were stalled by the legislatures on both sides delaying ratification of the START II agreement. The primary US instrument for broad economic, technological, and scientific engagement, the Gore–Chernomyrdin commission, languished as the two principals were engaged in the fight for the highest political office in their countries. Other issues that caused friction between Russia and the US included the enlargement of NATO and the US-led bombing campaign to defeat the Serbs in the Kosovo conflict.

When George W. Bush took office there was a lengthy pause in assessing where to go with Russia. Moscow had been roundly criticized by Bush and his advisers during the election campaign for human rights abuses in Chechnya and weapons proliferation to "rogue states." In the early months of the administration there seemed to be a conscious attempt to marginalize Russia. The Nunn–Lugar funds were reduced and Russia was denied any say over NATO enlargement. However, in the hope of securing Russia's acquiescence for a revision to the ABM treaty, that would allow the US to deploy a limited missile defense, Bush embarked on a wooing of President Putin at his first meeting with the Russian leader in Slovenia in June 2001. Bush claimed to have "looked into Putin's soul" and saw a man with whom he could do business. The September 2001 attacks brought a swift improvement in US–Russian relations as President Putin offered to share intelligence with the US, increase its support for the Northern Alliance (fighting the Taliban), and was willing to approve of the US using several former Soviet republics as bases for its military operations against Afghanistan. In return, Putin expected that the US would mute its criticism of Russian operations in Chechnya. When the two Presidents met in Texas, in mid-November 2001, there was no agreement on missile defense nor on the continued importance of the ABM treaty. Less than a month after that meeting, Bush stated his intention to withdraw from the treaty, a move that was "regretted" by Russia, but not met by any counter move. There has since been some concern in Washington at Putin's authoritarian moves, especially after the Beslan terrorist attack on a local school in 2004, his restrictions on the media and his continuing readiness to supply Iran with nuclear technology.

As regards Ukraine, the US was not enthusiastic about the prospect of its independence and President George H. W. Bush tried to argue against such a development in his "chicken Kiev" speech when he visited Ukraine in 1991. Since then, however, the US has been a strong supporter of the newly independent state and provided considerable assistance. It was one of Madeleine Albright's four key countries (the others were Nigeria, Colombia, and Azerbaijan) yet it has remained a disappointment to Washington. The lack of political and economic reform, as well as the scandals surrounding President Kuchma in Ukraine, has meant that the US has been unwilling to devote more resources and attention to Kiev. These were signs of a change in US policy after the 'Orange Revolution' in the Ukraine in December 2004 that brought the pro-western President Yustchenko to power.

US interests in Central Asia and the Caucasus are largely driven by oil and the related oil and gas pipelines plus seeking bases for the war on terrorism. The US has sought to protect Georgia from Russian bullying and to mediate an agreement (so far unsuccessfully) between Armenia and Azerbaijan on the disputed enclave of Nagorno-Karabakh. In Central Asia, US policy has been to try and bolster the independence of the five states in the region (Kazakhstan, Kyrgyzstan, Uzbekistan, Tajikistan and Turkmenistan) by political visits, military cooperation, and economic assistance, hoping to gain access to their rich supplies of energy and other resources. The September 2001 attacks brought a sudden new American interest in the region as it sought successfully to enlist their support in the fight against the Taliban regime in Afghanistan. This support included the use of military bases and in return the countries received substantial economic and financial assistance. There were, however, critics of this rapprochement with the Central Asian republics who argued that the US should not be engaging with such authoritarian, anti-democratic regimes and turning a blind eye to human rights abuses.

Asia

Notwithstanding US recognition of the importance of Europe, American security attention has gradually shifted from Europe to the Middle East and Asia. Hot spots

North Korea, Kashmir and China/Taiwan highlight how unstable and potentially explosive the region remains. US interests center on maintaining a balance of power in the region and ensuring that none of the above trouble spots flares up into open conflict. The US has security guarantees with five countries – Japan, South Korea, the Philippines (with a substantial number of troops stationed in all three countries), Australia and Thailand. It also has a strong political commitment to preserve Taiwan's freedom pending possible future reunification with China. The US also plays a prominent role in the Asia-Pacific Economic Cooperation Forum (APEC), a body with twenty-one diverse members representing half of global GDP, 40 percent of the world's population and three permanent members of the UNSC. Perhaps because of its very diverse membership, APEC has delivered very little in terms of economic cooperation. Although it is largely economic and consensus orientated it also has an important political element. At the Shanghai summit in October 2001, President Bush was able to gather support, including from China, for a strong anti-terrorist statement. Its key members use APEC meetings for bilateral discussions that might otherwise be difficult to organize. For example, in November 2004, President Bush used the occasion of the APEC summit in Chile to hold important bilateral meetings with several Asian leaders. As a result of the invasion of Iraq, a move that split Asia, US influence declined somewhat in the region.

The most important US relationship in Asia is with Japan, the region's dominant economic power. Having defeated Japan in 1945, the US helped the country establish a democratic political system and provided a security guarantee, essentially against China, backed up by the presence of 47,000 troops, of which over half are on the island of Okinawa. Although the US–Japan relationship has been close since 1945, it has not been without tension, particularly on the trade front. As the Japanese economy expanded it enjoyed a huge trade surplus with the US that led to resentment, anger, and even fear in the US. As a result, the US has continually pressed Japan to do more in terms of structural economic reform and to open its markets to American exports. It has often done so, however, in a hectoring tone that has not been appreciated in Tokyo. The US has also encouraged Japan to do more in terms of international security and was pleased that Tokyo agreed to send a small token force to Iraq.

US relations with China have steadily improved since the end of the Cold War. The collapse of communism in the Soviet Union was a profound shock for Beijing. The Chinese communist party leadership resolved to maintain a firm grip on political dissent while allowing some loosening of economic controls. Trade with the US increased sharply throughout the 1990s but at the same time there was continued American criticism over the human rights situation in China. According to one veteran American diplomat:

> the large overriding issue of the first half of the new century will be the relationship between the US and China. But I don't think it is a struggle that one has to win and the other has to lose. It will be the search for coexistence, in a way in which each country respects the other.
>
> (R. Holbrooke, *Financial Times*, 6/7 January 2001)

Since the normalization of relations between the US and China in the 1970s there has been a vast increase in trade and contacts between the two countries. But relations are still sensitive with Taiwan remaining a principal area of disagreement followed by human rights issues and weapons proliferation. President Bush caused a flurry of excitement when he told a television interviewer in May 2001 that "the US would do whatever it took to defend Taiwan" in the event of an attack by China. This statement appeared to depart from the previous policy, which had been to express strong support for Taiwan's territorial inviolability without an explicit commitment to Taiwan's defense. Administration officials, however, stated that there had been no change of US policy.

The declared policy of the Clinton administration toward China was "constructive engagement," a strategy aimed at integrating China into the world economy and thus helping to precipitate internal change there. This policy was sorely tested by the annual debates in Congress over most favored nation (MFN) status for China and by the accidental bombing of the Chinese embassy in Belgrade during the Kosovo campaign. But progress on WTO membership, including the granting to China of PNTR, and increased political exchanges to discuss North Korea and Taiwan put relations back on track. During the presidential election campaign George W. Bush had spoken of China as a "strategic competitor" and urged stronger ties with Taiwan. Some right-wing Republicans, such as Senator Jesse Helms, viewed China as "morally flawed" and an inevitable adversary. They argued that US policy should abandon the "One China" policy, support Taiwan independence and contain if not seek to weaken China. Relations between Washington and Beijing deteriorated almost immediately Bush took office following the collision of an American spy plane with a Chinese fighter plane off the coast of China and increased US arms sales to Taiwan. But a visit by Colin Powell in July 2001 helped smooth relations as did the growing trade between the two countries. The Chinese leadership is keenly aware of the importance of the US market for Chinese exports, a valuable source of hard currency at a time when they are trying to reform the economy. American business also regards China as a huge potential market and is reluctant to allow concern over human rights to spoil business prospects. US exports to China grew at an average rate of 13 percent in the 1990s; and American investment tripled there in the same period. It is also worth noting that there are more Chinese students studying in the US than any other nationality. In the long-term this could have a significant impact on Sino-American relations. The terrorist attacks of September 2001 provided an opportunity for an improvement in relations. President Jiang condemned the attacks and offered the US support in countering the terrorist threat. Since then there has been a steady improvement in US–China relations and several high-level visits in both directions.

In 1950 the US led a UN coalition of forces to repel the North Korean invasion of South Korea and after a bloody conflict, Korea was effectively partitioned along the 38th parallel. While relations with the North were frozen, the US provided the South with a security guarantee, backed up by the presence of 37,000 American forces in the country, and helped the country develop into a major economic power. As regards North Korea, a "rogue state" in American eyes, relations remain strained due to the North Korean nuclear weapons program, missile testing and proliferation, and threatening gestures toward the South. Under Clinton, the US worked out an "agreed framework" for dealing with North Korea, offering aid to replace North Korea's civil nuclear reactors with less dangerous plant in return for the suspension of their nuclear weapons program. It also offered other carrots (lifting of sanctions, economic cooperation) in return for North Korean restraint on exporting missile technology.

Toward the end of the Clinton administration there was a sudden thaw in relations between the two Koreas with President Kim Dae Jung being invited by President Kim Yong II to visit Pyongyang in June 2000. The visit led to a number of agreements and there was much optimism that the two states were set on a path of reconciliation that might lead to reunification. In the fall of 2000, Secretary of State, Madeleine Albright, became the most senior American official to visit Pyongyang and there was even speculation that President Clinton might visit North Korea. When George W. Bush took office, he ordered a freeze of relations with North Korea pending a review of American policy. This led the EU to send its own mission to North Korea in June 2001, a move that aroused some suspicion in Washington. A few weeks later, however, Bush agreed on a resumption of contacts with Pyongyang, although placing more emphasis on verification of North Korea's nuclear program. In January 2002, Bush's "axis of evil" speech led to a further freeze in relations between North Korea and the US and also halted progress in talks between the two Koreas. Gradually the Bush administration recognized the importance of having some channel of communication with North Korea and agreed to a new format of "Six Power Talks" aimed at resolving the nuclear issue. The question of Korean unification could pose some difficult problems for the US. It could lead to demands for the departure of American troops, and if this were to happen, it might have a knock-on effect on Japan that in turn could have wider ramifications. In 2004 Washington announced that it would reduce its troops in South Korea by a third. This was to allow the US to redeploy them to more unstable regions.

As regards India and Pakistan, the US tended to neglect both countries until they exploded nuclear devices. During the Cold War there was considerable suspicion of India's ties to Russia; and strong support for Pakistan as a base from which to support the Afghans (including Osama bin Laden!) in their struggle against the Soviet Union. More recently, the US has pressed New Delhi and Islamabad to refrain from further testing, an appeal which had little resonance in the wake of the Senate's rejection of the CTBT. Relations with Pakistan improved overnight when it granted the US permission to use its territory for operations against the Taliban regime in Afghanistan. Given Pakistan's previous support for the Taliban regime this was a major policy change that caused much internal anguish. As a result of Pakistan's support for the US, Washington agreed to drop most of the sanctions imposed against Islamabad after the nuclear test and the military coup. The US was also active in trying to press both India and Pakistan to resolve peacefully their differences over Kashmir.

Latin America

Few other regions of the world are so dependent upon and enjoy such complex relations with the US than Latin America. With an economy over five times that of the rest of the hemisphere combined, the US holds a dominant position in inter-American affairs. It is Latin America's leading trade partner and the largest source of investment capital. Brazil surpasses China with respect to trade and investment, and Venezuela and Mexico are two of the most important foreign oil suppliers for the US. Colombia supplies more than 80 percent of the cocaine that floods American streets. Moreover, US preferences affect the decisions of the IMF, World Bank, and Inter-American Development Bank (IADB) toward the region. The foreign and often the domestic policies of every Latin American and Caribbean country are shaped and constrained by its ties with the US. Partly because of this dependence and partly because of a long history of US interference in the region, relations between Washington and most countries of the region are not without problems.

During the Cold War, US policy toward Latin America focused on trying to prevent the communists or left-wing parties from coming to power. As a result the US often allied itself with repressive regimes that did not shrink from using brutal efforts to stamp out insurgencies. The US supported the Guatemalan military that killed over 100,000 civilians. In 1983 the US invaded Grenada to oust its pro-Castro government, backed the Contras seeking to overthrow the democratically elected Sandinista government in Nicaragua, and aided the extreme right in El Salvador's civil war. Another contemporary source of friction is the annual drug certification process demanded by Congress. The President must "certify" that each country is "fully cooperating" in the fight against drug trafficking, otherwise foreign aid will be denied. This certification process has been widely condemned by all Latin American countries as an infringement on their sovereignty. Some have suggested that the US should first deal with the huge demand for drugs within its own borders before turning its attention to the supply side abroad.

When the Democrats took over the White House in 1993 they hoped to turn a new chapter by strengthening US–Latin American relations and to shape a regional strategy, starting with the 1994 Summit of the Americas in Miami, which brought together the hemisphere's thirty-four elected presidents and prime ministers. At the summit, leaders endorsed the idea of negotiating a free trade area (FTAA) by 2005. The Clinton administration outlined an ambitious plan to improve relations with Latin America concentrating on promoting trade, sustainable development, strengthening democratic institutions and tackling the drug problem. Clinton vowed that "the 1990s would not be another 'lost decade' as was the 1980s." The confrontational north–south atmosphere that preceded the Miami summit gradually gave way to what even the Latin Americans called a "common language" on the integral nature of the problems facing the hemisphere. The US administration has supported the regional institutions tasked with the follow-up to the Miami summit. Both the OAS and the IADB are quietly but steadily implementing the summit process. While difficult domestic negotiations on trade issues and domestic ambivalence about the effects of NAFTA have remained in the background, the atmosphere has changed dramatically from the embattled antagonistic attitudes of the 1980s. But Clinton failed to implement his promise to Chile for early access to NAFTA and he ignored feelers in the same direction from Argentina.

There is no question that the most important US relationship in Latin America is with Mexico. Few other countries of the world affect the lives of Americans as much as Mexico, and no other country is more directly and intensely affected by US policies than Mexico. Relations between the two countries have taken a constructive turn since the signing of NAFTA in 1994 which meant that Mexico was one of only three countries (the others are Canada and Israel) enjoying free trade with the US. Mexico has since become the US's second largest trading partner (after Canada) and a major destination for US investment. Mexico sends more than 80 percent of its exports northward, while capital flows from the US, including remittances from Mexican workers, have fueled Mexico's economic recovery since the 1995 financial crisis. During the crisis the US provided Mexico with a $12.5 billion loan which Mexico repaid within two years. In addition to the large resident Hispanic population, approximately 350,000 Mexicans migrate each year to work (legally and illegally) in the US. Tensions over trade and other economic issues have not been resolved but are discussed within the NAFTA framework. Mechanisms are also in place to manage other contentious issues like migration, drug trafficking, environmental contamination, and water rights. Significantly, President George W. Bush made his first overseas visit to Mexico and in September 2001 invited President Fox to be his first official state visitor to the White House.

President Fox has also floated the idea of a customs union between Mexico and the US but the proposal met with a lukewarm response in Washington. Most Americans have an ambiguous attitude toward Mexico. They value the low-wage labor and its holiday resorts, but are concerned at the high levels of drug trafficking (highlighted in the film *Traffic*) and illegal immigration. Both problems are extremely difficult to resolve given the extended two-thousand-mile-long border and the huge disparities in wealth between the two countries. The per capita income in the US was $33,000 in 2004 compared to $6500 in Mexico. As a result of 9/11 and the need to tighten border controls there has been little progress in US–Mexican relations.

The US has one overriding interest in the Caribbean Basin – that this group of neighboring countries, with over fifty million people, is economically healthy, politically stable, and democratic. The US feels the consequences when any of the region's economies turn sour or the political situation turns violent. The Caribbean market is also important for the US as they buy more than half their imports from the US. Gradually trade and investment have replaced aid as the mainstay of the relationship. Two countries, Cuba and Haiti, pose particular problems. The former remains a bastion of socialism under Fidel Castro, the Cuban leader who has outstayed every American President since Kennedy. But dropping or even significantly modifying the US sanctions regime on Cuba has proved very difficult due to the activities of the Cuban-American lobby. The situation in Haiti, despite constant US prodding to reform, remains desperate. The economy is in ruins. Public institutions barely function and crime and violence are commonplace. The US fears that a further deterioration will lead to a new flood of "boat people" and create conditions for increased drug trafficking. Both Presidents Clinton and Bush had to authorize interventions in Haiti but as soon as the situation calms down US attention is diverted to other priorities. Critics argue that if the US cannot deal successfully with a failed state such as Haiti on its doorstep how can it deal with Afghanistan or Iraq.

Of all Latin American countries, the US is particularly concerned about the internal situation in Colombia. According to one expert, "Colombia is the most menacing foreign policy challenge in Latin America for the US" (Kissinger 2001: 90). In 2001, the US approved $1.3 billion in security assistance to Colombia, a nation of forty million people – the most, by far, for any country outside the Middle East. Colombia grabs US attention because it is the world's largest supplier of cocaine, much of which ends up on American streets. The US strongly supports "Plan Colombia" – an effort to defeat the guerrilla movement that controls most of the countryside where the illegal drugs are manufactured. Many critics of US policy, however, suggest that current US policy is focused too much on military efforts to interdict drugs and too little on helping Colombia to develop its economy and prevent human rights abuses. The US also faces a difficult situation in other Andean countries, Peru, Ecuador, and Venezuela, where political and economic stability is lacking, and there are voices critical of US policy (notably in Venezuela where the US was suspected of supporting the brief army coup against President Chavez in April 2002).

As the largest country in South America, Brazil has always exerted an important influence on regional affairs. Although there are no serious political and economic disputes between the US and Brazil, there are a number of trade disputes, as US barriers remain high to some of Brazil's most important exports. The US is also concerned about the depth of Brazil's commitment to the FTAA as Brazil has made no secret that strengthening the regional trade grouping, Mercosur, is its first priority. President Lulu has stressed that Mercosur is a more important priority than the FTAA. The Brazilian President has also been critical of American neglect of international institutions and pushed for greater involvement of development countries in the management of global affairs.

Middle East

For several decades the US has been the principal political, military, and financial supporter of Israel. With an eye on the powerful Israeli lobby in the US, successive administrations in Washington have rarely voted against Israel in the UN or sought to put real pressure on Israel to modify its policy on sensitive issues such as the settlements on the West Bank. While the US has been offering Israel quasi-unconditional support, it has also been closely involved in the elusive search for a Middle East peace agreement. Some argue that it is impossible to play the role of mediator while the US supports Israel so strongly. Others argue that only the US has the real clout to make any agreement stick. In recent years, there have been countless envoys, meetings, summits, photo opportunities on the White House lawn, negotiating sessions at Camp David. President Clinton invested an enormous amount of time and energy, particularly in his final six months in office, to secure a peace deal. He came close to pushing the former PLO chief, Arafat, and Israeli Prime Minister, Barak, to signing a deal but his efforts failed at the eleventh hour. The key divisive issues were the status of

Jerusalem and the return of Palestinian refugees to Israel. Most Americans blamed Arafat for the failure of the negotiations.

On taking office George W. Bush was not keen to repeat Clinton's hands-on efforts to secure a deal. In the face of increasing violence between Israel and Palestine, Bush preferred a wait-and-see approach, a strategy that was heavily criticized by some Europeans and by Sandy Berger (*Washington Post*, 8 September 2001). Despite indications that Bush was annoyed at Prime Minister Sharon's intransigence on the military occupation of Palestinian territory and on the settlements question (the illegal establishment of Israeli settlements on the West Bank and Gaza), he publicly supported the Israeli Prime Minister as a "man of peace" and gave his full backing to Israel. Bush's one-sided approach was criticized by many, including former Republican NSC adviser, Brent Scowcroft, who claimed that the President was "mesmerized by Sharon who has him wrapped around his little finger"(*Financial Times*, 14 September 2004). The US is part of the Quartet (US, UN, EU and Russia) seeking to give impetus to a Road Map for a Middle East peace. But the search for such a peace has proved elusive for over fifty years. In November 2004, after the death of PLO leader Arafat, President Bush, pushed by Tony Blair, promised to re-engage with the peace process but no one expected there would be swift progress.

The Middle East is also an area where the US often turns a blind eye to its normally forthright condemnation of states for human rights abuses or lack of democracy. According to one American diplomat, "The most striking thing about US human rights policy is its transparent selectivity – Israel, Egypt or Saudi Arabia are rarely criticized." As regards the Gulf States, the US has been ultra careful not to criticize their human rights records because of the economic importance of their oil exports for the American economy, and after September 2001, their usefulness in providing assistance for US military forces fighting against Afghanistan. The US reluctance to face up to the human rights abuses perpetrated by their allies in the Gulf has been under increasing criticism.

> To protect America's oil lifeline from the Gulf, Presidents from Franklin Roosevelt to George W. Bush have struck implicit Faustian bargains. American support for democracy and human rights in Saudi Arabia, Qatar and even Iraq has ranged from the non-existent to the tepid. Americans have a habit of shutting out things that they do not want to see – if these things conflict with predetermined policies, needs and opinions. Human rights and democracy have spread extensively throughout the world since the end of the Cold War – except in the Arab world. America's timidity in addressing this situation is a factor in perpetuating it.
>
> (J. Hoagland, *Washington Post*, 9 September 2001)

In the spring of 2004 President Bush announced a new wider Middle East initiative aimed at bringing democracy to the region. His initial proposals, launched without any reference to countries in the region, were deemed too radical and a watered-down version was presented to the G8 summit in Georgia. The proposals call for supporting civil society, greater education for women, supporting training of judges and journalists.

Critics argued that the initiative had little chance of success unless the US was seen to engage more in efforts to secure a Middle East peace deal.

Perhaps the most difficult and sensitive issue facing the second Bush administration will be preventing Iran developing nuclear weapons. The President made clear on several occasions that the US would not countenance such a move but it was equally not clear how the US could achieve its objective given the problems it encountered in Iraq. There were many hawks who argued, in the aftermath of the swift collapse of the Saddam Hussein regime, that the next step would be Teheran, then Damascus. By the end of 2004 there were few voices promoting a military option. As a result Washington increasingly turned to the Europeans to help seek a solution to the Iran nuclear issue.

Africa

Although President Clinton made two visits to Africa during his term in office and succeeded, at least partly, in turning Africa into a more important and visible issue, the "dark continent" remains a second-rank issue for US foreign policy. The Clinton strategy, largely taken over by Colin Powell, rested on two overarching goals: promoting the integration of Africa in the global economy, and the protection of the US and its citizens from transnational threats such as AIDS and drugs. Efforts to increase development assistance, however, have been largely thwarted by Congress. During the Cold War, US policy toward Africa was based on supporting "our guys" in the worldwide struggle against communism. Post-Cold War, US policy became more multifaceted and attracted the intermittent attention of leading politicians. But the fiasco of the military intervention in Somalia in 1993 and the bombing of the American embassies in Kenya and Tanzania in 1998 tended to overshadow some of the positive engagement.

The most visible symptom of the renewed American interest in Africa has been the many trips undertaken by Clinton (he spent two weeks there in 1998), Albright and Holbrooke before 2000, and Colin Powell after taking office in 2001. In terms of strategic interest the US largely focused its attention on Nigeria, an important source of oil and one of Albright's four priority nations, South Africa, Angola (minerals) and the countries around Sudan. As part of Clinton's aim of integrating Africa into the global economy he secured, despite opposition from domestic constituencies fearing increased textile exports, passage of the African Growth and Opportunity Act in 2000, that provided $500 million in support of economic development to countries embracing market economic forces.

Following the brutal ending of "Operation Restore Hope" in Somalia in 1993, the US was less willing than ever to send soldiers to war-torn Africa, for example, to prevent or mitigate the massive genocide perpetrated in Rwanda. However, pressures from the international community and the desire from the White House to take action did lead the US to support the African Crisis Response Initiative (ACRI), designed to foster self-reliance in peacekeeping. The US hopes the countries benefiting from this training will help and ultimately take the responsibility for peacekeeping operations over the continent.

Case study: the US and HIV/AIDS

The Clinton administration was instrumental in moving HIV/AIDS and other infectious diseases on to the international agenda. AIDS in Africa was the focus of the US presidency of the UNSC in January 2000 and it was the first time that a health issue had been considered in that body. Vice President Al Gore, in his opening statement, emphasized that "AIDS is not just a humanitarian crisis. It is a security crisis – because it threatens not just individual citizens, but the very institutions that define and defend the character of a society." The National Intelligence Council (NIC) also reported in January 2000 that "HIV/AIDS will endanger US citizens at home and abroad, threaten US armed forces deployed overseas, and exacerbate social and political instability in key countries and regions in which the US has significant interests" (Gannon 2000).

The NIC report stated that more people had died from HIV/AIDS over the last twenty years than from any other disease in human history. The devastation caused by the epidemic posed a clear and direct challenge to long-term US economic and security interests. HIV/AIDS was devastating whole societies and economies, depriving countries of the educated and skilled individuals required to build democratic governments, professional militaries, and free market economies. To meet this challenge, the US needed to implement, along with others, a long-term strategy to defeat AIDS. American leadership to increase funding, accelerate the search for a vaccine, expand access to medicines, and form partnerships with affected governments, businesses, and communities would be critical.

The report noted that of the more than twenty-two million people who have died from HIV/AIDS since the beginning of the epidemic, four-fifths of those deaths have occurred in sub-Saharan Africa. More than 70 percent of all people living with the disease, or twenty-five million HIV-positive individuals, live in Africa. A further 55 million people are projected to die of AIDS in Africa over the next two decades. Over 10 percent of the population are infected in sixteen African nations. HIV/AIDS is now the leading cause of death in Africa and deaths from the disease now exceed those from the global influenza pandemic of 1918–19 and the bubonic plague. Unlike influenza and plague, HIV/AIDS does not kill its victims for years, and most victims do not know they are infected. AIDS does not predominately kill the weak and elderly, but rather attacks the most productive adults, leading to distorted demographics in the hardest hit countries.

The loss of millions of working adults means not only the loss of the individuals, but the resources invested in them, and their knowledge. In some African countries more than 30 percent of the teaching and medical professions are infected by HIV/AIDS. Armies composed largely of young men who are far from home and frequently exposed to danger are at especially high risk for HIV infection. The US and other donor nations have begun training and equipping African militaries to improve their peacekeeping capabilities and to reinforce civilian control of troops. It is in the interest of the US and African nations to have healthy, professional militaries ready to carry out these roles, and HIV/AIDS threatens those interests. USAID estimates that by 2010 there will be more than forty million AIDS orphans in Africa with all the attendant social problems. The impact of the HIV/AIDS crisis on African economies is also worsening. Productivity losses, increased absenteeism, and rising insurance and training costs are hurting economies and businesses. An August 2000 study by the World Bank found that South Africa's GDP would be 17 percent lower in 2010 than it would have been without AIDS, costing the economy twenty-two billion dollars.

Under pressure from Colin Powell, the Bush administration has come to recognize the significance of the epidemic for US national security interests and started to commit resources to the long-term fight. The President announced in September 2003 a $500 million contribution to the UN AIDS campaign and committed the US to an active role in combating the disease. According to some estimates, a global effort would require $4 billion to $5 billion. Ultimately, HIV/AIDS will be controlled globally only when a vaccine has been found. The Bush administration has promised to increase funding for vaccine research focused on the strains of HIV/AIDS that most seriously affect Africa. At the same time, the US has supported the position of American pharmaceutical companies that insist countries use trademark drugs rather than cheaper generic drugs.

Despite the increased attention devoted to Africa there has not been a sizeable shift in funds for the continent although Madeleine Albright did manage to secure some extra funding for Nigeria to support "democratic practices." Development assistance budgets for Africa have declined steadily during the 1990s. In 2001 the Congress authorized $1.6 billion in aid, less than Americans spend each day on health care. Clinton also managed to secure congressional approval for his plan to offer debt relief, roughly $225 million, to Africa's poorest countries.

The increased US engagement with Africa is partly due to the lobbying efforts of the congressional Black Caucus and other Afro-American groups. Clinton took several members of the Caucus with him on his 1998 trip to Africa when he was the first President to admit that US policy toward Africa had been wrong in the past. In a reference to the Cold War, the Rwandan genocide and the lack of commitment to address African problems in a more prompt and efficient way, Clinton said that

> the United States has not always done the right thing by Africa. What we need to be doing today in South Africa and in the United States is dealing with the legacy of apartheid here and slavery and racial discrimination there, insofar as it still needs to be stamped out.

There was concern whether the increased US involvement in Africa would continue when Bush took over in 2001. As a candidate, Bush had said that "Africa did not fit into the national security interest." But in appointing two Afro-Americans as his main foreign policy advisers Bush also sent a strong signal that Africa would not be neglected. Colin Powell seemed far more interested in Africa than Rice. He made Africa one of his first priorities and stressed that he would continue to give Africa close attention. In a speech at the University of Witwatersrand on 25 May 2001, Powell pointed out

> that the US has almost 35 million citizens of African descent. In 2000 US–Africa trade approached $30 billion, and America was Africa's largest single market. The US was also the leading foreign investor in Africa and over 30,000 Africans were studying in the US.

In the aftermath of September 2001, it was inevitable that attention was diverted away from Africa, apart from countries such as Sudan that were charged with complicity in terrorism. It is also worth noting that the congressional Black Caucus does not attach as much importance to Africa as other ethnic groups, such as the Jewish-Americans, do to the Middle East. This leads to a certain imbalance in US foreign policy. As one staffer remarked to the author, "he who makes most noise and provides most campaign finance tends to get priority." There was no strong lobby in the US pushing to intervene in the face of genocide in Dafur, Sudan. The Bush administration, however, did provide $5 billion to launch the Millennium Challenge Corporation. This fund sets rigorous selection criteria for development assistance and evaluates governments on the quality of their economic policies, the level of their investments in health and education and their standards of governance.

Conclusion

The US has had to reassess its priorities following the end of the Cold War. Under Clinton, the US became closely involved in a new global agenda, even if he was unable to persuade Congress to ratify agreements on arms control, climate change, and the creation of the ICC. George W. Bush was less keen on this global agenda, but under prodding from Colin Powell, his administration slowly began to re-engage in multilateral fora, a process that was accelerated after September 2001. External spending has focused more on the military than non-military programs. Under Clinton, Europe was perhaps the top priority given the importance of issues such as NATO enlargement and the Balkans. Clinton also devoted considerable attention to the Middle East and paid more consistent attention to Africa than any previous President. When Bush came into office in January 2001 he declared that missile defense and the western hemisphere would be his top priorities. His defense officials also made no secret that Asia would be a greater priority than Europe in terms of security issues.

The 11 September attacks changed priorities overnight for the US and led to a solid bipartisan front in the effort to combat the terrorist threat. Immediately, states were judged on how they responded to the US demand for cooperation to fight terrorism. After 9/11 US attention focused more on the Middle East, Persian Gulf, and South Asia at the expense of Europe, Latin America, and Africa. This trend is likely to continue for some time. According to one NSC staffer, speaking to the author in December 2004, the next decade would see the US focusing on the "arc of crisis" from the Middle East and Caucasus to the Gulf and South Asia. With the invasion of Iraq the US lost support from many traditional allies, including France and Germany. As the US continued to debate its foreign policy priorities, there was a parallel debate on the extent to which the US should engage with the outside world. It is to this debate, with its historical connotations, that we now turn.

Selected further reading

The articles by Newhouse (2001) and Perry (2001) review the missile defense debate. The articles by Blinken (2001) and Wallace (2001) cover transatlantic relations as does

Haass (1997b) *Transatlantic Tensions* and Gompert and Larrabee (1997) *America and Europe*. The transatlantic rift over Iraq is well covered in Gordon and Shapiro (2004) *Allies at War*. US relations with its southern neighbor are covered in Dominguez and de Castro (2001) *The US and Mexico*, and Mazza (2001) *Don't Disturb the Neighbors*. Trade issues in the western hemisphere are covered in Schott (2001) *Prospects for Free Trade in the Americas*. A RAND (2001) study on "The US and Asia: Toward a New Strategy and Force Posture" looks at the region from a security perspective.

10

Hegemon and sheriff

Key facts

- The end of the Cold War did not lead to any new guiding principles for US foreign policy. 9/11 was a day that "changed America for ever" and as a result the war on terrorism became the new defining paradigm of US foreign policy.
- The debate on unilateralism versus multilateralism was within and between the political parties. There was a further debate on whether the US should seek to play an imperial role disregarding views of others or whether it should continue playing a leadership role within the international community. There is no danger of the US retreating into isolationism.
- The US has intervened in many trouble spots around the world since the end of the Cold War. It will continue to be called upon to intervene but as a result of Iraq it will do so only reluctantly unless its direct interests are threatened.
- The Bush administration's "new realism" doctrine is useful for sharpening public debate and portraying a black and white world. But it is of limited value in charting a new course for the US in the twenty-first century. One key issue is how the US responds to the deeper causes of terrorism. Another is whether the US will recognize the benefits and necessity of international cooperation in areas beyond terrorism?

Quid America?

Dean Acheson, the postwar Secretary of State, famously remarked about Britain that it had lost an empire but not yet found a role. At the end of the Cold War, a Russian professor, Georgi Arbatov, asked the US, "now that you have lost your enemy, what will you do?" The end of the Cold War deprived the US not only of an enemy but also its core organizing principles on which it had based its foreign policy for four decades. For many Americans in the huge foreign and security policy bureaucracy, it was difficult to come to terms with the end of the Cold War and, fearful of change, much of the Cold War rhetoric persisted throughout the 1990s and beyond. Some analysts suggested that:

> fear of alien ideas – once communism, now Islamic fundamentalism – permeates official thinking. The perceived need to combat threatening forces, once the Soviet Union, now Iran and Iraq, remains pervasive. And a preference for military intervention to achieve policy objectives continues.
>
> (Kegley and Wittkopf 1996: 7)

The continuity of American foreign policy during and after the Cold War, according to the same analysts, can be traced in part to the shared characteristics of the "self-selecting, self-recruiting and self-perpetuating foreign and security policy elite."

President Clinton did try and educate Americans to the emerging threats of a borderless world but ended up using traditional instruments of power – military might, covert action, sanctions and dollar diplomacy. Although there was no consensus on the future course and direction of US foreign policy there were many pundits and analysts prepared to criticize the policy void while refraining themselves from offering any prescription. According to one former national security adviser,

> The legacy of the 1990s has produced a paradox. On the one hand, the US is sufficiently powerful to be able to insist on its view and to carry the day often enough to evoke charges of American hegemony. At the same time, American prescriptions for the rest of the world often reflect either domestic pressures or a reiteration of domestic maxims drawn from the experience of the Cold War. The result is that the country's preeminence is coupled with the serious potential of becoming irrelevant to many of the currents affecting and ultimately transforming the global order.
>
> (Kissinger 2001: 18)

Until 11 September there was widespread complacency that the US will always get its way. Outside the specialist journals, there was little sign of intellectual fervor or debate seeking new directions. Academic output is often abstract and of little use to the policy community. The think tanks are productive but tend to produce papers only for immediate consumption. According to one observer, "the sound bite has triumphed over sound analysis resulting in an arid intellectual foreign policy landscape." The same analyst argues that US foreign policy has no guiding principles. It is simply running "on the fumes of the Cold War" (Kupchan 2002: 29).

Throughout history there are various sets of ideas driving US foreign policy including the Hamiltonian with its emphasis on strong government and support for business; the Wilsonian with its emphasis on America's democratic mission; the Jeffersonian stressing the importance of protecting American values at home; and the Jacksonian with its emphasis on military and economic strength. In this context, the Clinton administration demonstrated a mix of the Hamiltonian and Wilsonian approaches while the characteristics of both the Bush administrations were more a mix of the Jeffersonian and the Jacksonian.

One observer has suggested a novel way of looking at American foreign policy. He proposes "exemplarists" versus "vindicators." While both groups believe that the US has a peculiar obligation to better the lot of humanity they have very different approaches. Exemplarists hold that the US owes the world merely the example of a humane, democratic, prosperous society; meddling in the affairs of others would not only not do much good for the nations meddled in but could jeopardize American values at the source. Vindicators, on the other hand, contend that America must move beyond example and undertake active measures. Human nature is too recalcitrant for mere examples to have much lasting effect, and military might, even if it does not necessarily make right, certainly can restrain wrong. Over time these characterizations shift between the political parties and even individuals, during their own lifetimes, can embody both approaches (Brands 1999).

Unilateralism v. multilateralism

A continuing theme of US foreign policy is the debate between unilateralists, who in the grand tradition of George Washington and the Founding Fathers eschew entangling relationships, and internationalists, who advocate cooperation and see security relationships as effective instruments for controlling the behavior of partners (*World Policy Journal*, Summer 1995). Although the differences on this issue between Bill Clinton and George W. Bush are sometimes exaggerated, there was certainly a more profound orientation toward unilateralism in the Bush administration that caused concern at home and abroad. Unilateralists emphatically reject the loss of national autonomy in decision-making. They see no reason to accept any constraints when America is so powerful. The US should act as it sees fit, regardless of the views of others. The campaign against the Taliban in Afghanistan was a mix of the unilateral and multilateral. While appreciating the political and sometimes material support of the international coalition, the US made clear that it wished to carry out military operations largely on its own and not be limited by coalition politics, as in the Kosovo military campaign.

According to one noted political scientist,

> American foreign policy has tended, in this century, to move back and forth between the extremes of an indiscriminate isolationism and an equally indiscriminate internationalism or globalism. Both postures share the same assumption about the nature of the political world and the same negative attitudes toward foreign policy. They are equally hostile to that middle ground of subtle distinctions, complex choices, and precarious manipulations which is the proper sphere of foreign policy.
>
> (Morgenthau 1969: 15)

While there is some truth in Morgenthau's assertion, there has been rather little American isolationism in the twentieth century. The inter-war period of isolationism contrasts with American engagement in two world wars, four decades of global struggle to contain communism, and a remarkably internationalist 1990s final decade. Isolationism has a resounding negative connotation and is often used as an abusive term, particularly by Democrats about Republican members of Congress. There is, however, no simple inter-party split on foreign policy. There are unilateralists and multilateralists in both major parties, but on the whole there are more unilateralists in the Republican ranks and more multilateralists within the Democratic party.

Unilateralists, a different breed from isolationists, may be divided into two schools. The first school (neo-isolationists) advocates a fundamental retrenchment and a limited balancing role for the US. The second, and larger, school (primacists) seeks to preserve America's current hegemony and prevent any challenges from arising. Neither school sees any real gains from security cooperation. The neo-isolationists seek to protect the virtue of the US from the contamination of other less virtuous nations while the primacists are at best only prepared to contemplate *ad hoc* cooperation. The individualism promoted by the Protestant religion may account for some of these attitudes. Another reason is that, historically, many Americans distrust their own government so why should they wish to associate with foreign governments?

The former EU External Affairs Commissioner, Chris Patten, voiced his concern at the direction of US policy in a series of interviews in February 2002. He acknowledged that the US had more resources to go-it-alone than any other country but he doubted whether even the US could resolve the new security threats on its own. He contended that the US commitment to multilateralism had served it well in the last half of the twentieth century and the US had as much an interest as any other country in strengthening global institutions that provided a framework for the civilized resolution of disputes. US foreign policy was becoming "dangerously absolutist and simplistic." It was time European governments spoke up and stopped Washington before it went into "unilateral overdrive" (*Guardian*, 9 February 2002; *Financial Times*, 15 February 2002).

There was considerable speculation following the September 2001 terrorist attacks that the US would be a convert to multilateralism. Now that it had seen the benefits of international cooperation, it was argued, the US would change its approach on other issues. These hopes were soon dashed. The Bush administration did not change its policies on any of the issues of major concern to the international community such as Kyoto, the ICC, the CTBT and other arms control treaties. Indeed, in the midst of the campaign against the Taliban, Bush announced a unilateral withdrawal from the ABM treaty. An apt description of the Bush approach to international cooperation might be "utilitarian multilateralism." In other words, the US would be prepared to work with other countries if necessary to achieve a US foreign policy goal, but the general preference would be to operate without any international constraints.

Table 10.1. International agreements rejected by the US

Anti-Ballistic Missile Treaty (1972)
The Bush administration has decided that the ABM Treaty between the US and Soviet Union should be scrapped because it bans the testing and development of national missile defenses.

Biological Weapons (1995)
The administration abandoned a UN draft accord that sets out enforcement mechanisms for the treaty, which would limit germ warfare. US negotiators say the approach threatens industry and national security.

Comprehensive Test Ban Treaty (1996)
The treaty would ban all nuclear test explosions, but the administration says it would limit US research. The White House has held up submission of the treaty to the Senate, which refused to ratify it before in 1999.

Kyoto Protocol (1997)
Aimed at combating global warming, the protocol is backed by 178 nations. The White House has rejected it on the grounds that it would harm the US economy and exempt developing nations. President Bush promised to offer alternatives for dealing with the problem.

Land-mine Ban (1997)
The US rejects the treaty, which calls for the destruction of anti-personnel land mines, citing as one reason US commitments to defend South Korea from North Korea.

International Criminal Court (1997)
The treaty would create the first permanent international tribunal to prosecute war crimes, genocide, and crimes against humanity. The administration says the accord could infringe on US sovereignty and put US troops at risk. The White House has no plans to seek Senate ratification.

Small-arms Control (2001)
The administration agreed in principle to a UN pact to stem the illegal flow of small arms. However, US officials (under pressure from the National Rifle Association) blocked two key provisions: regulation of civilian ownership of military weapons and restrictions on trade to rebel movements.

The National Security Strategy of September 2002 set down the guiding principles of US foreign policy under President Bush. In line with American tradition, it stated that the US was a special nation with a special mission. No nation would be allowed to challenge US supremacy. The new global challenge was terrorism and the US would lead the fight against this evil, taking "pre-emptive action" when necessary. This phrase caused widespread international condemnation but simply stated openly what all American presidents would do if there was a serious threat to US vital national interests. Even Senator Kerry adopted a similar position in the 2004 election campaign.

Global hegemon

"We are the first global power in history that is not an imperial power," stated Sandy Berger in October 1999. He was disturbed, however, that many foreigners viewed America as a "hectoring hegemon." Berger criticized "those isolationists who refused to embrace any treaties because they imposed restraints on American sovereignty. The alternative is a world with no rules, no verification and no constraints at all."

Berger was right and wrong in his analysis. He was right to describe the picture of the US as a "hectoring hegemon" but he was wrong to depict the conservatives as iso-lationists. The conservative scene is highly complicated with only a small minority favoring isolationism. Indeed the majority of unilateralist conservatives could rally round the hegemon banner with the liberals, albeit for different purposes. Those arguing in favor of accepting US hegemony are usually found on the right-wing of the Republican party. Their flagship publications are the *National Review* and *The Weekly Standard*. Henry Kissinger is equally critical of the left and right in this debate.

> On the left many see the US as the arbitrator of domestic evolutions all over the world. For this school of thought, foreign policy equates with social policy. On the right, some believe that the Soviet Union's collapse came about more or less auto-matically through a new American assertiveness ... and based on this interpreta-tion of history, they believe that the solution to the world's ills is American hegemony.
>
> (Kissinger 2001: 19)

People who label the US "imperialist" usually mean it as an insult. But in conservative intellectual circles, there are many who argue that the US should accept and embrace an imperialist role. They argue that as the US is the major military power in every region of the world, the US should accept its new role and seek to impose its values as well as defend its interests. One of the leading advocates of this idea of enforcing a new "Pax Americana" is Thomas Donnelly, of the Project for the New American Century, who argues that policing the American perimeter in Europe, the Persian Gulf, and East Asia will provide the main mission for the US armed forces for decades to come. He contends that the Bush administration has tried to sidestep this reality, and instead is trying to formulate a more modest policy in the tradition of the "realist" or balance-of-power views associated with Henry Kissinger and Brent Scowcroft. This realist course is mistaken and the sooner the US government recognizes that it is managing a new empire, the faster it can take steps to reshape its military, and its foreign policy, to fit that mission (Kevin Baker, *The New York Times*, 9 December 2001).

One of Donnelly's supporters, Andrew Bacevich, professor of international relations at Boston University, argues that, like it or not, an imperial America exists and that maintaining American power globally already has become the unspoken basis of US strategy. He suggests that there is hardly a single prominent public figure who finds fault with the notion of the US remaining the world's sole military superpower until the end of time. The practical question, therefore, "is not whether or not we will be a global hegemon, but what sort of hegemon we'll be" (*National Interest*, 30 August 2001). Another analyst has suggested that one reason US hegemony has remained unchallenged is that the international structures created by the US during the Cold War have provided cover for American actions (Ikenberry 2001).

In the first Bush administration, the main figures in national security policy could all be described as conservatives. However, while sharing a belief in a strong military, they tended to differ on when that power should be used and whether, in principle, the US should seek allies for its main goals. On one side were neo-conservatives like Cheney, Rumsfeld, Wolfowitz, and outside advisers Richard Perle and William Kristol. Supported by intellectuals in the American Enterprise Institute, they favored a proactive foreign policy based on the unilateral use of US power, the maintenance of American hegemony as long as possible, and opposing the rise of alternative centers of power. On the other side were more traditional conservatives like Rice, Powell, and Hadley. They were far more cautious about using military power, believing that the US should not intervene in small, distant wars but rather keep its resources intact in order to focus on potential threats from major powers. Rice would describe this as "the new realism." Both sides believed in unrivalled American military power supported by an extensive network of alliances that essentially follow American demands and do not limit its freedom of action. President George W. Bush, who has never demonstrated any great interest in foreign policy, initially favored the conservative, do-less camp. But after 9/11 he swung behind the interventionist camp and held that America had a special mission to rid the world of terrorism. The Bush White House could be sure of broad support in Congress for a unilateral approach to foreign policy. A clear majority of members, mainly but not exclusively on the Republican benches, favor an America first approach and increasingly use congressional powers, such as the imposition of unilateral sanctions, to promote their agenda.

Within the conservative camp there is a division on whether the US can and should pay for this imperial role. The Republican pundit and Reform Party presidential candidate, Patrick J. Buchanan, has argued vehemently against the cost of such an imperial role (Buchanan 1999). Other critics believe that embracing an imperial stance would backfire precisely because of the foreign reaction it would provoke, or maybe already is provoking. One expert has argued that because the US is pursuing an imperialist course, "there are already coalitions forming left and right around the world to thwart it." He points to closer cooperation between Russia and China, to a united Europe that is becoming less of an ally and more of a competitor, and to the swift rise of the anti-globalization movement (Johnson 2000).

Samuel Huntington has described the present global situation as "uni-multipolar" to capture the temporary, sole, superpower status of the US. He agrees that the US cannot follow hegemonic impulses and that it must pursue international cooperation rather than unilateral action to promote its interests. Regrettably, the US has been acting more as a "rogue superpower" and pursuing a policy of "global unilateralism" with little reference to the interests of others. Unlike the situation during the bipolar Cold War, when many countries welcomed the US as a protector against the Soviet Union, American actions today are frequently resented by others powers, including long-standing allies (*Foreign Affairs*, March/April 1999).

Another academic and former senior Pentagon official argues

> That people who talk about "benign hegemony" and "accepting an imperial role" are focusing too much on one dimension of power and are neglecting the other forms of power – economic and cultural and ideological. Over-emphasizing US military strength ultimately would undercut those less tangible forms of power, and so curtail any effort to maintain an empire.
>
> (Nye 2002)

The conservative "imperialist camp" responds to these critics by arguing that most Americans have become used to the US running the world and would be very reluctant to give it up. On the other side of the political spectrum, critics suggest that the US should concentrate on solving its domestic problems rather than continue with its global agenda. Tackling poverty, illiteracy, crime, infant mortality, violence and homelessness should be the key issues. If the US is to inspire other countries with its values and achievements, "then it must be able to offer at least as much to its own people as those it seeks to guard" (Wittkopf and McCormick 1999: 5).

Despite the various labels attached to different groups or individuals it is not usually easy to observe any consistent behavior from those entrusted with the burdens of office. It is much easier to be consistent from an editorial office, a think tank or even a member of Congress. When confronted with "the facts that live in the office" and the realities of dealing with day-to-day, often unforeseen, events, policymakers rarely have time to ponder and frame decisions from an ideological perspective. But the Bush administration is different. It does operate from a set of clear ideological convictions. It remains to be seen whether the Iraq imbroglio will force it back toward the pragmatic middle ground. In early statements after his re-election in November 2004, President Bush promised to maintain "an aggressive foreign policy."

The reluctant sheriff

The debate over American hegemony and an imperial role raises the question as to the circumstances in which the US should intervene abroad. Should it play the reluctant sheriff as in Somalia or Kosovo, or the enthusiastic sheriff as in fighting the Taliban or ousting Saddam Hussein? Should it seek to impose its values as opposed to promoting its values? The military activism of President Clinton (an anti-Vietnam War protestor) that included invading Haiti to keeping peace in Bosnia, missile attacks on Sudan and Afghanistan, and bombing Yugoslavia was criticized by many Republicans. Yet many senior officials in the Bush administration were equally ready to use the military as a first resort to promote American interests. Although most Americans oppose a "globocop" role for the US, American interventionist policies enjoy broad cross-partisan support, even if there are disputes over what type of intervention the US should engage in. One commentator, however, is more skeptical. "When the American President today is faced with a military threat, his first question is not 'what strategy will work to fundamentally put an end to this threat?' Rather, his first question is 'how much do I have to pay to get this show off CNN so I can forget about it?'" (Friedman 2001: 467).

Deputy Secretary of State, Strobe Talbott, gave the reasoning for the activist interventionist policy of the Clinton administration.

> In an increasingly interdependent world, Americans have a growing stake in how other countries govern, or misgovern themselves. The larger and more close-knit the community of nations that choose democratic forms of government, the safer and more prosperous Americans will be, since democracies are demonstrably more likely to maintain their international commitments, less likely to engage in terrorism or wreak environmental damage, and less likely to make war on each other. That proposition is the essence of the national security rationale for vigorously supporting, promoting, and when necessary, defending democracy in other countries.
>
> *(Foreign Affairs*, November/December 1996)

Speaking to US troops in Macedonia on 24 June 1999, President Clinton went further in defending the American intervention in Kosovo.

> We can then say to the people of the world, whether you live in Africa, Central Europe, or any other place, if somebody comes after innocent civilians and tries to kill them *en masse* because of their race, their ethnic background or their religion, and it is within our power to stop it, we will stop it.

The Africans who were massacred in Rwanda might have wondered at the President's statement. This was clearly not a universal message like the Truman Doctrine or John F. Kennedy's famous 1961 inaugural address. For example, despite the critical importance of Pacific security to US interests, and the destabilization of Indonesia following the Asian financial crisis and the demand of East Timor for independence, the US was reluctant to become involved. At the time of the fight for independence, the US was pleased and relieved that the Australians took the lead in the UN peacekeeping force for East Timor. Although the US supplied some logistical assistance, a deeper military involvement would have been difficult to justify to Congress and the American public. Toward the end of her tenure, Madeleine Albright, speaking in Chicago on 17 January 2001, laid down some more concrete conditions that should be considered before using force. "Choices must be based on the gravity of US interests, the risks to our personnel, the likelihood of success, the willingness of others to do their share, and the consequences of inaction."

George W. Bush came into office less committed to such humanitarian interventions. As a candidate, Bush's main message was that he would be more selective than his predecessor in taking on foreign commitments. During the presidential debate in Boston on 3 October 2000, he said, "I would be guarded in my approach. I don't think we can be all things to all people in the world. I think we've got to be very careful when we commit our troops." But after the terrorist attacks of September 2001 that changed American politics in such a profound manner, he also argued for selective engagement, especially if it could be sold as helping to defeat terrorism. In speech after speech he promised to hunt down the terrorists wherever they might be hiding.

Richard Haass, Director of Policy Planning in State, and author of the doctrine of *à la carte* multilateralism, set out some guidelines for US intervention in a 1999 article. Haass began with the premise that US power is neither unqualified nor permanent. Rather than clinging to sole superpower status, Haass argued that the US should shape a multipolar system to its own advantage, based on cooperation and concert rather than competition and conflict. When cooperation failed, Haass advanced a number of propositions to guide interventions. Like his future boss (President Bush) Haass took a cautious approach, suggesting that interventions should be rare, as limited as possible, and only conducted for specific and realistic goals (*Foreign Affairs*, September/October 1999). These principles were scarcely different from those proposed by Albright in Chicago.

Whether the US is regarded as a proud or reluctant sheriff, past history would tend to suggest that it will more often opt for intervention than non-interference to secure its policy goals. Nearly every US intervention during the 1990s followed a similar pattern, whether Bosnia, Somalia, or the Mexican and Asian financial crises. First, there was an agonized debate and an initial determination not to become involved and second, a resigned acceptance of some US role (apart from Rwanda). One criticism of the US is that while it has prevailed in numerous conflicts since the 1980s, often spending considerable treasure and blood, on each occasion it has walked away as soon as the fighting was over without thinking about the consequences of its actions. The US abandoned Afghanistan (and Pakistan) when the Soviets retreated. It failed to provide any substantial assistance after the spate of direct and proxy wars it engaged in Central America. In Bosnia and Kosovo it was keen to get out as quickly as possible. Bush seems to have taken this criticism to heart. "We should learn a lesson from the previous engagement in the Afghanistan area, that we should not just leave after a military objective has been achieved" (*The New York Times*, 15 October 2001). The reality however was that the Bush administration was equally reluctant to commit the substantial resources necessary to ensure a stable Afghanistan.

The new realism

All post-Cold War Presidents have indulged to a greater or lesser extent in Wilsonian idealism. The Wilsonian idealists or internationalists seek to spread American values around the world. US intervention in the First World War and the Truman Doctrine were sold not in balance of power terms but as a struggle between good and evil, democracy and totalitarianism. During the Cold War, every American President held that this universal mission should be maintained regardless of the limits of American interests or power. President Carter, in his promotion of human rights around the world, was continuing in the tradition of Wilson. There was even a touch of Wilsonian rhetoric in President Bush's "new world order." President Clinton was accused by the Republicans of "excessive illusory Wilsonianism." Madelaine Albright, in her Chicago speech, contended that there was an overlap between idealists and realists.

> I hope never again to hear foreign policy in this country described as a debate between Wilsonian idealists and geopolitical realists. In our era, no President or Secretary of State could be taken seriously without finding a middle ground between the two.

This was indeed the position adopted by President Bush after 9/11. He came increasingly to view the importance of promoting freedom and democracy in order to reduce threats to the US. Meeting with Tony Blair in November 2004 after his re-election, Bush stated:

> The reason why I am so strong on democracy is democracies don't go to war with each other. I've got great faith in democracies to promote peace.

The prospects for the "new realist" approach of the Bush administration, however, are not particularly good. First, the term itself has never been defined by anyone in the Bush team. Rather it is used as a backdrop for the administration's foreign policy with the implied criticism that the Clinton administration was engaged in "romanticism." Second, by focusing almost exclusively on a traditional security agenda (rebuilding America's military power, deploying missile defenses, reinforcing long-standing alliances with Europe, Japan, and Taiwan, focusing on "rogues" and preparing for competition with China and Russia), the Bush team are neglecting several instruments that may be more relevant in tackling the world's problems. These include promoting human rights in a uniform manner, democracy building, sustainable development, economic integration, non-military foreign assistance, and support for a multilateral approach to world affairs.

Although the new realism may prove well suited to parts of the world in which the traditional security agenda is alive and well, such as the Middle East and Northeast Asia, it has much less to offer the rest of the world. European integration has demonstrated that mutual tolerance and interdependence have replaced the old balance of power politics of the continent. Similar trends are apparent in Latin America and Southeast Asia. Africa faces immense problems, but its problems stem from poverty and disease, not geopolitical rivalry. Most predictions suggest that the conflicts of the future are likely to arise from ethnic disputes, failed states, and struggles over scarce resources. The Bush team, however, made clear when it took office that it did not wish to become involved in "global social work." According to one analyst, "try as it might to make the world conform to a realist template, the Bush team will increasingly find that its approach to global affairs has become obsolete" (Kupchan 2002).

Realism does, however, offer political advantages in that it is easy to sell the concept to the public. For most Americans, it is easy to grasp because it portrays the world in clear, black and white terms. As President Bush remarked, you are either with the US in its crusade against terrorism or against it; there can be no ambivalence. Minor threats and the new security agenda are not America's business. According to one conservative commentator, the US should not get engaged in peacekeeping as it detracts from the principal tasks facing the world's finest fighting machine (Krauthammer, *Washington Post*, 9 December 2001). It is doubtful, however, whether the world will ever be so simple. Indeed the modern post-Cold War world is characterized by increasing complexity and for most problems there are no simple or swift solutions. Bush's new realism may help win support for a limited campaign against terrorism but it is an insufficient guiding principle for the challenges facing the US in the twenty-first century and its inevitable continuing involvement in world affairs. It may not always be easy or even possible to divide the world in black and white terms. Rather the administration will need to educate the public in Morgenthau's different shades of gray.

This will not be an easy task even if the administration was prepared to attempt it. No post-Cold War President has sought to educate the American public in the complexity of global affairs. Nor has there been any attempt to question the basic bureaucratic structures established at the onset of the Cold War. The US is struggling to find a role for NATO. There are some conservatives who prefer to circumvent alliances and avoid fighting wars by committee, a reference to the experience in Kosovo. Others believe NATO should be restructured to fight wars, under American leadership, outside Europe. Arguments over NATO were papered over during the first Bush administration. They may well resurface in the debate on further NATO expansion. The Prague summit of November 2002 accepted seven new candidates but several more, including a number of Balkan countries, would also like to join. How many new automatic defense guarantees is the US prepared to grant to countries that most Americans cannot find on a map?

It is doubtful whether the American public or the "new realists" would be prepared to accept the rise of alternate centers of power. Polling results reveal that most Americans fear the rise of alternate power centers, whether Japan, China, or Russia. Attitudes toward the EU were not tested although the EU is the most likely candidate to challenge the US at least in some areas. As noted above, the US, at least rhetorically, was a strong supporter of European integration. However, as was seen in its response to European efforts to create its own defense forces, the US was reluctant to sanction any development that might weaken American influence. The double-speak is most evident in Congress where many oppose any attempts to establish a European security and defense policy (ESDP) but at the same time urge the EU to take on more responsibility for peacekeeping in the Balkans. It will be a challenge for the US, having grown accustomed to calling the shots for so long, to accept that ceding some influence to other power centers, notably the EU, may indeed be in its long-term interests. As the US looks around the world and ponders the challenges of the twenty-first century, there are few alternative power centers, other than the EU, that share basic American values and are rich enough to make a decisive contribution to tackling global problems. The question is whether American elites are prepared to share influence in tomorrow's world. If the process is sold positively as reducing the global military and financial burden for the US then it may be successful. But if it is done reluctantly and is opposed by politicians seeking short-term credit, then it could lead to a serious split in trans-atlantic relations.

Conclusion

By historical standards the US is clearly a hegemonic power but a relatively benign one. Indeed, the above analysis would suggest that the US is a global hegemon *and* (despite Iraq) a reluctant sheriff. As the top dog in the international arena, the US has no wish to see radical changes in international relations. It talks about wishing to see more democracy in the Middle East but continues to seek close ties with the authoritarian regimes of the region. It prefers the status quo, hence no tampering with its alliance systems or the international financial and economic mechanisms that it helped establish. The US feels comfortable operating through NATO, the UNSC, the G8, the IMF, World Bank and, for most of the time, the WTO. This status quo mentality seems to inhibit, in many quarters, the development of a flexible mindset that is able to view the world in different shades of gray rather than black and white. The low-level debates about isolationism and internationalism, unilateralism and multilateralism are likely to continue without any consensus being reached. There were several articles after 11 September suggesting the US must now abandon unilateralism as its guiding foreign policy concept but there were no substantial policy changes. The present formula might be described as "utilitarian multilateralism," a variation on "*à la carte* multi-lateralism." Most members of the Bush administration would argue, however, that given that the US is seen and expected to have special responsibilities in the world, it is unrealistic to expect the US to accept a multilateralist discipline like other powers.

In 1992 a Carnegie Endowment report concluded "that the end of the Cold War was a rare opportunity and above all a time to change the way we think about the world and the way we conduct our affairs at home and abroad." Sadly, there was little sign of America's foreign and security policy elite engaging in any such reflection in the 1990s. Charge and counter charge were aimed at political opponents in an attempt to score points. In an era of seemingly unlimited American power, constraints on the use of that power are sometimes hard to endure. But if the US chooses to act alone in foreign policy, Americans should be careful that the independence gained outweighs the cooperation lost.

Selected further reading

The hegemony debate is covered in Holt (1995) *The Reluctant Superpower*, Petras and Morley (1995) *Empire or Republic?*, Steel (1995) *Temptations of a Superpower* and Tucker and Hendrickson (1992) *The Imperial Temptation*. Brzezinski (1997) *The Grand Chessboard* asserts that control of Eurasia is the key to control of the world. Buchanan (1999) *A Republic, Not an Empire* argues against foreign entanglements. Huntington (1996) *The Clash of Civilizations* predicts a clash between the Western Christian and the Islamic worlds. Johnson (2000) *Blowback: The Costs and Consequences of American Empire* looks at the cost of hegemony. Read (2001) *Special Providence* considers America's global reach while Nye (2002) *The Paradox of American Power* argues that the US cannot go it alone. Kupchan (2002) *The End of the American Era* suggests America needs a new internationalism. Kissinger (2001) provocatively asks *Does America Need a Foreign Policy?*

Conclusion

What kind of US leadership?

Key facts

- There are many actors involved in the making of US foreign policy. Who has decisive influence on any single issue depends on many factors, including the political importance of the subject and whether the White House is involved.
- The US will face an increasingly difficult international environment in the first quarter of the twenty-first century. Transnational issues such as the environment, energy, and water, plus the impact of hugely increased world population, are likely to dominate the agenda. Globalization will exacerbate the rich–poor divide.
- The US will need to modify its external spending and develop new instruments to deal with these new security threats. Past history suggests that the US will continue its global engagement. Foreign policy is likely to remain a political football, despite the bipartisan support in tackling the terrorist threat.
- The US arouses mixed reactions abroad. Many Europeans are concerned at the violence, gun culture, death penalty and trend toward unilateralism. On the other hand, there is still considerable admiration for American technology and culture. Although America may try and re-brand its image, as the only remaining superpower, it will continue to arouse emotions of envy and hatred.
- Whatever the outcome of the debates on foreign policy, the US will continue to be the key player in global affairs for the foreseeable future. But what kind of leadership will the US provide?

Who makes US foreign policy?

From this survey, it is clear that there are many different actors involved in the making of foreign policy. Their numbers are likely to increase as the barriers between foreign and domestic policy continue to erode. The executive and legislative branches both have constitutional authority to act in foreign affairs. A popular President, enjoying high public support, is in a much stronger position to take effective action than a weak, unpopular President. At the same time the occupant of the White House is constantly buffeted by external and internal forces that often severely limit his freedom of maneuver. America no longer has the financial and economic supremacy it enjoyed in the two decades after 1945. Its prosperity is linked to policies and developments in many other countries as well as decisions taken in international bodies such as the WTO. It is also dependent on foreign countries for mineral resources, markets for its goods and help in waging war on terrorism.

These factors lead to a certain consistency in American foreign policy despite the individual preferences of different Presidents. For example, Clinton exploited some policy differences with George H. W. Bush during the 1992 election campaign, but on taking office he stressed the essential continuity of American foreign policy and basically followed his predecessor's policies even in the areas of disagreement (China, Balkans). George W. Bush, on the other hand, came into office in 2001 determined to do exactly the opposite of his predecessor in foreign policy. His foreign policy team also contained many individuals who were prepared to abandon established routines of thought and action, the tradition of incremental change and the preservation of existing policies. But after several months of facing the reality of limited foreign policy options, President George W. Bush was forced to revert to the continuation of certain mainstream policies (engagement with Russia, China, and even North Korea). Pragmatism is as powerful a force as ideology in American foreign policy.

Although the President is underpinned by a large, executive bureaucracy, not all parts of the bureaucracy pull in the same direction all of the time. Turf wars and bureaucratic in-fighting are endemic in Washington. The battles between State (Powell) and the Pentagon (Rumsfeld) are documented in the books by Bob Woodward describing the preparations for the war in Iraq. In recent years, however, the NSC has come to play a key role in the formulation of foreign policy, a trend that reflects the increasing politicization of foreign affairs. The State Department has struggled to maintain its role and influence in the light of much larger and better, funded, executive agencies, and a rapidly changing foreign policy agenda. After a decade of decline in funding, Congress began to reverse this trend, notably as a result of Colin Powell's charisma and stature. The Pentagon has not had any funding problems and there was no sign of any decrease in its influence. Although Rumsfeld was unable to introduce his radical proposals for a major transformation of the military, he did set out guidelines in the 2001 QDR that were meant to lead to a leaner, more mobile, and efficient fighting force. The importance of fighting terrorism also led to new priorities, and increased funding, for the military and the intelligence services.

At the same time, there has been a marked increase in the influence of interest groups who are more vocal and more visible on the Washington scene than ever before. America's regions are also making their voice felt more than before as are the media and public opinion. The war on terrorism also led to a more supportive Congress, keen to demonstrate its patriotism in speedily passing anti-terrorist legislation, accepting the lifting of sanctions on countries that were helping the American war effort and unblocking a number of agreements with third countries. This behavior in the fall and winter of 2001–2 was in marked contrast to the attitude of Congress during the last years of the Clinton administration. When the patriotic fervor diminishes, it is likely that there will be a reversal to the now traditional struggle for power between Congress and the White House. The Republican control of both houses, however, should make it easier for George W. Bush in implementing his foreign policy. The media and public opinion were very supportive of the war on terrorism, particularly as the campaign in Afghanistan to topple the Taliban regime cost almost no American lives. But we have seen how fickle public opinion can be and a prolonged conflict in Iraq, accompanied by further terrorist acts and more American casualties, could lead to changed attitudes.

The world in 2015

What kind of world will the US face in the twenty-first century? How should it respond to the new threats and challenges? What resources will be required? There is never any shortage of material from commissions, think tanks, and other experts to guide administration in the formulation of US foreign policy. In 1999 and 2000 a number of major reports were compiled by leading foreign policy practitioners and analysts that assessed the future international environment in which the US would have to operate. The reports all provided excellent reviews of the problems, including terrorist attacks, that the US would likely face in coming years. Prior to the attacks of September 2001, their analysis and recommendations were hardly noticed. Afterwards, the authors were rarely off the lecture circuit and the talk shows.

The first report, or series of reports, was produced by the United States Commission on National Security in the 21st Century, led by former Senators Gary Hart and Warren B. Rudman. The first report stated that America's homeland would become increasingly vulnerable to hostile attack from more challenging adversaries, so much that military superiority and excellent intelligence would not entirely protect the US. It also suggested that the US would be more susceptible to security threats because of the rapid advances and proliferation of information and bio-technologies, as well as the vulnerabilities of the evolving international economic infrastructure. Borders will be more porous and the sovereignty of states will come under pressure. Fragmentation or failure of states will occur with destabilizing effects on neighboring states. Energy will continue to have major strategic significance, and space will become a critical and competitive military environment. It concluded that the US will be frequently called upon to intervene militarily during a time that will require different military and other national capabilities.

The report put forward a number of priorities for US national security:

- defend the US by maintaining nuclear, homeland security, conventional, expeditionary/intervention, humanitarian relief, and constabulary capabilities;
- maintain America's social cohesion, economic competitiveness, technological ingenuity, and military strength;
- assist the integration of key major powers, especially China, Russia, and India, into the mainstream of the emerging international system;
- promote the dynamism of the global economy and improve the effectiveness of international institutions and international law;
- adapt US alliances to a new era in which America's partners seek greater autonomy and responsibility;
- help the international community tame the disruptive forces of globalization.

The second major report, "Global Trends 2015," prepared under the direction of the US National Intelligence Council (NIC), identified and analyzed the key drivers and trends that will shape the world of 2015. The key drivers identified were demographics, natural resources and the environment, science and technology, the global economy and globalization, national and international governance, future conflict, and the role of the US. Between now and 2015, the US will face three important challenges: managing relations with non-state actors, combating criminal networks, and responding to emerging and dynamic religious and ethnic groups. US global economic, technological, military and diplomatic influence will be unparalleled among nations as well as regional and international organizations in 2015. This power will not only ensure America's pre-eminence, but will also cast the US as a key driver of the international system.

Given the remarkable consistency in analysis in all these reports, it is worth examining how the administration responded to their recommendations. Little was done before 11 September but afterwards a number of recommendations were followed, particularly the blueprint for homeland defense. There was a reluctance, however, to engage in a significant reorganization of the foreign and security policy bureaucracy and to devote more resources to "soft security" issues. In the aftermath of September 2001, the administration and Congress preferred increasing the defense budget and the budgets of the intelligence agencies rather than devoting more money to technical and development assistance programs (apart from the new frontline states in the fight against terrorism). Nor was there any sign of a change in attitudes toward global issues such as the environment and poverty. Yet if the US is not seen even to consider tackling these problems it could well provoke further resentment among the "have nots" of the world.

Former President Clinton did attempt to address these issues in his 2001 BBC Dimbleby lecture. He argued that the US had a duty, which coincided with its national interest, to take a lead in tackling some of the problems that arose from globalization. It was indefensible that half the world's population earned less than two dollars a day and a third had no access to clean water. The fact that Clinton did not give these issues his full attention when in office demonstrates how difficult it will be to change the mindset of most American politicians who have very different priorities. There are few members of Congress with the vision to see the wider security picture. There are even fewer prepared to campaign for a more internationalist approach and for increased funding to address the problems of global poverty and sustainable development.

Is the past a guide to the future?

Is there anything that we can learn from the history of American foreign policy that might provide a guide to US behavior in future? It is important to note that the global role of the US is a relatively new phenomenon, essentially spanning the last half of the twentieth century. During the first century after independence the US was overwhelmingly concerned with domestic issues, including a devastating civil war. It played little or no role in international affairs and the only armed conflicts it engaged in were against Britain, Mexico, and native Americans. At the end of the nineteenth century, the US began to play a greater world role. After some hesitation, it intervened decisively in both world wars and after 1945 established a consensus in favor of a global role to defeat communism.

Having won the Cold War it was by no means inevitable that the US would maintain its global engagement. Some argued that the US, and others, had paid a high price for American involvement around the world. It would be prudent to retreat if not into isolationism then to a more modest role. These voices struggled for a hearing in both parties. Those that did argue for such a change, as Pat Buchanan, were roundly defeated at the ballot box. Although the Cold War consensus fueled by the Soviet threat was not replaced by a comparable policy or ideological framework, the majority view was that America had widespread global interests and that the US should thus maintain its global engagement. The mainstream debate after the Cold War was thus limited to the size and nature of American engagement, not the engagement itself.

Interestingly, in the aftermath of the September 2001 terrorist attacks, there were virtually no voices calling for the US to retreat into isolationism. This might have been an understandable reaction on the basis that global engagement, especially in places such as the Middle East, had brought the US mainly trouble and strife. Instead, there was a broad consensus across the political spectrum that the US should remain engaged globally – even if there was no consensus on what global posture the US should adopt. There were almost no voices arguing against America's sole superpower position. The question, rather, was how best to maintain this unique position in world affairs. Should the US seek to act unilaterally, multilaterally or "pick and mix" in order to maintain its hegemonic position?

The outcome of the Iraq War will certainly be a very important element in how America develops its foreign policy in future. The neocons were certainly chastised by the Iraq experience. David Brooks, a leading right-wing commentator, accused Bush and Rumsfeld of entering Iraq with a "childish fantasy" and asserts that the US is now "a shell shocked hegemon." Tucker Carson, a conservative pundit on CNN's *Crossfire*, said, "I supported the war and now I feel foolish. I'm just struck by how many people like me who were instinctively distrustful of government forgot to be humble in our expectations." Another critic, Samuel Huntington, agreed, stating, "we just didn't realize how totally different the culture is in Middle Eastern countries. We might defeat Saddam but we cannot defeat the Iraqi people."

Bush shrugged off such criticism, emphasizing religion and values as his driving forces. He told Bob Woodward, "There is a human condition that we must worry about in times of war. There is a value system that cannot be compromised – God-given values. Freedom is not America's gift to the world. Freedom is God's gift to everybody in the world." Richard Clarke confirms Bush's simplistic attitude stating that "Bush looked for the simple solution, the bumper-sticker description of the problem." There is something attractive in a leader that makes a decision and then sticks to it through thick and thin. But at what point does tenacity become obstinacy?

Bush came into office opposed to US involvement in "nation building." These were dirty words associated with Clinton and the UN. But American-led "regime change" was another matter. In contrast to previous American interventions, President Bush stated that the US was prepared to engage in "nation building" after the defeat of the Taliban regime. But neither the White House nor Congress seemed ready to devote the necessary resources to nation building even though this is likely to be the main foreign policy task for the next twenty years.

The ugly American

Americans have always considered themselves a nation with a mission. In the early years of the republic Alexis de Tocqueville wrote:

For 50 years, it has been constantly repeated to the inhabitants of the United States that they form the only religious, enlightened, and free people. They see that up to now, democratic institutions have prospered among them; they therefore have an immense opinion of themselves, and they are not far from believing that they form a species apart in the human race.

American exceptionalism is also linked to American nationalism. But as one observer notes, this is not easy to define as there are two competing strands.

On the one hand, a generous and encompassing nationalism that celebrates tolerance, diversity and liberty. On the other hand, a wary, intolerant suspicion, even paranoia that finds any manifestation of otherness threatening and contemptible.

(Lieven 2004)

How, then, are these Americas viewed by the outside world? Senator Kerry charged President Bush during the 2004 election campaign with "having divided America and divided the world." Quoting an array of polls, Kerry said that more people around the world hated America now than ever before. For most of the Cold War period, American leadership of "the free world" had been accepted without question. Since the end of the Cold War, the US has often been perceived as a bully, threatening to punish others if it did not get its way, or to withdraw, or not to pay its dues. Madeleine Albright may have been right in describing the US in 1996 as "the indispensable nation" but few foreigners enjoyed being lectured at by a nation that did not pay its UN dues and chose selectively what international agreements it would join. There is no question that America's image worsened dramatically during the first George W. Bush administration. Many were shocked at the administration's defiance of world opinion on a whole range of global issues. US action on Iraq and Bush's rejection of the Kyoto Protocol were perhaps the two biggest shocks. The 2004 poll results of European attitudes toward the US were dramatic. A substantial majority (57 percent) of Europeans were hostile to American leadership while nearly 80 percent disapproved of Bush's foreign policy. According to one observer, "the growth in anti-American feeling is one of the biggest threats confronting the world" (Moisi, *Financial Times*, 2 June 2004). Another commentator wrote, "No nation in history has ever squandered so much respect and trust, hence so much political capital in so short a time" (Joffe, *Time*, 29 November 2004).

In the run up to the 2004 election, both Democratic and Republican foreign policy experts emphasized the importance of the US taking steps to improve its public diplomacy (see articles by Samuel Berger and Chuck Hagel in *Foreign Affairs*, May/June and July/August 2004). As one European Foreign Minister told the author in March 2004, "we are witnessing a phenomenon without precedent. We have never seen such disdain from Washington. Not only is there a complete absence of consultation, but there is an exaltation of unilateralism and the militarization of foreign policy thinking." This resentment could be costly to America in the future. Certainly America's size and geographical situation has made it easier to ignore those proclaiming the necessity of global interdependence. US military and economic superiority has also made many Americans reluctant to accept that there might be an alternative to doing it "my way." But going-it-alone also carries a price.

In the post-Cold War period, there was also increasing criticism of many aspects of American society and culture. Felix G. Rohatyn, a former US ambassador to France, wrote that "in Europe, and elsewhere, the death penalty, guns and violence in society cast a large cloud on America's moral leadership" (*Washington Post*, 20 February 2001). But this is not the whole image. Many aspects of American society and culture are widely admired. Its universities attract the top brains from around the world. Silicon Valley is a veritable united nations of software designers and IT specialists, all imbued with an entrepreneurial spirit lacking in most other countries. The Senate may never hold confirmation hearings on Mickey Mouse, Madonna, Britney Spears, Tom Cruise or Microsoft but in many ways they are also seen as American ambassadors. The rest of the world has adopted many bits of Americana – from MBA programs to MTV programs, from Big Macs to computer Macs. There is little sign that the world's fascination with America will decline.

The end of the post-Cold War era?

The 11 September terrorist attacks signified the end of the post-Cold War era in dramatic fashion. The post-Cold War era was characterized by pragmatic internationalism in US foreign policy. The new era is characterized by a single obsession – the war on terrorism. 9/11 transformed George W. Bush and imbued him with a new sense of purpose. Given the horrendous nature of the terrorist attacks many Americans relinquished critical judgment and acquiesced in policies they would otherwise have abominated. 9/11 also provided a golden opportunity for the hawks in the administration to push for regime change in Iraq and elsewhere.

9/11 also helped the US improve ties with its main Cold War adversaries, Russia and China. Relations between the US and Russia made significant progress with both sides willing to seize the opportunity of a fresh start. Although the distrust did not vanish overnight, President Bush seemed prepared to establish a close personal relationship with President Putin, paying him the compliment of inviting him to his ranch in Texas. In response to Moscow's assistance in the war on terrorism, Washington muted its criticism of Russian behavior in Chechnya. Russia was invited to join a new consultative forum with NATO and it in turn muted its criticism of NATO enlargement. The two sides agreed to disagree on missile defense. Despite this improvement in relations there remains some suspicion of Russian motives, especially on weapons proliferation, among Pentagon officials. There is also considerable resentment of the US in Russia, especially among the older foreign and security policy elite. On balance, however, the prospects for a permanent improvement in US–Russian relations have increased significantly since 11 September.

There has also been an improvement, albeit not to the same extent, in relations with China. The suspicions about China remain high within the Bush administration and many consider that the hidden agenda behind missile defense is the construction of a shield that would protect the US from a potential Chinese attack if the US came to the assistance of Taiwan. The supporters of Taiwan are influential within the right-wing of the Republican party and are likely to make life difficult for any President wishing to move rapidly to improve relations with China. At the same time, it was a Republican President (Nixon) who made the breakthrough in establishing relations with China in the 1970s. It is not inconceivable, especially given Bush senior's close ties to Beijing, that there might be a similar dramatic improvement in Sino-US relations.

The continuing Cold War mindset among many members of the foreign and security policy elite in Washington is most apparent in discussion of "rogue states." The easy victory over the Taliban forces in Afghanistan encouraged the proactive conservatives in their view that the US should use military force to bring about a regime change with other rogue states. Despite the difficulties in Iraq, the fear of the outside world and the apparent need for an enemy is still apparent in right-wing circles in America.

Others saw the 11 September 2001 terrorist attacks as an opportunity for new thinking.

> The attacks underline the irrelevance of America's dominant security policies, which are still rooted in Cold War attitudes and structures. The failure to move away from the Cold War mentality has its roots not only in various forms of inherited bigotry but also in very strong interests within the US security establishment. A terrorist operating out of a tent in Afghanistan may do more to spur changes in the US armed forces than several decades of blue-ribbon panels, commissions and reports.
>
> (Anatol Lieven, *Prospect*, November/December 2001)

The failure of the US to win broad support for its campaign against Iraq was criticized in a *Financial Times* editorial of 12 March 2003: "The measure of the US diplomatic fiasco is that a perfectly arguable case about one of the most despicable regimes of modern times was so mishandled that international public opinion came to worry more about the misuse of American power than about Saddam Hussein."

The war on terrorism has thus become the single defining issue for US foreign policy. If there were further terrorist attacks on the US, there could be a renewed angst in the population and a siege mentality might develop similar to that during periods of the Cold War. This might lead to suspicion of foreigners in general and Muslim-Americans in particular. But if the US is perceived as having "won" the war on terrorism, then it may lead to a more expansive foreign policy that would include increased resources to tackle some of the problems associated with globalization. America could lead a new international coalition that would have on its agenda a reduction in poverty, protection of the environment, access to clean water and an attack on infectious diseases. There are many private American foundations already active in these fields but at present the US government is perceived as unwilling to really engage on these issues. It is not only a question of increased resources. There needs to be changes to the present organization of the international system. Rightly or wrongly the US is widely regarded as running the system for its own benefit. Critics allege that not only does the US have a controlling position in the UNSC, the G8, NATO, the IMF, World Bank and WTO, but it also benefits disproportionately from globalization. There is a strong case for the above international organizations becoming more inclusive in order to give more stakeholders a voice in global governance. But change will not happen unless the US takes the lead.

The great debates over foreign policy in American history have focused mainly on identifying and constructing optimal security relationships for the US and have been driven by differing assessments of the gains from cooperation, especially the likely constraints on America's own freedom of action. In the post-Cold War world, however, there has been no fundamental national debate on the aims and goals of American foreign policy. As one critic observed,

> To the extent that there is any discussion of the shared national interest today, it's all about whether we can define a new common threat and not a new common mission. The "big enemy" is still the organizing principle for American internationalism, not "the big opportunity"; or "the big responsibility." The US needs to build a new coalition of software writers and human rights activists, Iowa farmers and environmental activists to push for free trade and internationalism.
>
> (Friedman 2001: 437)

Partly because of the absence of a national debate, US foreign policy since the end of the Cold War has lacked any clear direction. The internationalist momentum left behind by the Cold War and America's stark preponderance of power kept the US globally engaged virtually by default. Instead of the communist dragon, other dragons have taken their place, notably "rogue states," terrorists, and drug traffickers. While there is little prospect of the US retreating from a world from which it benefits significantly, there may be adjustments to American foreign policy that could force its partners, notably in Europe and Asia, to an increased share of global responsibilities.

A few observers have attempted to define the post-Cold War era. Francis Fukuyama has argued that as liberal democracy has triumphed we can now enjoy "the end of history." Samuel Huntington, in contrast, has suggested that the new geopolitical dividing lines are cultural and that a clash of civilizations is imminent. The popularity of his thesis increased dramatically after 11 September 2001. Another view is that put forward by Thomas Friedman, namely that globalization is the one big thing that has changed the nature of world politics. Yet another view, from Charles Kupchan, is that the fundamental, inescapable, geopolitical feature of the moment is uncontested American power and not democracy, culture, or globalization. There are powerful parts to all these viewpoints. Liberal democracy has indeed been on the march in the 1990s and the world has never been more "democratic." There is a growing gulf between fundamental adherents of Islam and Christian societies. But the gulf is not beyond repair. Globalization has had a greater impact so far on economic policy than foreign policy. American power is undisputed at present. But is it the right mix of power ingredients? Is it not too much focused on hard, compared to soft, power? How long can it last?

Number one – for how long?

The prospects facing the US as number one power in the world in the short- to medium-term are good. There are no obvious internal threats to its security and the external threats, mainly from terrorism, may injure but cannot defeat the US. American technological and economic predominance shows no sign of being challenged. The gap between its military capabilities and that of other powers continues to grow. It may no longer need them but it shows no sign of giving up its worldwide network of military alliances and bases that allows the US to project power to every part of the globe. Yet, as Joe Nye has pointed out, military power alone cannot produce outcomes that Americans want on many issues that matter to their safety and prosperity. However justified, the doctrine of the early use of force poses enormous problems for the stability of the international system.

Furthermore circumstances can change fast. In 1900, Britain still ruled the waves and yet within two decades, despite growing global inter-dependence, it was fighting for its very existence. In 1945, Canada and Argentina were on a par in terms of per capita GDP. In 2002, Canada was four times richer per head than Argentina. America has enjoyed a wonderful half-century as top dog. But there is nothing inevitable in it being able to continue in this position for the next fifty years. America's present standing rests largely on a decade of impressive economic growth. If this were to end, as has happened in Japan, and budgetary and fiscal problems were to increase over the coming years, then the threat of imperial over-stretch would return. America is already heavily dependent on foreigners to finance its budget deficit. It also faces major problems in coping with an ageing population that will demand greater budget shares than in the past. At the same time the prognosis for America retaining its top dog status into the foreseeable future is very good providing American leaders operate with wisdom and understanding of the concerns of others. A foreign policy that holds America to be invincible and that combines unilateralism, arrogance and parochialism could be very dangerous. Contrary to what Condoleezza Rice stated in 2000, there is no contradiction between promoting the national interest and a commitment to the interests of a far-from-illusory international community. It can indeed be argued that since the end of the Cold War the US has gained power but lost influence.

President Bush during his first term in office held a simple "black and white" view of the world divided into "friends and enemies," "good guys and bad guys." The center-piece of his 2004 re-election campaign was "steady, strong leadership" and he promised to continue with a similar assertive foreign policy in his second term. Although he talked of the importance of the US being "a humble nation" during his first election campaign there was little sign of humility when in office. Indeed, arrogance is the word most people associate with the Bush White House.

But Bush considers that 9/11 gave him – and the US – a mission to change history (*Time* magazine, 6 September 2004). He believes that in a dangerous world the best way to ensure America's security is to shed constraints imposed by alliances and international bodies. He also believes, unlike one of his predecessors, John Quincy Adams, that the US should go "in search of monsters to destroy." From the results of the 2004 elections it would seem that a majority of Americans share, or at least support, his world outlook. If the US continues to try and use its impressive military power to change the world it will inevitably run into serious trouble. But if the humble approach is followed, then neither America nor the rest of the world has anything to fear for the foreseeable future. There is an important difference between power and authority. Power is the ability to compel by force and sanctions; authority is the ability to lead and requires legitimacy – and the US depends upon it for almost everything it tries to do.

An explicit American hegemony may appear preferable to the messy compromises of the existing order but if it is nakedly based on military power and commercial interests it will lack all legitimacy. Terror will continue and worse there may be widespread sympathy with terror. But American power placed at the service of an international community legitimized by representative institutions and the rule of law, accepting its constraints and inadequacies but continually working to improve them, that is a very different manner. This is essentially the path followed by America up until 9/11, a path that won it respect and admiration throughout the world. If that respect is to be regained, then America must cease to think of itself as a heroic lone ranger in a never-ending war against "evil" and reconcile itself to a more modest leadership role in a flawed but still indispensable system of cooperative global governance.

Glossary

Al Qaeda network The radical Islamic terrorist network controlled by Osama bin Laden, responsible for the 11 September 2001 terrorist attacks.

Cold War The name given to the struggle between the West, led by the US, and the communist countries, led by the Soviet Union, from 1946 to 1991. The two camps comprised the bipolar world of the Cold War era.

Containment The policy of firmly resisting the communist threat during the Cold War.

Dayton agreement The venue of an air force base in Ohio where the US brokered a peace deal between the Serbs, Croats, and Bosnians in 1995.

EXIMBANK The Export-Import Bank of the United States supports the financing of US goods and services and maintains and creates US jobs.

Focus groups Selected members of the public, chosen by polling experts as a representative sample of the population, to offer opinions on current political issues.

Founding Fathers The name given to the politicians who met and drafted the constitution of the US.

G8 The group of seven leading industrialized nations (US, Germany, France, Britain, Italy, Japan, Canada) that meet annually at summit level to discuss economic and political affairs. Russia, the eighth member, participates in the political part. The European Commission is also a full participant.

Idealism The policy, associated with President Wilson, which favors open diplomacy, disarmament, collective security and strong international organizations. Idealists also seek to promote democracy and human rights around the world.

Inside the beltway A term used to denote the Washington policy elite (the beltway is the ring road around Washington DC).

Internationalism Support for active American engagement in world affairs.

Islamic fundamentalism Those who use the Islamic religion as cover for violent actions, including terrorism, usually directed against the US.

Isolationism The desire to isolate the nation as much as possible from international affairs, usually accompanied by a lack of interest in the outside world.

Kyoto Protocol   The 1997 agreement in Japan when nearly all countries in the world – with the conspicuous exception of the US – agreed on cuts in greenhouse gas emissions.

Manifest destiny   The belief that the US had a special mission to expand (across North America) and promote its values abroad.

Marshall Plan   The provision of substantial US economic and financial assistance to Western Europe after the Second World War.

Military-industrial complex   The phrase used by President Eisenhower to warn of the dangers of excessive power in the hands of defense contractors, the Pentagon, and defense officials.

Monroe Doctrine   A doctrine proclaimed by President Monroe in 1823 asserting US supremacy in the western hemisphere and warning other powers not to interfere.

Multilateralism   A policy choice that prefers working with other countries and/or international institutions.

Mutual Assured Destruction   MAD refers to the policy of each superpower having so many offensive nuclear weapons that if one side were to launch an attack it would invite inevitable retaliation leading to both sides being destroyed.

Neocons   The name given to the group of neo-conservatives that advocated acting unilaterally and using American military power first and foremost to achieve foreign policy goals. Many neocons occupied high-level positions in the George W. Bush administration and were very influential in the decision to invade Iraq.

New realism   A term used by some Republicans to describe their *realpolitik* views of how to deal with the world – it implies criticism of the Democrats for their alleged idealistic or romantic approach to international affairs.

New world order   The term coined by President George H. W. Bush after the collapse of communism to explain his optimistic view of world affairs.

Powell Doctrine   A policy associated with Colin Powell, when he was chairman of the Joint Chiefs of Staff, which states that the US should only commit its armed forces when there is a clear political objective, and the military should use overwhelming force to achieve a rapid victory.

Protectionism   An economic term for policies such as raising tariffs or imposing quotas on imports to protect domestic industries.

Rogue states   The name used to describe countries such as Iraq, Iran, North Korea, Libya. An attempt to rename them "countries of concern" in 1999 failed to stick.

Sanctions   An attempt to influence the behavior of third states by imposing restrictions on trade or other contacts with the country.

Staffer   The name given to someone working on the staff of a government agency or for a senator or congressman or for a congressional committee.

Sustainable development   The concept of marrying economic development with environmental concerns.

Unilateralism   A policy choice that prefers going-it-alone in foreign policy.

Uruguay Round   The name for the international trade negotiations that were launched in Uruguay in 1986 and concluded in 1994. A further round was launched at Doha in November 2001.

Selected key dates

1776	Declaration of Independence
1812–15	War against Britain
1861–5	Civil War
1898	War with Spain over Cuba
1917–18	US involved in First World War
1941–5	US involved in Second World War
1945	Founding of the United Nations
1947	Truman Doctrine, Marshall Plan
1949	US agrees to establishment of NATO
1950–3	Korean War
1962	Cuban Missile Crisis
1964–73	Vietnam War
1979–80	Fall of US-backed Shah of Iran; Ayatollah Khomeini takes power; rise of fundamentalism; Iran hostage crisis
1986	Iran-Contra affair
1988	George H. W. Bush elected President
1989	Fall of Berlin Wall
1990	Reunification of Germany
1991	Collapse of Soviet Union
1990–1	Gulf War
1992	Bill Clinton elected President
1993	US involvement in Somalia, Haiti
	Oslo Middle East Peace Accords
1994	NAFTA signed
1995	US-sponsored agreement on Bosnia at Dayton
1999	Kosovo air campaign – US bombing of Serb targets
2000	Camp David Middle East peace talks sponsored by Clinton
	George W. Bush elected President
2001	Terrorist attacks on New York and Washington DC
	US military campaign against Taliban regime in Afghanistan

Appendix 1

US participation in major international organizations and treaties

United Nations (UN) established 1945, the US is one of the five permanent members of the UN Security Council (UNSC).

North Atlantic Treaty Organization (NATO) established 1949, NATO is a collective defense organization with 19 members. A further enlargement was foreseen at the Prague summit in November 2002. The US plays the leading role in NATO.

World Trade Organization (WTO) is an international trade organization established under the Uruguay Round to promote trade and to regulate disputes between its members.

Group of Eight (G8) established 1973, this is a self-appointed exclusive club of northern industrial democracies – the US, Canada, Japan, the UK, Germany, France and Italy (plus Russia). There is an annual meeting of leaders plus other meetings of Foreign and Finance Ministers. The EU also participates through the Presidency and European Commission.

International Monetary Fund (IMF) established after the Second World War to provide financial support to its members in economic difficulty.

World Bank established after the Second World War to provide financial assistance to developing countries (NB the President of the World Bank has always been an American; and the Managing Director of the IMF a European).

Rio Pact established 1948, the pact provides for the collective defense of all Latin American countries (except Cuba).

ANZUS defense pact signed in 1951 linking Australia, New Zealand, and the US. New Zealand was suspended from ANZUS in 1986 following a dispute with the US over whether visiting American ships should declare if they carried nuclear weapons.

South East Asia Treaty Organization (SEATO) established 1955, the organization was dissolved 1977, but collective defense arrangements remain – members include the US, UK, France, Australia, New Zealand, Thailand and the Philippines.

North American Free Trade Agreement (NAFTA) established 1994, provides for closer economic collaboration between the US, Canada, and Mexico.

Asia-Pacific Economic Cooperation Forum (APEC) established 1989, provides an annual meeting for 21 Pacific Rim countries to discuss mainly economic cooperation. Operates on consensus basis. The US finds it a useful venue for bilateral meetings.

Free Trade Area of the Americas (FTAA) negotiations started in 1994 to seek a free trade area for all the countries of the western hemisphere. The aim is to complete the FTAA by 2005.

Appendix 2

Key players during the post-Cold War period

George H. W. Bush administration (1989–93)

Vice President: Dan Quayle
National Security Adviser: Brent Scowcroft
Secretary of State: James Baker III
Secretary of Defense: Richard B. (Dick) Cheney

William J. Clinton administration (1993–2001)

Vice President: Al Gore
National Security Adviser: Anthony Lake (1993–7); Sandy Berger (1997–2001)
Secretary of State: Warren Christopher (1993–7); Madeleine Albright (1997–2001)
Secretary of Defense: Lee Aspin (1993–4); William J. Perry (1994–7);
    William S. Cohen (1997–2001)

George W. Bush administration (2001–2004)

Vice President: Richard B. (Dick) Cheney
National Security Adviser: Condoleezza Rice
Secretary of State: Colin Powell
Secretary of Defense: Donald Rumsfeld

George W. Bush administration (2005–2008)

Vice President: Richard B. (Dick) Cheney
National Security Adviser: Stephen Hadley
Secretary of State: Condoleezza Rice
Secretary of Defense: Donald Rumsfeld

Bibliography

Books

Abelson, D. E. (1996) *American Think Tanks and Their Role in US Foreign Policy*, New York: St Martin's Press.

Acheson, D. (1969) *Present at the Creation*, London: Hamilton.

Albright, M. (2003) *Madam Secretary*, New York: Miramax.

Allison, G. and Zelikow, P. (1999) *Essence of Decision: Explaining the Cuban Missile Crisis*, 2nd edn, New York: Addison-Wesley.

Alperovitz, G. (1994) *Atomic Diplomacy: Hiroshima and Potsdam: The Use of the Atomic Bomb and the American Confrontation with Soviet Power*, 2nd edn, Boulder, CO: Pluto Press.

Alterman, E. (1998) *Who Speaks for America? Why Democracy Matters in Foreign Policy*, Ithaca: Cornell University Press.

Ambrose, S. E. and Brinkley, D. G. (1997) *Rise to Globalism*, 8th edn, New York: Penguin.

Andrew, C. M. (1995) *For the President's Eyes Only: Secret Intelligence and the American Presidency from Washington to Bush*, New York: HarperCollins.

Anonymous (2004) *Imperial Hubris: Why the West is Losing the War on Terrorism*, New York: Brasseys.

Arlen, M. (1982) *Living-Room War*, New York: Penguin.

Art, R. J. J. and Jarvis, R. (1999) *International Politics: Enduring Concepts and Contemporary Issues*, New York: Addison-Wesley.

Augelli, E. and Murphy, C. (1988) *America's Quest for Supremacy in the Third World*, London: Pinter Publishers.

Baker, J. (1995) *Politics of Diplomacy: Revolution, War and Peace, 1989–1992*, New York: Putnam.

Bamford, J. (2001) *Body of Secrets*, New York: Doubleday.

—— (2004) *A Pretext for War: 9/11, Iraq and the Abuse of America's Intelligence Agencies*, New York: Doubleday.

Barnett, T. P. M. (2004) *The Pentagon's New Map: War and Peace in the Twenty-First Century*, New York: Putnam.

Barone, M. (2001) *The New Americans*, New York: Regnery.

Berry, N. (1990) *Foreign Policy and the Press*, Westport, CT: Greenwood.

Beschloss, M. and Talbott, S. (1993) *At the Highest Level: The Inside Story of the End of the Cold War*, New York: Little, Brown.

Bhagwati, J. (2001) *The Wind of the Hundred Days: How Washington Mismanaged Globalization*, Cambridge, MA: MIT Press.

Bildt, C. (1998) *Peace Journey*, London: Weidenfeld and Nicolson.

Blechman, B. M. (1990) *The Politics of National Security: Congress and US Defense Policy*, New York: Oxford University Press.

Blix, H. (2004) *Disarming Iraq*, New York: Pantheon.

Blum, W. (2003) *Killing Hope: US Military and CIA Interventions Since World War II*, London: Zed Books.

Booth, K. and Zalewski, M. (eds) (1995) *International Theory: Positivism and Beyond*, New York: Cambridge University Press.

Boren, D. and Perkins, E. (eds) (2000) *Preparing America's Foreign Policy for the Twenty-First Century*, Norman: University of Oklahoma Press.

Boughton, J. M. (2001) *The Silent Revolution – the IMF 1979–89*, Washington DC: International Monetary Fund.

Brands, H. W. (1999) *What America Owes the World*, Cambridge, UK: Cambridge University Press.

Brewer, T. (2000) *Globalizing America: The USA in World Integration*, Cheltenham, UK: Edward Elgar.

Brown, S. (1994) *The Faces of Power: Constancy and Change in United States Foreign Policy from Truman to Clinton*, New York: Columbia University Press.

Brzezinski, Z. (1997) *The Grand Chessboard: American Primacy and its Geostrategic Imperatives*, New York: Basic Books.

—— (2004) *The Choice: Global Domination or Global Leadership*, New York: Basic Books.

Buchanan, P. J. (1999) *A Republic, Not an Empire: Reclaiming America's Destiny*, Lanham, MD: Regnery Publishers.

Bush, G. H. W. (1999) *All the Best*, New York: Scribner.

Bush, G. H. W. and Scowcroft, B. (1998) *A World Transformed*, New York: Knopf.

Callahan, D. (1994) *Between Two Worlds: Realism, Idealism and American Foreign Policy After the End of the Cold War*, New York: HarperCollins.

Carter, J. (1982) *Keeping Faith: Memoirs of a President*, New York: Bantam.

Chase, R. et al. (eds) (1998) *The Pivotal States: A New Framework for US Policy in the Developing World*, New York: W.W. Norton.

Chomsky, N. (2000) *Rogue States: The Rule of Force in World Affairs*, Cambridge, MA: South End Press.

—— (2003) *Hegemony or Survival: America's Quest for Global Dominance*, New York: Metropolitan Books.

Christopher, W. (1998) *In the Stream of History: Shaping Foreign Policy for a New Era*, Stanford: Stanford University Press.

—— (2001) *Chances of a Lifetime*, New York: Scribner.

Clark, W. (2001) *Waging Modern War*, New York: Public Affairs.

Clarke, R. A. (2004) *Against All Enemies: Inside Americas's War on Terrorism*, New York: Free Press.

Clinton, B. (1996) *Between Hope and History*, New York: Random House.

—— (2004) *My Life*, New York: Random House.

Cohen, W. (ed.) (1993) *Cambridge History of American Foreign Relations*, New York: Cambridge University Press.

Coll, S. (2004) *Ghost Wars: The Secret History of the CIA, Afghanistan, and bin Laden: From the Soviet Invasion to September 10, 2001*, New York: Penguin Press.

Cooper, J. M. (2001) *Breaking the Heart of the World – Woodrow Wilson and the Fight for the League of Nations*, New York: Cambridge University Press.

Crabb, C. et al. (2000) *Congress and the Foreign Policy Process: Modes of Legislative Behavior*, Baton Rouge: Louisiana State University Press.

Daalder, I. (1999) *Getting to Dayton: The Making of America's Bosnia Policy*, Washington DC: Brookings Institution Press.

Daalder, I. and Lindsay, J. M. (2003) *America Unbound: The Bush Revolution in Foreign Policy*, Washington DC: Brookings Institution Press.

Destler, I. M., Gelb, L. H., and Lake, A. (1984) *Our Own Worst Enemy: The Unmaking of American Foreign Policy*, New York: Simon and Schuster.

Dobbs, M. (1999) *Madeleine Albright: A Twentieth-Century Odyssey*, New York: Henry Holt.

Dominguez, J. I. and de Castro, R. F. (2001) *The US and Mexico: Between Partnership and Conflict*, New York: Routledge.

Doyle, M. W. and Ikenberry, J. G. (eds) (1997) *New Thinking in International Relations Theory*, Boulder, CO: Westview Press.

Dryden, S. (1995) *Trade Warriors: USTR and the American Crusade for Free Trade*, New York: Oxford University Press.

Dumbrell, J. (1997) *Making of US Foreign Policy*, 2nd edn, New York: Manchester University Press.

Ferguson, N. (2004) *Colossus: The Price of Americas's Empire*, New York: Penguin Press.

Friedman, T. (2001) *The Lexus and the Olive Tree*, New York: Anchor Books.

Fukuyama, F. (1992) *The End of History and the Last Man*, New York: Maxwell Macmillan International.

Garfinkle, A. M. (1995) *Telltale Hearts: The Origins and Impact of the Vietnam Antiwar Movement*, New York: St Martin's Press.

Gergen, D. (2002) *Eyewitness to Power*, New York: Simon and Schuster.

Giddens, A. (2000) *Runaway World: How Globalization is Shaping Our Lives*, New York: Routledge.

Gompert, D. C. and Larrabee, S. F. (eds) (1997) *America and Europe*, Cambridge, UK: Cambridge University Press.

Gordon, P. H. and Shapiro, J. (2004) *Allies at War: America, Europe, and the Crisis Over Iraq*, Washington DC: Brookings Institution Press.

Gruff, P. (1999) *The Kosovo News and the Propaganda War*, Washington: International Press Institute.

Haass, R. N. (1997a) *The Reluctant Sheriff*, New York: Council on Foreign Relations.

—— (1997b) *Transatlantic Tensions*, Washington DC: Brookings Institution Press.

—— (1999) *Intervention: The Use of American Military Force in the Post-Cold War World*, Washington DC: Brookings Institution Press.

Haass, R. N. and O'Sullivan, M. L. (eds) (2000) *Honey and Vinegar: Incentives, Sanctions and Foreign Policy*, Washington DC: Brookings Institution Press.

Halberstam, D. (1983) *The Best and the Brightest*, New York: Penguin.

—— (2001) *War in a Time of Peace*, New York: Simon and Schuster.

Halliday, F. (2000) *The World at 2000*, London: Palgrave.

Halper, S. and Clarke, J. (2004) *America Alone: The Neo-Conservatives and the Global Order*, Cambridge, UK: Cambridge University Press.

Hastedt, G. P. (2000) *American Foreign Policy: Past, Present, Future*, Upper Saddle River, NJ: Prentice Hall.

Helms, J. (2001) *Empire for Liberty: A Sovereign America and Her Moral Mission*, Lanham, MD: Regnery Publishers.

Henehan, M. (2000) *Foreign Policy and Congress: An International Relations Perspective*, Ann Arbor: University of Michigan Press.

Hersman, R. (2000) *Friends and Foes: How Congress and the President Really Make Foreign Policy*, Washington DC: Brookings Institution Press.

Hippel, K. (2000) *Democracy by Force: US Military Intervention in the Post-Cold War World*, New York: Cambridge University Press.

Hirst, P. Q. and Thompson, G. (1999) *Globalization in Question: The International Economy and the Possibilities of Governance*, Malden, MA: Polity Press.

Hoffman, S. (1968) *Gulliver's Troubles or the Setting of American Foreign Policy*, New York: McGraw-Hill.

Hoge, J and Rose, G. (2004) *How Did This Happen? Terrorism and the New War*, New York: Public Affairs.

Holbrooke, R. (1998) *To End A War*, New York: Random House.

Holsti, O. R. (1996) *Public Opinion and American Foreign Policy*, Ann Arbor: University of Michigan Press.

Holt, R. (1995) *The Reluctant Superpower: A History of America's Economic Global Reach*, New York: Kodansha.

Huntington, S. P. (1996) *The Clash of Civilizations and the Remaking of World Order*, New York: Simon and Schuster.

—— (2004) *Who Are We? The Challenge to America's National Identity*, New York: Simon and Schuster.

Hyland, W. (1999) *Clinton's World: Remaking American Foreign Policy*, Westport, CT: Praeger.

Ikenberry, J. G. (2001) *After Victory, Institutions, Strategic Restraint and the Rebuilding of Order After Major Wars*, Princeton: Princeton University Press.

Jentleson, B. (2000) *American Foreign Policy: The Dynamics of Choice in the 21st Century*, New York: Norton.

Johnson, C. (2000) *Blowback: The Costs and Consequences of American Empire*, New York: Metropolitan Books.

—— (2004) *The Sorrows of Empire: Militarism, Secrecy, and the End of the Republic*, New York: Metropolitan Books.

Kagan, R. and Kristol, K. (eds) (2000) *Present Dangers: Crisis and Opportunity in American Foreign and Defense Policy*, San Francisco: Encounter Books.

Kaplan, R. (1998) *An Empire Wilderness*, New York: Vintage Books.

Kegley, C. W. and Wittkopf, E. R. (1996) *American Foreign Policy: Pattern and Process*, New York: St Martin's Press.

Kennan, G. F. (1984) *American Diplomacy*, expanded edn, Chicago: University of Chicago Press.

—— (1997) *The Cloud of Danger: Some Current Problems of American Foreign Policy*, Boston: Little, Brown.

Kennedy, P. (1993) *Preparing for the Twenty-first Century*, London: HarperCollins.

Kennedy, R. (1966) *Thirteen Days*, London: Macmillan.

Kessler, R. (1992) *Inside the CIA: Revealing the Secrets of the World's Most Powerful Spy Agency*, New York: Pocket Books.

Kirkpatrick, J. M. (1996) *Good Intentions: Lost on the Road to the New World Order*, Washington DC: American Enterprise Institute.

Kissinger, H. (1979) *White House Years*, Boston: Little, Brown.

—— (1982) *Years of Upheaval*, Boston: Little, Brown.

—— (1995) *Diplomacy*, New York: Touchstone Books.

—— (2001) *Does America Need a Foreign Policy? Toward Diplomacy for the 21st Century*, New York: Simon and Schuster.

Klare, M. T. (1995) *Rogue States and Nuclear Outlaws: America's Search for a New Foreign Policy*, New York: Hill and Wang.

Kramnick, I. (1987) *The Federalist Papers*, New York: Penguin.

Krenn, M. L. (1998) *The African American Voice in US Foreign Policy since World War II*, New York: Garland Publishers.

Kull, S. and Destler, I. M. (1999) *Misreading the Public: The Myth of a New Isolationism*, Washington DC: Brookings Institution Press.

Kupchan, C. A. (2002) *The End of the American Era*, New York: Knopf.

LaFeber, W. (ed.) (1965) *John Quincy Adams and the American Continental Empire*, Chicago: Times Books.

—— (2002) *America, Russia and the Cold War, 1945–2000*, Boston: McGraw-Hill.

Lake, D. A. (1999) *Entangling Relations: American Foreign Policy in its Century*, Princeton: Princeton University Press.

Larson, T. (2001) *The Race to the Top – The Real Story of Globalization*, Washington DC: Cato Institute.

Lessor, I. (ed.) (1999) *Countering the New Terrorism*, Santa Monica: RAND.

Lewis, B. (2004) *From Babel to Dragomans: Interpreting the Middle East*, New York: Oxford University Press.

Lieven, Anatol (2004) *America Right or Wrong*, Oxford: Oxford University Press.

Lindsay, J. M. (1994) *Congress and the Politics of US Foreign Policy*, Baltimore: Johns Hopkins University Press.

Lippman, T. (2000) *Madeleine Albright and the New American Diplomacy*, Boulder, CO: Westview.

Litwak, R. (2000) *Rogue States and US Foreign Policy: Containment After the Cold War*, Baltimore: Johns Hopkins University Press.

Lodal, J. (2001) *The New Weapons of Mass Destruction and Their Challenge to American Leadership*, New York: Council on Foreign Relations Press.

Low, P. (1993) *Trading Free: The GATT and US Trade Policy*, New York: Twentieth Century Fund Press.

MacKinnon, M. (2000) *The Evolution of US Peacekeeping Policy under Clinton: A Fairweather Friend*, Portaland: Frank Cass.

McInerney, T. and Valleley, P. E. (2004) *Endgame: The Blueprint for Victory in the War on Terror*, Washington DC: Regnery.

Mann, T. (ed.) (1990) *A Question of Balance: The President, the Congress and Foreign Policy*, Washington DC: Brookings Institution Press.

Mazza, J. (2001) *Don't Disturb the Neighbors: The US and Democracy in Mexico, 1980–1995*, New York: Routledge.

Melanson, R. (1996) *American Foreign Policy Since the Vietnam War: The Search for Consensus from Nixon to Clinton*, 2nd edn, Armonk, NY: M.E. Sharpe.

Morgenthau, H. J. (1969) *A New Foreign Policy for the United States*, New York: Praeger.

Mosler, D. and Catley, B. (2000) *Imposing Liberalism on a Recalcitrant World*, New York: Praeger.

Neustadt, R. (1960) *Presidential Power: The Politics of Leadership*, New York: Wiley.

—— (1990) *Presidential Power and the Modern Presidents: The Politics of Leadership from Roosevelt to Reagan*, New York: Maxwell Macmillan.

Nixon, R. M. (1981) *RN: The Memoirs of Richard Nixon*, New York: Warner Books.

Nye, J. S. (1999) *Understanding International Conflicts: An Introduction to Theory and History*, New York: Addison-Wesley.

—— (2002) *The Paradox of American Power: Why the World's Only Superpower Can't Go It Alone*, New York: Oxford University Press.

O'Hanlon, M. (2000) *Technological Change and the Future of Warfare*, Washington DC: Brookings Institution Press.

Owen, D. (1995) *Balkan Odyssey*, New York: Harcourt Brace.

Oye, K. A., Lieber, E. O., and Rothchild, D. (eds) (1992) *Eagle in a New World: American Grand Strategy in the Post-Cold War Era*, New York: HarperCollins.

Petras, J. and Morley, M. (1995) *Empire or Republic? American Global Power and Domestic Decay*, New York: Routledge.

Piller, P. (2001) *Terrorism and US Foreign Policy*, Washington DC: Brookings Institution Press.

Powell, C. (1995) *My American Journey*, New York: Random House.

Prestowitz, C. (2004) *Rogue Nation*, New York: Basic Books.

Read, W. R. (2001) *Special Providence: American Foreign Policy and How it Changed the World*, New York: Knopf.

Reagan, R. (2001) *Reagan in His Own Hand*, New York: Free Press.

Rice, C. and Zelikow, P. (1997) *Germany Unified and Europe Transformed: A Study in Statecraft*, Cambridge, MA: Harvard University Press.

Roberts, P. (2004) *The End of Oil: On the Edge of a Perilous New World*, Boston: Houghton Mifflin.

Rosenau, J. N. (1997) *Along the Domestic–Foreign Frontier: Exploring Governance in a Turbulent World*, New York: Cambridge University Press.

Rosenblum, M. (1993) *Who Stole the News?*, New York: Wiley.

Rubin, B. (1985) *Secrets of State: The State Department and the Struggle over US Foreign Policy*, New York: Oxford University Press.

Ruggie, J. G. (1996) *Winning the Peace: America and World Order in the New Era*, New York: Columbia University Press.

Schott, J. J. (2001) *Prospects for Free Trade in the Americas*, Washington DC: Institute for International Economics.

Scott, J. M. (ed.) (1998) *After the End: Making US Foreign Policy in the Post-Cold War World*, Durham, NC: Duke University Press.

Sefarty, S. (ed.) (1991) *The Media and Foreign Policy*, New York: St Martin's Press.

Seib, P. (1997) *Headline Diplomacy: How News Coverage Affects Foreign Policy*, Westport, CT: Praeger Series in Political Communications.

Shapiro, R. Y. and Page, B. I. (1992) *The Rational Public: Fifty Years of Trends in American Policy Preferences*, Chicago: Chicago University Press.

Shoemaker, C. C. (1992) *The NSC Staff: Counseling the Council*, Boulder, CO: Westview.

Simon, J. D. (2001) *The Terrorist Trap – America's Experience with Terrorism*, Indiana: Indiana University Press.

Smith, J. A. (1991) *The Idea Brokers: Think Tanks and the Rise of the New Policy Elite*, New York: Free Press.

Smith, P. M. (1991) *How CNN Fought the War*, New York: Birch Lane.

Smith, T. (2000) *Foreign Attachments: The Power of Ethnic Groups in the Making of American Foreign Policy*, Cambridge, MA: Harvard University Press.

Snow, D. M. and Brown, E. (1997) *Beyond the Water's Edge: An Introduction to United States Foreign Policy*, New York: St Martin's Press.

Spanier, J. and Hook, S. W. (1998) *American Foreign Policy Since World War II*, 14th edn, Washington DC: Congressional Quarterly.

Stearns, M. (1996) *Talking to Strangers: Improving American Diplomacy at Home and Abroad*, Princeton: Princeton University Press.

Steel, R. (1995) *Temptations of a Superpower*, Cambridge, MA: Harvard University Press.

Strobel, W. P. (1997) *Late-Breaking Foreign Policy: The News Media's Influence on Peace Operations*, Washington DC: Washington Institute of Peace.

Suskind, R. (2004) *The Price of Loyalty*, New York: Simon and Schuster.

Talbott, S. and Chanda, N. (2004) *The World After September 11*, New York: Basic Books.

Tanter, R. (1999) *Rogue Regimes: Terrorism and Proliferation*, New York: St Martin's Press.

Tucker, D. (1997) *Skirmishes at the Edge – The United States and International Terrorism*, Westport, CT: Praeger.

Tucker, R. W. and Hendrickson, D. C. (1992) *The Imperial Temptation: The New World Order and America's Purpose*, New York: Council on Foreign Relations.

Tyler, P. (1999) *A Great Wall: Six Presidents and China*, New York: Public Affairs.

Unger, C. (2004) *House of Bush, House of Saud: The Secret Relationship Between the World's Two Most Powerful Dynasties*, New York: Scribner.

Vance, C. (1983) *Hard Choices: Critical Years in American Foreign Policy*, New York: Simon and Schuster.

Van Hippel, K. (1999) *Democracy by Force: US Military Intervention in the Post-Cold War World*, New York: Cambridge University Press.

Viotti, P. R. and Kauppi, M. V. (1999) *International Relations Theory: Realism, Pluralism, Globalism, and Beyond*, Boston: Allyn and Bacon.

Walker, M. (1996) *The President We Deserve: Bill Clinton, His Rise, Falls and Comebacks*, New York: Crown Publishers.

Waltz, K. (1979) *Theory of International Politics*, Reading, MA: Addison-Wesley.

Weber, C. (2001) *International Relations Theory: A Critical Introduction*, London: Routledge.

Wildavsky, A. (1975) *Perspectives on the Presidency*, Boston: Little, Brown.

Wittkopf, E. R. and McCormick, J. M. (1999) *The Domestic Sources of American Foreign Policy*, 3rd edn, Lanham, MD: Rowman and Littlefield.

Woodward, R. (1994) *The Agenda: Inside the Clinton White House*, Accord, MA: Wheeler.

—— (1999) *Shadow: Five Presidents and the Legacy of Watergate*, New York: Simon and Schuster.

—— (2004) *Plan of Attack*, New York: Simon and Schuster.

Zakaria, F. (1998) *From Wealth to Power: The Unusual Origins of America's World Role*, Princeton: Princeton University Press.

Zimmerman, W. (1996) *Origins of a Catastrophe*, New York: Random House.

Articles

Beatty, J. "The real roots of terror," *Atlantic Monthly*, December 2001.

Berger, S. R. "A foreign policy for the global age," *Foreign Affairs*, November/December 2000.

——— "Five easy pieces for the next administration," *Peace Watch*, February 2001.

——— "Foreign policy for a Democratic President," *Foreign Affairs*, May/June 2004.

Bergsten, C. F. "The dollar and the euro," *Foreign Affairs*, July/August 1997.

——— "America and Europe: clash of the titans?" *Foreign Affairs*, March/April 1999.

——— "America's two-front economic conflict," *Foreign Affairs*, March/April 2001.

Blinken, A. "The false crisis over the Atlantic," *Foreign Affairs*, May/June 2001.

Blumenthal, S. "The return of the repressed: anti-internationalism and the American right," *World Policy Journal*, Fall 1995.

Bolton, J. "Kofi Annan's UN power grab: US foreign policy doesn't require the permission of the Security Council," *The Weekly Standard*, 4 October 1999.

Bowman Cutter, W., Spero, J., and D'Andrea Tyson, L. "New world, new deal: a democratic approach to globalization," *Foreign Affairs*, March/April 2000.

Chege, M. "What is Clinton's international legacy?" *The Washington Quarterly*, Spring 2001.

Daalder, I. H. "Are the United States and Europe heading for divorce?" *International Affairs*, Summer 2001.

Eagleburger and Barry, "Dollars and sense diplomacy: a better foreign policy for less money," *Foreign Affairs*, July/August 1996

Garrick, U. "The shrinking of foreign news, from broadcast to narrowcast," *Foreign Affairs*, March/April 1997.

Goodby, J. E. and Weisbrode, K. "Back to basics: US foreign policy for the coming decade," *Parameters: US Army War College Quarterly*, Spring 2000.

Haass, R. "Foreign policy by posse," *The National Interest*, Fall 1995.

——— "Globalization and its discontents," *Foreign Affairs*, May/June 1998.

——— "What to do with American primacy," *Foreign Affairs*, September/October 1999.

——— "The squandered presidency: demanding more from the commander-in-chief," *Foreign Affairs*, May/June 2000.

Hagel, C. "A Republican foreign policy," *Foreign Affairs*, July/August 2004.

Hamilton, L. "Can foreign policy be bipartisan?: looking ahead," *The Washington Quarterly*, Spring 2001.

Howard, M. "What's in a name?: how to fight terrorism," *Foreign Affairs*, January/February 2002.

Huntington, S. "The lonely superpower," *Foreign Affairs*, March/April 1999.

——— "The erosion of American national interests," *Foreign Affairs*, March/April 2002.

Ikenberry, J. "American grand strategy in the age of terror," *Survival*, Vol 43, No 4, 2003.

Kurth, J. "The adolescent empire: America and the imperial idea," *The National Interest*, Summer 1997.

Lancaster, C. "Redesigning foreign aid," *Foreign Affairs*, September/October 2000.

Lavin, F. L. "Asphyxiation or oxygen? The sanctions dilemma," *Foreign Policy*, Fall 1996.

Lindsay, J. "The new apathy: how an uninterested public is reshaping foreign policy," *Foreign Affairs*, September/October 2000.

Mandelbaum, M. "Foreign policy as social work," *Foreign Affairs*, January/February 1996.

——— "A perfect failure: NATO's war against Yugoslavia," *Foreign Affairs*, September/October 1999.

Mann, J. "Not your father's foreign policy: the faces are familiar, but the dilemmas are new. Is the Bush team framing the right choices?" *The American Prospect*, 9 April 2001.

Maynes, W. "The perils of (and for) an imperial America," *Foreign Policy*, Summer 1998.

Nairn, M. "Redefining American leadership: grading President Clinton," *Foreign Policy*, Winter 1997/98.

Newhouse, J. "The missile defense debate," *Foreign Affairs*, July/August 2001.

Nye, J. S. "Redefining the national interest," *Foreign Affairs*, July/August 1999.

O'Hanlon, M. "Come partly home, America: how to downsize US deployments abroad," *Foreign Affairs*, March/April 2001.

Perry, W. "Preparing for the next attack," *Foreign Affairs*, November/December 2001.

Pfaff, W. "The question of hegemony," *Foreign Affairs*, January/February 2001.

Powell, C. "A Strategy of Partnerships," *Foreign Affairs*, January/February 2004.

Powlick, P. and Katz, A. "Defining the American public opinion/foreign policy nexus," *Mershon International Studies Review*, May 1998.

Quinlan, J. and Chandler, M. "The US trade deficit: a dangerous obsession," *Foreign Affairs*, May/June 2001.

Reilly, J. "Americans and the world: a survey at century's end," *Foreign Policy*, Spring 1999.

Rice, C. "Promoting the national interest," *Foreign Affairs*, January/February 2000.

—— "Forging foreign policy for a new age," *Peace Watch*, Summer 2001.

——"A balance of power that favors freedom," *US Foreign Policy Agenda*, December 2002.

Rieff, D. "Whose internationalism, whose isolationism?" *World Policy Journal*, Summer 1996.

Rubin, B. "Legacy of State," *Foreign Service Journal*, September 1989.

Spiro, P. J. "The new sovereigntists," *Foreign Affairs*, November/December 2000.

Talbott, S. "Globalization and diplomacy: a practitioner's perspective," *Foreign Policy*, Fall 1997.

Tucker, R. W. "Alone or with others," *Foreign Affairs*, November/December 1999.

Walker, M. "The new American hegemony," *World Policy Journal*, Summer 1996.

Wallace, W. "Europe, the necessary partner," *Foreign Affairs*, May/June 2001.

Wallace, W. and Zielonka, J. "Misunderstanding Europe," *Foreign Affairs*, November/December 1998.

Walt, S. M. "Two cheers for Clinton's foreign policy," *Foreign Affairs*, March/April 2000.

Waltz, K. "Globalization and American power," *The National Interest*, 23 June 2000.

Weinstein, M. M. and Charnowitz, S. "The greening of the WTO," *Foreign Affairs*, November/December 2001.

White House, "United States of America National Security Strategy," Washington DC, 2002.

Williams, C. "Principled hegemony," *World Policy Journal*, Fall 1997.

Wolf, M. "Will the nation-state survive globalization?" *The Cato Journal*, Winter 2001.

Zoellick, R. B. "A republican foreign policy," *Foreign Affairs*, January/February 2000.

Reports (accessed 11 April 2005)

Clarke, J. G. (2000) "A Foreign Policy Report on the Clinton Administration, Cato Institute," report 382, 3 October 2000.

Gannon, J. C. (2000) "The Global Infectious Disease Threat and its Implication for the United States, January," available *www.cia.gov/cia/publications/nie/report/nie99–17d.html*

German Marshall Fund – for public opinion results, *www.gmfus.org*

Kugler, R. L. and Frost, E. (eds) (2001) "The Global Century: Globalization and National Security," Washington DC, National Defense University Press.

Pew Research Center – for analysis of public opinion, *www.pewresearchcenter.org*

RAND (2001) "The US and Asia: Toward a New Strategy and Force Posture," Santa Monica: RAND.

World Bank Policy Research Report (2001) "Globalization, Growth and Poverty," Herndon, VA: World Bank Publications.

Websites, journals and media sources (accessed 11 April 2005)

The US government has numerous websites relevant to foreign and security policy. Among the more useful are *www.whitehouse.gov*, *www.state.gov*, *http://usinfo.state*; *www.defenselink.mil*; *www.odci.gov*; *www.cia.gov*; *www.fbi.gov*. The two main Congressional committees dealing with foreign policy have the following websites: *www.senate.gov/~foreign*; *www.house.gov/international_relations*

There are numerous journals dealing entirely or partly with foreign policy issues. Among the most useful are *Foreign Affairs*, *Foreign Policy*, *The National Interest*, *World Policy Journal*, *World Politics*, *SAIS Review*, *International Security*, *Congressional Quarterly*. Many of these journals have websites including *www.foreignaffairs.org*; *www.foreignpolicy.com*; *www.americans-world.org*; *Foreign Policy in Focus*, *www.foreignpolicy-infocus.org*. *The Globalist*, an online think tank, also has a good website at *www.theglobalist.com*

Most of the leading think tanks have good websites, e.g.:

American Enterprise Institute, *www.aei.org*
American Foreign Policy Council, *www.afpc.org*
Brookings Institution, *www.brookings.org*
Carnegie Endowment for International Peace, *www.ceip.org*
CATO Institute, *www.cato.org*
Center for Defense Information, *www.cdi.org*
Center for Strategic and International Studies, *www.csis.org*
Council on Foreign Relations, *www.cfr.org*
Foreign Policy Association, *www.fpa.org*
Henry L. Stimson Center, *www.stimson.org*
Hoover Institute, *www.hoover.org*
Institute for International Economics, *www.iie.com*
Middle East Institute, *www.mideasti.org*
National Endowment for Democracy, *www.ned.org*
RAND, *www.rand.org*
The Heritage Foundation, *www.heritage.org*
US Institute of Peace, *www.usip.org*
Washington Institute for Near East Policy, *www.washingtoninstitute.org*
Woodrow Wilson Center, *www.wwics.si.edu*

The New York Times and the *Washington Post* have good websites with archived material on US foreign policy. Among the foreign press, the *Financial Times*, *The Economist*, the *Frankfurter Allgemeine Zeitung*, *Le Monde* and *El País* have regular quality coverage of US foreign policy.

Index